X

Violence: Theory and Ethnography

Violence: Theory and Ethnography

Pamela J. Stewart and Andrew Strathern

continuum
LONDON • NEW YORK

Continuum
The Tower Building, 11 York Road, London, SE1 7NX
370 Lexington Avenue, New York, NY 10017–6503

First published 2002

© Pamela J. Stewart and Andrew Strathern 2002

British Library Cataloguing-in-Publication Data
A catalogue record for this book is available from the British Library.

ISBN 0-8624-6007-0 (hardback)
     0-8264-6008-9 (paperback)

Typeset by YHT Ltd, London
Printed and bound in Great Britain by Biddles Ltd, Guildford and King's Lynn

364.0195

Contents

Acknowledgments

We wish to thank Brian Southam for originally giving us a contract for this book with the Athlone Press. Also, we warmly thank Continuum International Publishing Group for working with us on this project during 2001 and 2002. We wish to thank the government and people of Papua New Guinea for research permissions and research collaborations on the topics we discuss in Chapter 4. A part of this chapter is derived from a conference presented at the symposium session on exchange at the 2001 meeting of the Association for Social Anthropology in Oceania, organized by Maria Lepowsky and Paula Brown. A section of Chapter 5 ("Roads of Violence") derives in part from a paper published earlier in *Anthropology and Humanism* 24(1): 20–31, as cited in the chapter, and our summary of these matters appears here with permission from that journal.

This volume is dedicated to Ndamba and Ongka, two leaders in Mount Hagen, Papua New Guinea, who saw the opportunities for peace and used them well.
And to those who try to understand and accept the diversity of humankind.

CHAPTER 1

Violence as a Construct

Violence. A term written, seen, and heard everywhere on a daily basis. A problem seen as perennial or escalating. A kind of action imputed to both anarchists and to state authorities. A category in between peaceful disputing, and major planned warfare and fighting that fills newspaper pages and television screens. A propensity that some scholars say is rooted in the biology of mammals such as humans, while others argue that it is produced by particular social and historical conditions. A term that is contested both in its meanings and applications. An enduring phenomenon that is a part of our lives and cannot be ignored, yet has proved difficult to understand and analyse. This is the phenomenon that is the topic of this book.

Our purpose is not to propose a single new theory to replace existing ones, nor is it to produce a complete synthesis of viewpoints. It is, rather, to assess the present state of knowledge and perspectives on violence, particularly in terms of the contributions made to these perspectives by anthropology. In taking this approach, we do not reject biology and psychology. Rather, we recognize the "layered" quality of all explanations of, or discussions about, human behavior, from molecular biology to metaphysics. Forms of behavior can be reduced to underlying structures and processes that relate to biology, for example, or they can be philosophized in terms of metaphysics. Explanations and discussions belong to specific scientific or discursive realms. Anthropology in the broadest sense includes many kinds and levels of such realms, ranging from physical anthropology, evolutionary psychology, archaeology and prehistory, to social and cultural anthropology. Our own focus is on the last two categories, and we take our cue from the ethnographic records – the numerous

1

particular studies of practices in different parts of the world that constitute the database for attempts to comprehend the world in its complexities and to see broad patterns running through these complexities. The predominant approach here is empirical. We can use the ethnographic record to test general propositions about human cultural behavior, for example. Our own aim will be to present case histories that illustrate how certain factors do come together that enable us to make sense of patterns of violence within their own contexts. This does not mean we espouse cultural determinism or cultural relativism. It does mean that, in line with ethnographic work, we think that contexts, and especially historical contexts, are important. It is only on the basis of a detailed understanding of such contexts that we can arrive at broader propositions.

At the same time, the examination of a series of ethnographic cases can simply leave us with an impression of the bewildering diversity of materials, without overall or comparative understanding. A framework for the selection and presentation of such materials is therefore needed. The framework need not depend on a unitary theory of causes. Rather, it can consist of a number of approaches to the phenomena, and the questions that can be asked in their analysis. In the study of violence the major questions that have been broached include: What part does violence play in human social behavior in general? Should we analyse violence in terms of its contribution to social control and order, or as a form of behavior that is destructive of order and represents anarchy? Under what circumstances is violence particularly likely to be prevalent? What is its place in wider processes of conflict and settlement? In relation to these questions there are two broad sociological approaches. The first, and most widely known, is a functional approach. This sees violence in terms of its relationship to "law and order" and tends to define it as subversive of order, and therefore itself in need of control by coercive restraints. The second approach is symbolic. In this, investigators look for the subjective and cultural meanings associated with violent acts and how these impel or induce the actors to commit acts of violence. While these may be subversive of order in one sense, they are constitutive of it in another. Violence can be seen as either destroying order or creating it.

This apparent paradox is easily resolved if we realize that order is a subjective concept. What constitutes order and how it is to be attained or maintained vary according to people's positions in society and according to their own personal perceptions. As anthropologists or sociologists we may tend to construct models of systems in which order is implicated as an objective, ongoing property. However, these are indeed only models, and they may contain ideological or value-driven components that in fact reflect the subjective preferences or perceptions of dominant classes in society. If we divest ourselves of these models for a moment, we can look at the question of order from within the perceptions of social actors themselves, without imputing that these represent "the whole society." Take the example of protesters against the political meetings of international powers at which decisions about patterns of world trade are made. From the viewpoint of those attending these meetings, and the governments that host them, disruption of the meetings is disorder, and a violation of laws. From the viewpoint of the protesters, their actions are justified attempts to institute a different kind of world order than that entertained by the powers that hold these meetings. In a further complication there is often dissent within the body of the protesters, between those who wish to protest peacefully and those who wish to use violence, that is, to attack the police, to destroy property, and to threaten the physical safety of delegates.

Delegates and peaceful protesters may then unite in condemning the violent actions of those relatively few who espouse violent action as a means to achieving their ends. These few are likely to be seen, and perhaps to self-identify, as anarchists, who are in fact opposed to concepts of order that are shared by the protesters at large and their wider society. The issue of violence turns on the question of whose perception of order is at stake. Violence pinpoints the differences between people's perceptions of what is proper and appropriate in different contexts of conflict. This explains why it is praised by some and condemned by others. The perception of what is violence may also be subjective. Alternatively people may agree on what constitutes violence but disagree on whether it is appropriate or justified.

It is in the sphere of this subjectivity, then, that we build the framework for this book. We are interested in understanding processes of agreement and disagreement about the justification for violence. We take this central point from David Riches's proposition that "the performance of violence is inherently liable to be contested on the question of legitimacy" (Riches 1986: 11). Riches was interested in creating what we may call a transactional model of violence, in which subjectivity is a fundamental component. He developed an idea of the "triangle of violence" in which the viewpoints of performer, victim, and witness are distinguished. The performer may see a violent act as justified and therefore legitimate. The victim is likely to see this same act as unjustified and illegitimate. The witness or witnesses will have a different range of views depending on relations with either the performer or the victim or both. This model satisfactorily takes into account the subjectivity of

3

violence as a category of action. It needs to be broadened, however, in order to move it from the context of individual actions to collective contexts. Performer, victim, and witness may be pluralities rather than singular actors. And especially since witnesses may be diverse and may also be directly or indirectly involved in the issues at stake, the category of witness is potentially extremely complex. Further, witnesses, depending on their reactions or positions, may themselves turn into performers or victims, or both. Giving a temporal dimension to Riches's model, then, we can see that a given configuration of performer, victim, and witness may be only one moment in a larger process.

Moreover, in some contexts, it may be hard to single out a performer and a victim. This is the case for contexts we may wish to call warfare or organized fighting. At one point in his wide-ranging discussion Riches notes that he treats warfare "simply as violence that is subject to a certain level of organization" (1986: 24). Warfare is therefore subsumed as a special category of violence, collectivized from the original transactional model. But warfare involves two performing sides. Each may claim simultaneously to be a "victim," for example of injustice, aggression, or exploitation. Or each may be motivated by considerations of negative reciprocity, i.e. revenge, feeding into their images of victimage. Warfare is a special case of violence that in these ways stands outside a simple performer–victim relationship. In particular, revenge is an extremely important form of motivation, consideration of which again goes to the heart of the central point about contested legitimacy, and also the question of social order. Riches's model can be applied to contexts of revenge, but it does not encompass or explain them. Here we want to examine this point a little further. It is particularly relevant to our discussions throughout this book of conflict, organized fighting, and violence in Papua New Guinea; but revenge as a theme in a broad sense is shared very widely in many societies, including large-scale centralized contemporary polities.

In Mount Hagen, Papua New Guinea, and in many other places, killing another person sets up an irrevocable chain of circumstances, whether the killing is intentional or not. The chain is retributive. The killing must be balanced either by a killing in response or by a restitutive payment of compensation. While these processes have no doubt arisen historically and have certainly varied over time, the principle involved has remained fairly stable regardless of the situation in the law of the wider nation-state. The balancing involved is what the Hageners recognize as justice, that which is right, fair, appropriate, legitimate (*kapokla*). Revenge killings were considered legitimate in this sense in pre-colonial times; but the method of settling by compensation was also firmly established prior to colonial control, which dated from the 1930s through to 1975. Compensation payments are always seen both as the currently appropriate or "modern" way of settling conflict over killings and also as a means of warding off the ever-present possibility of a revenge killing, seen as rooted in people's inclinations. The threat to kill in revenge is the sanction behind the obligation to pay compensation. And in certain cases a killing and counterkilling can lead to wider conflicts, escalating into organized fighting. Hageners therefore also see the outbreak of fighting as a constant possibility, in spite of the fact that their society has changed greatly since the 1930s when the Australian colonial power first entered their region; almost everyone has some affiliation with a Christian church and a realization of belonging to a nation-state. The church affiliations often effect a redefinition of new political groupings within the communities which can lead in itself to violence even though church teachings may be explicitly against the use of force. The threat of organized fighting is also a sanction, therefore, in maintaining a certain adherence to pro-social behavior, in addition to any fears of being brought to trial for a killing or being put in jail. Reciprocal violence, or the threat of it, is a basis for order, as well as disorder.

And the basic impulse behind such violence is that of revenge. Revenge produces a situation that is *kapokla*, even though it does not in fact necessarily end a sequence of negative interactions but may rather provoke them. It is seen as *kapokla* by those who have most recently killed one of the other side. Each side in a sense sequentially feels that it is the victim of the other's violence; each also feels that it is *kapokla* to exact vengeance. We have to accept this impulse as fundamental, and recognize the political genius which has historically substituted compensation payments for revenge killings. In other words, it is revenge which sets Riches's model into motion in these cases, not the reverse.

Revenge, however, may take more than one form. It may encompass what anthropologists have called "mystical violence": killings by magic, sorcery, or witchcraft. This can happen in social contexts where people are close kin and it is not thought appropriate to strike someone down physically. Revenge may be sought by occult means. Deaths may be attributed to such acts, whether there is, from the people's viewpoint, clear evidence or not. The aggrieved person may be said to have practiced the magic personally or to have hired a sorcerer to do so. Witches may be thought of as practicing their killings outside of the nexus of revenge, but to be brought into it by those involved in processes of revenge. Accused witches may be made in turn the object of revenge attacks, physical or "mystical" (the distinction is one that people may make, but not in terms of an epistemology that excludes magical killings as a possibility). Physical and "mystical" killings may form historical chains in people's minds. Indeed, the potentiality of a switch from one to the other helps to ensure the constant reproduction of fears of violence between categories of people over time. Such fears also depend on the ideology of revenge. Of course, the practical enactment of revenge depends on pragmatic matters. We do not argue that it is a primordial impulse that cannot be contained. Clearly it is contained in many contexts. Contained responses to violent situations are as much a biologically driven response as violent responses can be. We do think, however, that revenge cannot be argued away as an epiphenomenon of other, more fundamental matters, or as a factor that has simply withered away and is no longer relevant to contemporary societies. The struggle to transcend violence (and ideas of revenge that often underpin violence) is one that appears to be a persistent challenge in human societies at all times. We can see the impulse either in psychological or social terms, as one of the conditions of humanity in which social behavior has been developed. In either case, it is basic.

Herein lies an element of contention that surrounds Riches's own transactional model. In his treatment of violence there is a tendency to see the phenomenon in terms of rational action. To do justice to the subtleties of his treatment, we must recognize that he writes that "*with equal efficacy* [Riches's emphasis], violent acts fulfill both instrumental and expressive functions" (1986: 25). The reference to expressive functions here allows his model to encompass matters of emotion as well as of practical intention. Emotionality, however, is not foregrounded. First, Riches argues, "the instrumental function may be the more fundamental, for the 'core' purpose of violence, tactical pre-emption, implies instrumentality" (p. 25). He in fact goes on to say that "if an act of violence has no instrumental aim, it would not be performed" (ibid.). Second, the expressive functions he refers to are presented in social, rather than emotional, terms. Writing of the "expressive functions" of British football hooliganism, he suggests that the hooligan "engaged in fighting against a rival group of fans offers to his group a statement about his own worth as an associate, to the rival group a statement about his own group's political and social capabilities, and to the watching middle classes a 'sceptical' view of working-class opinions about middle-class values" (p. 25). We can make two observations here. First, there is the by now familiar point that the same act constitutes "order" (to the hooligan's associates) and "disorder" (to the putative middle-class witnesses who see it, perhaps, on television). Second, these expressive functions might as well be called "instrumental," since they have to do with specifically intended, if second-order aims. The emotional dimension is therefore largely elided. We are suggesting here that it should be kept in focus. In sociological terms, Riches's analysis of hooligan behavior may be accepted. However, its *impact* is emotional, and this is because of its imputed emotional roots. It shocks the viewer, not just because it is deviant but because it is threatening and is perceived as being "out of control." Similarly with ideas of revenge. If these are seen as emotionally motivated, they are all the more threatening. And if a society's discourse itself is constructed around "the passions," as Hallpike (1977: v) has observed for the Tauade of Papua New Guinea, we certainly cannot ignore the modality of emotion, since it itself is both personally and socially articulated.

This point may also help us to appreciate a further one, that actions have consequences that go beyond their original intentions, and therefore an analysis of violence as a form of *rational* action has its limitations. As we have seen, Riches stresses the instrumentality of violence as a means to an end. Indeed, his analysis is striking because he highlights the efficacy of violence as a form of action and argues further that its core purpose is pre-emption. We must comment here that it may fail in such a core purpose and may unleash consequences far worse than those that its performer had intended. In fact, this is a common result of violent action in contexts that lead to wider conflict and ultimately organized fighting; not to mention attracting the punitive actions of local and state authorities and the vituperation or dislike of networks of neighbors. That performers so often engage in violent acts *without* reckoning on these likely consequences might be taken as evidence for the *irrationality* of violent action in these respects.

One of the problems in making use of Riches's theory is that he grounds it, at least primarily, in what he calls an Anglo-Saxon viewpoint, encapsulated in the English language. Nevertheless, he also claims that its application is cross-cultural and does not depend on the presence or absence of particular terms in a given language. Social processes may exist even if they are not labeled, he argues. The "core" purposes he outlines are therefore meant to be taken as generally applicable. Here he develops a picture of the political relations between performers on the one hand and victims and witnesses on the other. He imputes to the performer an aim, which he agrees may not be met, of persuading the victim and witness of the legitimacy of his act. This, he argues further, may be attempted by claiming that the act was one of tactical pre-emption, carried out in order to curtail certain activities of the victim. Riches seeks to illustrate this argument by reference to the "violent acts associated with rape," which he says performers may justify (to themselves?) as a means of pre-empting a physical response by the victim. But the rapist is simply using further violence to complete the violent act perpetrated against the victim. Riches reduces violence in general to pre-emptive self-defense. While some instances may fall into this category, it is unlikely that all will do so, and the choice of rape as an example begs the question of whether the meaning of the violence is really just a kind of strategic pre-emption or rather has to do with deeper emotional tendencies and aims, including forms of hatred, punitive elements, and fantasized projections. In other words, the idea of rationality is clearly difficult to apply here.

It is difficult to know how much weight to place on this part of Riches's argument. Clearly, it is not one that we wish to make central to our own discussions. He himself notes (1986: 7) that the "primary meaning" of violence may not be tactical pre-emption other than in a "minority of instances," and "many ambitions can stimulate acts of violence" (p. 7). Still he argues that it amounts to "a necessary condition of violence since the performer uses it to justify the acts of violence themselves" (ibid.).

Perhaps we can separate these rather *a priori* arguments from the substantive propositions Riches provides on the phenomenology of violence itself which seem more amenable to use. First, there is his claim that violence is subject to contested legitimacy. Second, he argues that people usually agree on the meanings of violent acts even if they disagree about their legitimacy. Third, this is partly because the practice of violence is highly visible. And last, he suggests violence does not depend on specialized equipment, but only on the use of the body to harm others. He offers these observations as a part of the reason why people choose violence even when they are not compelled to do so. In our work here, we accept all of these observations as productive ones, without arguing that they are absolute in every instance. For example, people may actually not agree at all on the "meaning" of a violent act. And many forms of violence do depend on the development of specialized equipment. Still, the fundamental point – that in many instances of violence the body is the prime tool – is a useful one to bear in mind. Perhaps it helps to explain why the body is also often made an object of torture or is actually maimed in acts of violence. Cutting off children's hands, supposedly to stop them later holding guns, might be taken as illustrative of Riches's general theory. It also leads us into a consideration of the specific forms that violence takes and the reasons for them.

Conclusions and further pointers

Violence is a topic that preoccupies many social commentators today, writing from diverse disciplinary perspectives including anthropology, sociology, history, criminology, psychology, and political science. Indeed, concern with this topic has increased rather than decreased since the supposed end of the Cold War, partly because of the numerous interethnic and inter-regional conflicts that have emerged around the world in the last decade of the twentieth century. Our aim in this book is not to give a complete conspectus of problems relating to violence from all disciplinary viewpoints, since that would be too great an undertaking. Rather we wish to explore the specific contributions that anthropology can make to the topic, and to show how these can feed into approaches made through other disciplines.

Definitional questions are at the heart of this enterprise. David Riches, as we have noted, is an anthropologist who has broached the issues involved most explicitly (Riches 1986). Riches pointed out that the perspectives of the performer, the victim, and the witness all differ, and that the definition of what constitutes an act of violence may also be contested. Violence is a term used rhetorically, not analytically, and its most constant meaning is that it signals acts whose legitimacy is itself an object of conflict. Riches adds another point: violence is effective and is accessible to anyone, hence it is likely to be resorted to frequently in disputes by parties who cannot gain their ends by other means (Riches 1986: 11). Riches's propositions regard violence from a situated, pragmatic perspective, seeing it as a form of rational action directed towards certain ends, rather than as prompted by passion or irrational impulse, or as conditioned by genetically based tendencies towards aggression.

It is clear that Riches's rational action approach is only one among a number of possible anthropological approaches to the question of violence. In terms of phenomenology, however, we highlight three aspects of his argument that are significant. The first is that the topic of violence marks out an arena of contested legitimacy. The second is that violent action is accessible to a wide range of people, although in practice some may have more access to it than others. The third is that violence is effective – it gains people's attention. But, while the first two propositions are by and large true, the third hides many complications. For example, we have to distinguish between short-term and long-term effects. An act of violence may succeed in producing a short-term gain but in the longer run it may provoke a more severe and injurious set of losses for its perpetrators.

9

Further approaches to violence, in addition to the phenomenological-motivational theories of Riches, are largely historical in character, and have to do with causation and antecedents, as well as with the consequences of violent action These two classes of approaches belong to the social sciences, and our discussion will relate to them. Debates on species-level proclivities will on the whole not concern us. Given the plasticity of human mental tendencies, it seems clear that people can, in different contexts, be both highly pro-social (even altruistic) and also highly violent. For example, behavior on behalf of one's own group may be said to exhibit "love." This same behavior may involve killing members of other groups. It is not possible to argue that humans are simply peace-loving nor that they are simply violent by nature, since they appear to be both; and it appears that "love" itself can lead to violence against others in the putative defense of one's own people. This surely is the discursive basis of what is called patriotism in situations of war or collective fighting, leading protagonists in war often to portray their actions as necessary forms of pre-emptive self-defense, precisely in the way that David Riches has delineated. The justification given by the Japanese Prime Minister, General Tojo Hideki, for the attack on Pearl Harbor that brought the United States into World War II is a case in point. The "unintended consequences" of the attack were, of course, precisely the opposite, in the longer run, of his declared intentions.

Using as a focus David Riches's notion that violence pertains to arenas of contested legitimacy, we will use a number of case studies to examine how such arenas develop, how violence is escalated or controlled, and what the longer term, emergent effects are that proceed from these arenas. Although in an earlier era anthropologists succeeded in showing how processes of conflict were controlled and managed in societies they called "tribal," it is evident that today there is a general perception that violent and deadly forms of conflict are becoming harder to control, and that this situation results from the complex interactions between populations which are gestured towards in the term "globalization." We will try to give more specific, historically based meanings to this term through our case studies. In this context we will also examine arguments that attribute patterns of violent conflict to the long-term results of colonialism in the Third World. These arguments are pervasive in the literature and are often strongly motivated in political terms. For our purposes, it is important to recognize that in all cases a multiplicity of interacting causes is at work. Colonialism is only one part of the picture, albeit one that is obviously significant in historical terms.

From the standpoint of causes, then, we may delineate those features that are likely to lead to violence. These include basic features of social structure, cultural perceptions, power distributions, the emergence of "narratives of opposition" in which two sides nurture mutual distrust, and disputes over material resources. These factors can operate at all scales of social relations, from the inter-personal to the interstate, and are intertwined with complex strands of both psychology and history. The ground we cover here is fairly well recognized, but we use discussion of it to move on to a con-sideration of the consequences, and of ways of avoiding the con-sequences of violence by making peace. Our interests in this context include the phenomenology of violence, rhetorical uses of the term violence itself, and arguments about its effectiveness, all of which in fact dovetail with a consideration of violence's consequences. It is here also that we believe the strongest implications can be drawn from ethnographic materials on the societies of New Guinea, espe-cially those of the New Guinea Highlands. These were dubbed in the 1960s as violent societies, seen as such in comparison with some African peoples, such as the Nuer of the Sudan studied by the well-known anthropologist Edward Evans-Pritchard (see e.g. Barnes 1962). At the same time it soon became apparent that these societies often had impressive ways of settling hostilities and making peace, and therefore exhibited a kind of spiraling between violent and non-violent phases of interaction which some saw as their "normal" state. Since then it has further become apparent that such cycles are not timeless but are in fact artifacts of historical processes. This realization returns us to the theater of history as the major site of our observations and reflections on violence. History, in fact, provides a neutral arena in which we can examine events and results over suf-ficient runs of time to test generalizations about the so-called violent or peaceful tendencies of people.

The New Guinea Highlands societies provide arenas also for the discussion of a range of themes relating to violence and ritual, vio-lence and gender relations, the symbolic transcendence of violence, and violence and reciprocity, particularly revenge. Discussions of the blood-feud and revenge practices were a stock in trade of earlier British social anthropology (Evans-Pritchard's work on the Nuer comes to mind once again; see Evans-Pritchard 1940). Subsequently the topic has been seemingly "deconstructed," or has gone out of favor (but see Abbink 2001). This is regrettable because, as we have argued, the imperative of revenge is general to human societies.

One set of arguments regards revenge in terms David Riches would recognize as belonging to rational action theory: violence, far from being simply a cultural imperative or the result of passion, is seen as contingent, situated, political, based on calculations of advantage and disadvantage. Where this viewpoint is empirically substantiated, as for example in R. Brian Ferguson's discussion of Yanomami warfare (Ferguson and Whitehead 1992, Ferguson 1995), it is certainly illuminating and helps us to turn "timeless practice" into history. However, it is a mistake to treat the argument here in either/or terms. One of the best rounded studies of the blood-feud, in spite of inevitable limitations in its data, is Christopher Boehm's book on blood revenge in historical Montenegro, prior to the creation of the Montenegro state in the mid-nineteenth century (Boehm 1984). Boehm's sensitive portrayal makes it quite clear both that high passions were engaged in feuds because of issues of honor and shame, and that in spite of this there was much rational calculation and careful thinking, for example about how and when to bring a feud to a settlement.

A second viewpoint regards revenge as an archaic phenomenon, transcended by and irrelevant to contemporary political processes. Revenge is devalued or discounted as a political process of contemporary significance. One version of this argument relocates violence back to the narrow field of discussion of societies said to be like the Nuer, or like the Melpa of Mount Hagen in Papua New Guinea or the Dani of Irian Jaya. This viewpoint is profoundly mistaken. First, there is abundant evidence that themes of revenge deeply permeate interethnic conflicts today, as witness the case of Kosovo in the Balkans next door to Montenegro and Albania. Here we are dealing with old ideas recycled through new political circumstances and themselves changing rapidly as a result, often becoming heightened rather than disappearing. The significant point here is to see a set of cultural ideas in transformations as they dialectically encounter alterations in the scale of political relations and in the identities of players in the political arena (A. J. Strathern (1992: 245), drawing on the work on Kohistan by R. Lincoln Keiser (1986) and comparing this with materials from Mount Hagen, Papua New Guinea). Materials of this kind are relevant to the understanding of the expanded scale of fighting in Afghanistan, and the part played in this by Islamic ideas which brought the Taliban to power in Afghanistan (see the earlier studies by Barth 1959 and Ahmed 1976).

Second, the societies that are relegated to this category of the archaic past are popping up everywhere as parts of a re-emergent present. One of the fundamental implications of Ferguson and Whitehead's edited volume on *War in the Tribal Zone* (1992) was that states create arenas of "neo-tribalization" at their borders and the tribes so constituted impinge strongly in turn on the states, forming spatio-temporal areas of ambiguity and flux that are from time to time stabilized. This is exactly how we need to see the topic of revenge today. More and more contexts have developed in which political relations are in flux. Within these revenge flourishes as an ideology and a practice because it is one way of pursuing interests and exercising power, but also because it is fueled by strong feelings that emerge out of the domains of kinship and senses of identity. Revenge, and its occasional transcendence, is therefore a vital element to study in any broad contemporary consideration of violence. Revenge does not enter as an "archaic" element destabilizing modern processes of conflict settlement. It is itself reconstituted in the contemporary context; and once this happens, because it is not well recognized or taken into account, conflicts are much harder to settle than they were in earlier historical formations in which feuding took place. In these formations ways of settling feuds went hand in hand with feuding itself. In contemporary contexts by contrast the killings are often tragically cut off from the possibility of settling them. We will pursue this argument with examples from New Guinea, the Balkans, Northern Ireland, and Africa. It is, in effect, the result of the existence of state structures and the mutual impingement of local and national processes that feuding systems cannot realize their own larger cyclicities of violence and peace-making.

It is here too, in our view, that a beginning can be made on the problem of ethnocide. This term is heavily loaded with contested subjective meanings and emotions. People are either keen to label a situation as ethnocide or to deny the validity of such a label. Ethnocide is violence whose legitimacy is contested by almost all external witnesses to it. It is an extreme label. And yet, the processes that make it up are not unusual, but partake of the same elements that cause violence generally. Our argument here, following that of many others (for example on Rwanda and Burundi), is that state structures produce categorical identities that are given positions of unequal power and are not relieved by the operation of cross-cutting ties that are found in tribal contexts. In these circumstances Max Gluckman's "the peace in the feud" (Gluckman 1955) becomes instead "the war in the feud," and once killings have escalated beyond a certain point all controls are lost. Revenge is universalized, along with fear: compensation and reconciliation cannot then operate. In this case, in addition to old ideas leading to monstrous results in new contexts, many old ideas simply cannot operate at all; they become extinct. It is this mix of circumstances, then, that can lead to ethnocide, or the intended categorical destruction of persons labeled in a particular way, whether this involves a few hundred or many thousands of actual deaths and whether the percentage of a population in fact wiped out is 10 percent or 80 percent. Here we come full circle back to David Riches's approach: it is the intentions of the actors that are central here, what they are aiming to do. It is up to the varying roster of witnesses whether the label ethnocide will be applied, and if applied will stick, but in analytical terms intentionality is central, bringing us back to the phenomenological–motivational approach and uniting it with the study of causes and consequences. Intentionality in turn has to be inferred from narratives, and these narratives come to constitute contested histories. In the next chapter we will look at a classic case of such histories, in the context of Rwanda-Urundi, the former colonial territory now divided between the independent states of Rwanda and Burundi.

CHAPTER 2

History and Histories

In asking what kinds of history they should write, some anthropologists have argued that we need to represent the histories that the peoples we study make for themselves. History thus becomes the ethnography of indigenous histories. This we may call an internalist perspective. Externalist perspectives, by contrast, bring to the topic the standpoints and particularly the explanatory theories of the outside observer.

Interpretive anthropology aims at understanding meanings, not at establishing causes and functions, and these meanings are the indigenous cultural conceptualizations. If such meanings, in their cultural relativity and specificity, are the object of ethnographic work, then it follows that historical writing must also take its cue from these meanings, since these are the "realities" we suppose to exist. The meanings may be fragmentary, partial, and situational as postmodernist writers declare, but they are still "there" and can be studied. A problem arises, however, if this viewpoint is applied to historical circumstances when peoples with sharply different sets of meanings meet and interact, especially in colonial contexts where the anthropologist is positioned as a member of the colonizing or ex-colonizing society, and the people studied are those colonized. This is the problem of "epistemological switch." To take an example from New Guinea, when European explorers first entered the Highlands of Papua New Guinea from the 1930s onwards they were widely regarded as spirits. In some places, such as among the Huli and Duna peoples in the Highlands region, they were seen as *tama* spirits who had emerged from holes in the ground and who heralded the end of the world, a cataclysmic event. The anthropologist who writes about this history "knows" (or believes) that this set of indigenous perceptions is not true, and while as an ethnographer he or she may be content to report this indigenous view of history, it may not feel comfortable to leave the matter at that. The historical fact of the outsider entering into the indigenous world forces an epistemological switch of viewpoint in which insider views become phenomenologically "bracketed" (see Taylor 1999: 55–97). Interpretive anthropologists faced with this situation have responded by making a further set of interpretations. Indigenous notions are now seen as being "really" metacommentaries on, or reflections of, wider external realities such as the impingement of colonialism, capitalism, power, exploitation, and the like. An internalist perspective thus dissolves into and is transcended by an externalist one. Indigenous "reality" is after all obviated in favor of an outside perspective.

With those who set out from externalist perspectives the problem is quite different. Here the viewpoints and schemes of analysis are already there. The analyst is likely to consider indigenous accounts as either not very relevant or at any rate as "mystifications" of realities (not the same as metacommentaries). How, then, to make use of indigenous testimonies with this kind of approach? Such testimonies can only be unconscious witnesses to the realities the observer brings to bear on the situation. Yet history is certainly also the study of conscious acts and thoughts that motivate people, so there is a problem also of what to do with the meanings associated with people's own historical consciousness. Faced with this difficulty, the theorist working in the externalist mode has to come to terms with indigenous meanings after all.

Internalist and externalist perspectives thus blend into each other, though at the outset they appear radically different, if not opposed. Both also suffer from difficulties: interpretive approaches reach for the ready-made categories of externalist analysis in order to complete their hermeneutic circles, but do not in themselves question these categories; while externalist theories have at least to take into account indigenous meanings but again do not offer much by way of studying them.

We propose an approach that does away with these difficulties. In encounters between people both sides construct narratives of meanings, and they use these to interpret each other, to come to terms, resist, dominate, collaborate, and so on. These competing narratives are continually tested in events and are reinforced or shattered and remade. As much misunderstanding is involved as understanding, and struggles emerge on the basis of these misfits or "disjunctures" as well as because of conflicting interests and values. History, then, in a composite sense, is the narrative of the interaction of narratives. It exists in the interplay between people based on these narratives and in the changes of narrative over time. Since the narratives influence each other they exist dialectically and their history is a dialectical history; and since such narratives are also often statements about identities, history becomes a story of how such identities emerge dialectically and are subject to change.

An approach of this kind allows us freely to make use of both internalist and externalist insights while insisting that "meanings" are distributed across the spectrum and are constantly subject to negotiation. The application of this approach to the study of violence can be shown very clearly from one such study, by Liisa Malkki, on conflicts between the Hutu and Tutsi peoples in Burundi. These conflicts have led to a series of mass reciprocal killings in both Burundi and neighboring Rwanda since 1972. Malkki worked with Hutu refugees at a camp called Mishamo in Tanzania in 1985–6 and found that the Hutu had developed a remarkable narrative history of the violence between themselves and the Tutsi rulers of Burundi, and a pejorative stereotypical picture of the Tutsi as an ethnic group. Malkki calls such narratives and pictures a mythico-history (Malkki 1995: 52–104). The narrative is clearly one-sided, and a Tutsi narrative would surely be quite different. It is in the disjunction between such historical narratives that the greatest potential for lethal conflict emerges. In pursuing an approach to violence, therefore, it becomes particularly significant to examine the roles, often decisive, played by such divergent narratives in the production of violence. Often, for example, both sides see themselves as victims and the other side as the oppressors; or each side thinks of itself as a minority faced by a majority. Questions of meaning are therefore paramount, but the meanings themselves are contested as a part of the overall contests of legitimacy that both lead to and surround acts of violence. Conversely, when narratives of events are more closely in agreement, the possibilities for settlement are greater. Negotiations between opposing sides in fact often involve a struggle to come to a reasonable level of agreement on the history of events themselves prior to seeking a settlement.

The point made here, about divergent narratives and their role in the genesis or reproduction of violence, is not intended to represent the only strand of a historical approach to the topic, since narratives are just a constituent part of a much larger set of processes involving causes and consequences. However, at every point in a sequence, such causes and consequences are themselves turned into narratives that then feed into the overall processes at work. Narratives also represent historical consciousness and its permutations, and therefore strongly affect, as well as reflecting, intentions and agency. For this reason it is not possible to make a clear-cut distinction between history as it is "scripted" and history as it is "enacted," because scripting takes place continuously alongside experience, and looks both backward and forward. The Hutu mythico-histories developed in the camp at Mishamo were not, nor were they intended, simply as retrospectives, but also as prospectives, giving motivation to the refugees to achieve their aim of returning to and reclaiming their homeland from Tutsi domination as they perceived it. For some purposes, no doubt, it may be valid to make the script/event distinction, but it is important to remember that in life these feed into and off each other, and therefore there is no true dichotomy between them.

Liisa Malkki's study of Hutu refugees in a relocation camp is startling for the clarity with which it brings out both the construction of ethnic stereotypes and the ways in which these stereotypes are geared to the experiences and the production of violence. As such, this study can be taken as paradigmatic of similar circumstances elsewhere. Far from being simply primordial, the stereotypes were generated in quite specific historical circumstances. They drew, however, on longer standing elements of perception and experience, stretching back to colonial and pre-colonial times. A limitation of the study is that it presents only a Hutu viewpoint, although it does make a valuable contrast between the attitudes of Hutu in the camp at Mishamo and those living outside of the camp in the town of Kigoma. We will counterpose Malkki's discussion with that of another ethnographer, Christopher Taylor (1999), whose standpoint partly reflects the ideas of the Tutsi people. Both Malkki and Taylor are concerned with the problem of ethnocide as an extreme case of violence projected onto a collective level. The people whom Malkki studied in 1985–6 were living in Burundi until 1972, when "the Burundi army, controlled by members of the minority Tutsi ethnic group, initiated mass killings of the majority ethnic group, the Hutu, in response to an attempted Hutu rebellion" (Malkki 1995: 2). Malkki says that "these massacres were part of a long history of oppression and inequality between Hutu and Tutsi in Burundi" (ibid.). Groups of Hutu fled the killings as refugees, and some were settled by the Tanzanian government at Mishamo, "a carefully planned physically isolated refugee camp." There, Malkki found many years later, "its inhabitants were continually engaged in an impassioned construction and reconstruction of their history as 'a people'" (1995: 3). By contrast, the Hutu refugees in the town at Kigoma did all they could to blend in with others and to avoid being seen as Hutu at all. This shows how much historical and ethnic consciousness is conditioned by circumstances rather than any innate ethnic feelings.

This introduction to Malkki's narrative presents us immediately with a modern situation, in which an army, controlled by the members of a dominant group, massacres a large number of people (*c.* 100,000 or 3.5 percent of the total population) belonging to the Hutu category, and many of those remaining flee across a national border to a refugee situation in another state whose government, presumably, wishes to contain the conflict and not allow it to spill over into its own area, while still offering a refuge to those who have fled and to obtain international aid in doing so (Malkki 1995: 2). This explains the enclavement and isolation of Mishamo, and the ambivalent relationships that developed between the Hutu there and the Tanzanian authorities. Second, we are informed that the massacre was the culmination of a long history of oppression. Jack David Eller (1999), at the end of his reconsideration of history in Rwanda and Burundi, tells us that we must realize that, while these two areas show many similarities in social and political structures, there were differences between them. In both, the category of those who were Tutsi was seen as holding political power and privilege; but in Burundi there was a further development of "a special class of nobility that came very close to evolving into [a] distinct ethnic group in its own right" (Eller 1999: 240). If this is correct, it might help to explain a part of the "history of oppression" to which Malkki refers.

The historical description of society in both Rwanda (Ruanda in the spelling previously used) and Burundi is made moot by the fact that the units of description themselves have been contested. Jacques Maquet, dealing with Ruanda (the northern part of the Belgian colony of Ruanda-Urundi), says that his fieldwork was carried out in 1950–51, but was directed at establishing an account of the society as he believed it to have been some 40 years earlier, in about 1910, prior to "significant modifications due to European influence" (Maquet 1961: 1). He also tells us that much of his picture of the political organization of the past was based on a kingdom-wide questionnaire administered to some 300 respondents, with a list of 100 questions. He goes on to say that "as might have been expected, the more competent persons on political organization were Tutsi, and in fact more than ninety percent of our informants were Tutsi. Since the number of Hutu and Twa was too small to be of any significance, their interviews were not taken into account in the computation of the results" (p. 3). Given the fact that Maquet's account is avowedly a reconstruction, and that it presents an almost completely Tutsi view of the society, it seems highly likely that it is ideologically biased in certain ways, and that these ways must have corresponded to the interests and circumstances of the Ruandan Tutsi in 1950–51, and to how they perceived Maquet and his

19

indigenous research assistants (who were probably Tutsi). This should be borne in mind when we refer to Maquet's findings. From a historical viewpoint, those of his observations relating to the actual time of his fieldwork would be the most valuable of all. From the perspective of his reconstructive exercise, however, these were largely elided, as were also the views of the Hutu on their contemporary place in the social structure at large. For example, when we read that "the Tutsi migration [as cattle-keeping pastoralists from the north into the territory of agricultural people] seems to have been gradual and peaceful, an infiltration rather than a conquest," we must recall that these are probably derived from the words of Tutsi informants, and prominent ones among these. Maquet does go on to note here that the Tutsi's cattle needed ever more grazing land and Hutu farmers "had to move from the most fertile soils, in the bottom of valleys, because during the dry season these places were the only ones where cattle could find fresh grass" (Maquet 1961: 12). When we consider the meaning of the term "had to move," we are bound to ask what made this obligatory, what form of coercive control was at work? Maquet also dates all of these processes to at least four centuries ago, so we are definitely in the realm of speculation here, as we also are in considering where the Tutsi came from in the first place, although Maquet suggests, presumably on the basis of physical similarities and oral traditions, that they are related by origin to Ethiopian populations, perhaps Somali.

Malkki issues a warning about these forms of categorization for Burundi. She says that it is problematic, in fact, to narrate "the history of Burundi as a story featuring fixed categorical actors ('the Hutu', 'the Tutsi', 'the Twa') conceived as separate and self-perpetuating collectivities" (1995: 21). She recognizes, nevertheless, that this is how the history has in fact been narrated, and that this narration has in turn influenced the historical consciousness of the people she studies. This point supports our argument that history as it is inscribed cannot be separated from history as it is experienced, since experience reflects prior inscriptions while also transforming them. In the study of the production of identities and of how these can lead to violent interactions the point is fundamental.

Malkki herself resorts to Maquet's account of Ruanda in summarizing "scholarly consensus" on the history here. The Twa are a small minority, seen as forest-dwelling potters, hunters, and iron-workers, also singers and dancers; they form less than 1 percent of the population and are "politically marginal" (Malkki, p. 21). Christopher Taylor, however, suggests that some thousands of Twa were also killed in Rwanda in 1994 (Taylor 1999: 95). The Hutu are thought to have settled in Burundi as artisans and cattle keepers as well as cultivators, perhaps from the fifth century B.C. onward. The Tutsi in Burundi belong to two subcategories, the Tutsi-Abanyaruguru and the less wealthy Tutsi-Hima; while the recognized royal family, the Abaganwa "princes of the blood," "are not generally considered to be Tutsi" (Malkki, p. 22). This is the source of Eller's remark about the special characteristics of social stratification in Burundi. However, Malkki goes on to note that the Tutsi-Hima actually emerged as the dominant group within the army and were active in the 1972 massacre (ibid., drawing on an unpublished manuscript by Lemarchand). This seems to be a significant observation. It was those Tutsi in Burundi (who were most closely tied in with the Hutu, and who as a result most energetically sought to dissociate themselves from Hutu connections and to improve their status by entering the army) who allegedly were prominent in the killings.

Malkki, also following Lemarchand, further notes that in Burundi a fairly high number of Hutu were themselves chiefs who held offices in the royal domains (p. 24). This fact might also explain jealousy and resentment on the part of Tutsi-Hima against Hutu of this category. In order to explain the more long-term patterns involved, however, we need to look at further aspects of history. Lemarchand, for example, indicates that there was a sharp evaluative difference in status between the Tutsi-Hima and the Banyaruguru: "Compared with the Hima, whose traditional social image evoked disdain if not outright contempt, the Banyaruguru (literally 'the people from above') enjoyed considerably higher status" (Lemarchand 1994: 11). This in turn was because of their connections to the monarchy. Lemarchand further observes, "That the most violently anti-monarchical elements among the Tutsi in the early 1960s happened to be of Hima origins is perhaps not entirely coincidental" (ibid.). This shows very clearly that, in Burundi at least "Tutsi" was not in fact a unitary category.

The overall question of how a minority of pastoralists could come to exercise control over a much larger number of agriculturalists tends to be answered in terms of the institution of clientage, called *buhake* in Rwanda and *bugabire* in Burundi, sometimes described by observers as a kind of feudal vassalage. All commentators agree that this institution was pivotal. One reason for a Hutu to enter into it as the client of a Tutsi cattle owner was that his patron would then defend him against the possible depredations of other Tutsi (Taylor 1992: 53). Maquet describes *buhake* as follows for Ruanda. An individual (he says this could be either Hutu or Tutsi) who was less wealthy in cattle than another asked protection from a person of higher status, offering in return his services. He offered beer or a honey drink to the wealthier man and ritually asked from him milk and riches, and likened their relationship to that of father and child. The patron then gave this new client usufruct over cattle and their produce and offspring. The client could in turn at a later stage lend these out to his own clients, thus setting up a hierarchy. The patron was supposed to support the client in lawsuits, to help him with bridewealth payments, and to give him a hoe and meat or hides if needed; also to claim compensation on his behalf if he was murdered and to help look after his widow and family. The client in return had to travel with his patron, including on military expeditions, to help rebuild his settlement from time to time; and to present him with beer and also cattle if the patron needed them. Hutu clients, as opposed to Tutsi ones, might be required to work in the patron's fields.

The relationship was perpetuated by succession. The heirs of the client inherited his relationship to the patron's family at the will of the patron himself, who could accept or reject them. He could also select the best of the clients' cows at this time. A client could also end the *buhake* relationship. Maquet thinks that in the period up to about 1920, a client who ended his clientage in this way could keep any cattle that did not come from the patron's family; but that after this time the client's whole herd became forfeit. History enters Maquet's account rather suddenly here, for he tells us in a flurry of facts that, around this time, the administrative chiefs of the Belgian colonial power increased their standing vis à vis the king and the army chiefs, and modified custom "by establishing the principle of the merging of the cows received from the lord [patron] with those acquired independently" (1961: 132). Colonialism and its vicissitudes enter here. Perhaps at this time also other flexibilities that may have been in play disappeared. Recognizing that identities were normally inherited patrilineally through lineage affiliations, Maquet says that nevertheless "the son of a rich Hutu cattle owner and of a Tutsi woman was sometimes regarded as a Tutsi" (p. 135) even though this was unusual. When we come to the times of genocide it was precisely this kind of issue that generated bitterness. Hutu extremist leaders sometimes took Tutsi wives or mistresses, who were regarded as desirable. The children of these liaisons were, however, killed by other Hutu in circumstances of ethnic conflict, precisely because they were seen as Tutsi, or simply because they were of mixed parentage, referred to as "Hutsi" (Taylor 1999: 32). Maquet himself, writing of a much earlier period before the times of ethnocide, notes that although marriages between Hutu and Tutsi were not banned "they were neither favored nor frequent." Further, "marriages between Twa and the two other groups were prohibited" (p. 136).

Maquet concludes from his study of *buhake* that it "granted a minority the means to live ... by the moderate and clever exploitation of the majority" (p. 141). The Tutsi maintained a "pretense to a natural superiority" and assisted poorer members of their category with cattle in order to keep up this appearance. Maquet estimates the Tutsi were never more than 10 or 15 percent of the population, making their level of exploitation supportable. This was also particularly so because the land did not produce much surplus food. Perceptions of membership of the Hutu or Tutsi categories were supported by stereotypes of appearance: "for the Tutsi to be slender, tall, and light-skinned; for the Hutu, to be short, and stout with coarse features" (p. 146). (Here we may ask if these were stereotypes maintained at that time by both sides. Questions about appearances are not among the 100 questions used in Maquet's overall survey. Presumably these were floating stereotypes, proverbially maintained.)

Returning to the theme of colonially-induced changes, the most significant alterations of the system, perhaps in both Rwanda and Burundi, were ones that made social relations more rigidly hierarchical by establishing indirect rule through the existing elites (Malkki 1995: 27). The German and Belgian colonial authorities themselves found it convenient to rationalize the order of local society as natural and essential, using expressions of bodily hexis (i.e. physical appearance and comportment) as the symbols of this order. The colonial experience itself "coarsened" and simplified pre-existing hierarchies and divisions in the direction of rigidly defined ethnic strata. Ethnicity in this sense was a creation of colonization; but a creation, we must note, that had its basis in the indigenous status hierarchy. This hierarchy's historical "naturalization" in colonial times became the basis for the putatively "primordial" identities invoked in post-colonial conflicts. What was altered from the past was not so much the categories of perception as their political validation. Here is another fundamental way-station on the path to understanding ethnocide as it later developed.

Rwanda and Burundi became two separate states as a result of independence arrangements made in 1962. Prior to that they were joined as Ruanda-Urundi under first German, then Belgian colonial rule, from about the end of the nineteenth century (1890). Musinga, a Ruandan king who had usurped the position of a half-brother and was in a weak position, accepted German protection in 1897 and allowed Roman Catholic missionaries in from 1900, encouraging them to settle in areas where his own influence was weak in the hope of consolidating his power (Taylor 1992: 52). The result was the opposite: the missionaries increased their own influence at the expense of his. The working missionaries in the field often "sided with the dominated Hutu majority against the dominant Tutsi (p. 53). While the German government officially supported the king, these French-speaking missionaries from Alsace were engaged in their own processes of establishing influence, sometimes giving cattle to Christian Hutu to care for which the Hutu saw in clientage terms, and offering monetary employment and trade goods. Tutsi patrons complained that their Christian Hutu clients were selling off cattle rather than keeping them in the traditional *buhake* arrangement (p. 55). Hence the Hutu found a way out of the old patterns of domination by joining the church (and its own forms of clientage and gift logic). Taylor writes that "by 1904 mission stations had become small fiefdoms," with their own Hutu clientele, actively resented by the king and his Tutsi chiefs. The king joined with the Germans in defeating a resistance movement led by a priestess in the north where pre-colonial Tutsi royal influence had been weaker and so centralizing control of the kingdom, which passed to the Belgians after World War I under a League of Nations mandate (p. 58). Educated Hutu continued to benefit from the mission system, but Tutsi also joined the church and took up modern education. When Musinga was deposed and replaced by his son, backed by the church, a single hierarchy of civilian Tutsi chiefs was created, as mentioned by Maquet. Since Tutsi now controlled the Catholic church, Hutu began switching to Protestantism (p. 60). The king repudiated approaches to him from the Hutu in 1958, and ethnic violence first broke out in 1959. The United Nations intervened and entered Rwanda in 1960 to oversee elections, which resulted "in an overwhelming victory for the Hutu parties" and the abolition of the Tutsi monarchy, with independence in July 1962. Taylor notes that as a part of this process "tens of thousands of Rwandan Tutsi were killed," and many more fled elsewhere as refugees (p. 61).

The reference to ethnic violence here is sudden. That tensions grew between Hutu and Tutsi as these categories were rigidified and pressed into a coercive state structure in Tutsi control but with an educated and dissident mass of Hutu, is clear. It is also clear that the introduction of a democratic structure of voting led to the collapse of minority power. It is less clear why violence also took place at this time. Perhaps we have to remember that the kingship (based in the southern or "sacred" part of the kingdom) had been supposed to provide a sacred principle of unity for the whole society, and when this principle was breached there was more scope for the physical expression of resentments. According to Taylor, from this time onwards the process of reverse discrimination set in. Authorities measured the fingers and noses of school students; those with thinner fingers and narrower noses were declared to be Tutsi and beaten (p. 61). However, the new military government that took over in 1973 after the collapse of democratic rule discouraged this persecution and the Catholic church's position was also upheld.

Malkki, in commenting on the events in Rwanda from a Burundi viewpoint, suggests that "the violence and fear" in Rwanda propelled "the political imagination of two irretrievably opposed categorical actors" from Rwanda southwards into Burundi (Malkki 1995: 31). There were Hutu uprisings in 1965, 1968, and 1969 which prompted purges and thousands of killings, leading up to the more extensive massacres of 1972, with estimates of the death toll varying from 80,000 to 250,000. Both Malkki and Taylor point out that Hutu intellectuals were particularly targeted in these killings. The Burundi authorities discouraged further involvement by Catholic missionaries, whom they saw as pro-Hutu (Taylor 1992: 62). In Rwanda the Catholics first established themselves in the north, where they favored the Hutu. The first violence against the Tutsi rulers began also in the north of Rwanda where Tutsi control largely stemmed from recent colonial history; and the military government formed in 1973 predominantly represented the Hutu of the north. In his later book Taylor notes that the violence in the north actually began with the supporters of ethnically defined political groups (1999: 4). The Tutsi government of Burundi no doubt perceived in all this a pan-Hutu threat, leading it to engage in what Malkki and Lemarchand call a "selective genocide" (Malkki 1995: 34, quoting Lemarchand and Martin). All Hutu, if not killed, were excluded from the government and from armed service.

Subsequent events in both countries have escalated in complexity, with many further episodes of violence and mass killings in which both sides have been reciprocally involved. Malkki (1995: 259–97), working from published documents, outlines these as they apply to Burundi, mostly cases where the Tutsi authorities killed more Hutu. She highlights (p. 286) not only the scale of these killings but also the range of atrocities committed by soldiers, which were reminiscent of stories of similar atrocities from 1972. The cases she cites are those where Tutsi soldiers inflicted these atrocities on Hutu victims. She refers to them as instances "of a ghoulish repertory of violence" (ibid.).

It must be recalled here that in Rwanda the opposite political outcome had prevailed from that in Burundi. In Rwanda from 1973 a Hutu-dominated northern-based military government came to power after the killings of large numbers of Tutsi. In Burundi the government and army remained Tutsi-dominated, and continued to kill large numbers of Hutu on successive occasions. Malkki's whole study is conceptualized in terms of the Hutu in the Burundi situation, and she highlights the horror of the killings and the continuing plight of very large numbers of mostly Hutu refugees. Taylor, by contrast, writing on Rwanda and in the aftermath of the large-scale killings of Tutsi there in 1994, details the situation of Tutsi refugees in Uganda from 1961 onwards and how refugee camps there contributed to the resurgence of Tutsi military power in the Rwandan Patriotic Front. Both studies show the political role of refugee camps. The whole narrative also demonstrates the influence of historical particularities. Violence spread out from the north of Rwanda to the whole region of the two ex-colonial states, and the violence itself was in part a product of history, since the "Tutsi domination" in the north had been more recent than in the south and Taylor tells us that "the last Hutu polity had remained independent" there until 1928 (1992: 62). A ripple effect therefore proceeded from northern Rwanda through to Burundi, with wide and tragic effects. Such a historical narrative helps to dispel any simplistic version of ethnic conflict in the region. It does not, however, do away with the problem of explaining violence, other than to show that those who undertook it probably did see it as either justified or politically necessary in most instances.

With the large-scale violence we are dealing with here, we have to be able to understand it on the one hand as a product of a kind of collective paranoia; on the other, it was also a product of hierarchical, militarized societies marked by intense competitions for power at their centers, and correspondingly intense efforts to stifle opposition to power. These structures of power were compounded both from earlier indigenous patterns of centralization and from newer arrangements brought into being by colonial administration and post-colonial democracy followed by military takeovers, together with the availability of weapons. But from an anthropological viewpoint, it is the construction of stereotypes that is most telling of all at the level of popular psychology.

Here Malkki's work provides a unique perspective. The Hutu refugees from Burundi living in Mishamo camp had developed a complex "mythico-history" of their identity, which largely consisted of depicting the Tutsi as evil. These narratives amounted to a cosmology of good and evil, in which the Tutsi were demonized. (We might wonder here if this bifurcated epistemology owed something to those very teachings of the Catholic missionaries which the Burundi Tutsi rulers saw as threatening to them because they had been imparted to Hutu pupils. The Christian world view does presuppose a clear distinction between good and evil. Of course, we do not mean to suggest that the Catholic priests preached any intentional ethnic message.)

Malkki describes and analyses the mythico-history in a number of ways. First, there is the refugees' own history of "the Hutu." One element in this is an alliance between the Hutu ancestor and the Twa, since the male incoming ancestor supposedly married a Twa woman as well as a woman of his own Bantu people (Malkki 1995: 61). Nothing of such a myth appears in Maquet's account of Rwanda. This may be because there was only one Twa among those he questioned and we are never told what this Twa said.

The refugees also declared that the Hutu had their own king, who was said to be like a mole who could pass through the earth and emerge elsewhere (a metaphor for the indigenous spread of the Hutu long before the Tutsi came) (p. 62). They repudiated what they said was an official Tutsi version of origins, compulsorily taught in schools, to the effect that Kigwa, an ancestor from the sky, had three sons, Rututsi the eldest, Ruhutu the middle son, and Rutwa, the youngest (a story that certainly does give an appearance of taking a particular line) (p. 65).

The refugees went on to declare that the Tutsi had come from Somalia and had stolen their country. They came looking for pasture for their cows, and the Hutu ancestors gave them land where there was room. Then the Tutsi gave Hutu women dung as manure to help their trees grow, and asked them to come and look after their own children. They gave Hutu men cows and required the Hutu to look after these and guard their own cows (the *buhake* relationship). So it came to be that the Hutu worked for the Tutsi. In this narrative the Hutu are presented as innocents, tricked into servitude by the malign cleverness of the Tutsi (p. 70). The very word Hutu is said to mean servant (p. 71). But the refugees used it proudly to mean "autochthon" (an example of what anthropologists call parodic appropriation, the adoption of a previously stigmatized identity as a proud marker of self).

In another "cluster of themes" the Belgian colonial government was presented as a protector of the Hutu, by comparison with the Tutsi, who behaved tyrannically after independence. The Belgians, they said, punished both Hutu and Tutsi equally if they did wrong, they instituted their form of justice. Here the Belgians represented knowledge and power outside of the Tutsi domination, a sphere of relations to which the Hutu could gain access through education. Belgian knowledge is projected as benign by contrast with the malign knowledge of the Tutsi. The Catholic Belgian mission figures largely here. The Hutu children were declared to have been pioneers in trusting the Belgians. Later, from 1961, the refugees declared, the Tutsi had blocked this road of education, preventing Hutu from entering school (p. 77). And the Tutsi had chased the missionaries away.

Along with these historical narratives went those of bodily stereotypes, seen as linked with moral characteristics. The stereotypes of the body were exactly those we have already met from the early work of Maquet, and were closely related to those put out by early German administrators. The Tutsi were said to be tall, thin, and beautiful, unable to do painful chores; whereas the Hutu were said to be vigorous, and capable of hard work, unlike the rather delicate Tutsi: "It is we who cultivate the fields, it is we who nourish the Tutsi," they said. "They eat our sweat" (p. 80).

In explaining how this servitude came into being the refugees suggested that a lazy Tutsi father in need of wealth would tempt a Hutu man with cows into a marriage with his daughter. Educated young Hutu men were said to be seduced into such an arrangement because "the Tutsi girls are much more beautiful than the Hutu girls" (p. 82). But the Tutsi wife is said to be lazy, and the Hutu have to work hard to support her and her family. The children take the form of their mother and so this bodily form is desired (p. 83). Here we must comment that this narrative is emphatically not a representation of an ordinary *buhake* relationship. It is a modern myth of contemporary relations, up to the time of the massacres of 1972. We may recall Maquet's observation that intermarriage between Hutu and Tutsi was infrequent in the past, and that the groups were largely endogamous.

The refugees had complete body maps, remarking on a continuous range of Hutu–Tutsi differences, and stressing Tutsi arrogance. These maps were also related to stories of atrocities, which Malkki calls "necrographic maps" (p. 89), minute descriptions of what could be done to body parts: descriptions of how Tutsi split Hutu into two, how they forced mothers to eat the fingers of their babies, or how Tutsi girls pushed bamboos into the vaginas of Hutu girls up into their mouths (p. 91). The powers of the mind and the reproductive powers of the body are highlighted in these descriptions, which are mementoes of, if not recipes for, ethnocide. The refugees declared that the Tutsi wanted "to equalize the population" (p. 91), a clear reference to "ethnocide."

These stark accounts make it clear how, once stereotypes of good and evil are created and are mapped on the body, the violence of ethnocide becomes thinkable and doable. Here such violence is imputed to the Tutsi. Clearly it could in principle work either way. In Rwanda in 1994 this came about, generating narratives of atrocities which mirrored those from Burundi but with a reversal of agency. Christopher Taylor's second book (1999) records, and reflects on, this side of the overall picture. His account, fueled by personal experience of the events involved and his own enmeshment in them, stresses both history, discourses, and notions of the body and being which were important in his earlier (1992) book. He also discusses gendered aspects of violence. We have already seen how stereotypes of beauty, desire, and trickery persistently entered the cosmology of the Hutu refugees, and Taylor implies that violence against women has been a significant part of what has happened (see also Declich 2001 on rape during the civil war in Somalia). He also foregrounds the activities of the *Interahamwe*, youth attack parties organized by the political party of Rwanda's Hutu president Habyarimana. He says these were vigilantes who set up roadblocks, beat people, and used machetes, clubs studded with nails, and grenades (1999: 33). This aspect reminds us of similar youth organizations which have been developed as political tools of violence elsewhere, for example in Sri Lanka. When we are considering the genesis of extreme violence, it is important to realize that much of it emerges from the militarization or paramilitarization of youth groups who are specifically trained by their political superiors to kill others, and who seek group prestige and personal advancement by doing so. Taylor (p. 84) points out that the *Interahamwe* became "death squads."

The history of events in both Rwanda and Burundi underlines this point more generally since it indicates that large-scale killings are carried out mostly by military and paramilitary personnel. In theoretical terms this is significant since it speaks to the issue of contested legitimacy. Naming a conflict "a civil war" or "a fight between two political factions" or "an interethnic confrontation" means in each case that a claim to legitimacy is being staked. If the conflict is called "war" this may make it more justifiable, and therefore possible, to kill civilians who are identified with the military enemy. Calling a struggle "political" appeals to different political visions and ideologies, and so also gives it an aura of justification. And calling it "ethnic," as has often been pointed out by analysts, also dignifies violence by appealing to putatively primordial forms of identity. As we have seen, forms of identity may indeed be rooted in the past, but their political valorization, and even their fundamental lineaments, shift with the politics of power in general.

Taylor illustrates this last point with reference to Rwanda and Burundi myths of origin. He cites a Tutsi version of a myth from early colonial times. In this the legendary first king of Rwanda, Gihanga, had three sons Gatutsi, Gahutu, and Gatwa. Gihanga entrusted a full pot of milk to each son, asking him to guard it during the night until his return (Taylor 1999: 75). Gatwa drank the milk and fell asleep. Gahutu became tired and dozed off, spilling some of his milk by accident. Only Gatutsi stayed vigilant and kept his pot full, so Gihanga gave him the right to rule Rwanda and to own cattle. The claim made here for the Tutsi is not like the claims made against them by the Mishamo camp refugees, that they are clever but malign; rather, the claim is that they were faithful and competent, and so deserved their superior status. The Burundi refugees' version of this story was that the Tutsi claimed that the ancestor Kigwa descended from the sky and had three sons, the eldest Rututsi, the next Ruhutu, the last Rutwa, and that by the mere fact of genealogical primogeniture the Tutsi claimed to be superior (Malkki 1995: 65). Other versions of origin stories deny that the three categories had a single origin at all. Taylor's analysis makes it clear that such variations depended on the political expediency of the moment. Until 1958 most of the Tutsi leaders in Rwanda adhered to a story of separate origins, while Hutu politicians, keen to obtain a stake in national politics, claimed a single origin. After the Belgians began replacing the hitherto favored Tutsi with Hutu appointees, Tutsi nationalists now abandoned their version of separate origins and declared that appointments should be on the basis of education alone. This was at a time when more Tutsi than Hutu were educated. In this way Taylor constantly tacks backward and forward between the "Hamitic hypothesis" of the separate origins and later arrival of the Tutsi in Rwanda and Burundi, and the political exigencies and vicissitudes of modern times. He takes a nuanced stand. Differences between these groups did and do exist; but the picture from physical anthropology, linguistics, and oral traditions is complex and often confusing. Nevertheless, it is important to recognize, he says, the ideological ways in which these complexities have been used, and to point out their role in the genesis of extreme political stances leading to ethnocide.

Turning back for a moment to some aspects of history that have a longer background than the traumatic events stemming from independence, we find that Maquet gives yet another version of an origin myth that is concerned only with the category of the Tutsi themselves. In this the first king of Ruanda-Urundi was called Nkuba, a name that means lightning. He lived in the sky with his wife Nyagasani, their two sons Kigwa and Mututsi, and their daughter Nyampundu. The three children fell from the sky and settled on a hill, where Kigwa married his own sister, and later Mututsi married his niece, the daughter of his brother and sister. The descendants of these marriages became the two royal clans, who married each other, and formed a kingly line seen as divine (a pattern commonly found in the other parts of East Africa). This myth justifies the rule of a particular set of Tutsi. It does not even mention the Hutu and Twa, though we can recognize them in the name of Kigwa, who has appeared in versions we have given earlier (Maquet 1961: 108). We have therefore a clear demonstration of how myth changes over time.

Further, in Ruanda, the kingdom was in pre-colonial times defended by an army, under an army chief, stationed in the northern borders of the kingdom. The army was recruited along lines of clientship. The king or *mwami* asked his own Tutsi clients to bring their sons to court for military training. They were then trained and stayed permanently in service; and membership of the army also continued patrilineally over time, so that whole patrilineages of people became units within the army. The army itself was divided into warriors and cattle herders. Its members had to present cattle to the king on his accession and to provide the court with milk. The army also sought to expand the king's domains, and the kingdom was constantly engaged in annexing and looting other areas (Maquet 1961: 109–17). These details graphically reveal that Ruanda was an expanding militaristic state with a sacred king at its center (compare Southall 1956 on the Alur of Uganda). Surely this militaristic and Tutsi-based ethos was not entirely absent in the context of colonial and post-colonial events.

There was, however, another dimension at work. Taylor's earlier book provides this. The king's body was itself a symbolic focus expressing the relationship between Tutsi and others in terms of an idea of communicational flow (see also Taylor 1999: 119–26). The term for the king, *mwami*, had connotations of spreading out, being well known, fruitfulness, and lactation (Taylor 1992: 25); also of fluids of fertility, and urine seen as a source of fertilizing rain (p. 27). Taylor suggests that some of these elements of meaning were taken over from earlier Hutu kings by the Tutsi monarchy, who imitated Hutu rituals of rainmaking. Cattle themselves were represented in myth as having emerged from lakes, primordial sources of fertility linking sky and earth. (The same is true for pigs in some New Guinea myths.) The flow of cattle between persons was seen as ensuring the reproductive process in general (another familiar theme with echoes from the Nilotic region, see Evans-Pritchard 1940 on the Nuer people). Blockage of the pathways of this process was seen as inimical to social relations, leading to sterility and extinction. Royal rituals emphasized "the importance of liquid aliments" (Taylor 1992: 36). In one ritual cycle, called the Path of Inundation, the king's ritual experts were instructed to capture a Twa woman past childbearing age from the forest just outside the kingdom, and to shed her blood along with that of other animals colored black (for death) in order to remove blockages of the flow of fertility in the kingdom at large. The Twa woman's body, Taylor says, represented disorder. Her sacrifice was a means of re-establishing order. Taylor notes that the Twa "have perennially been denigrated by the Tutsi and the Hutu" (p. 38). Taken as a whole, these details help us to see that there was a cultural and ideological basis for Tutsi hegemony, based on cattle, which blended Tutsi and Hutu cosmological ideas, and also encompassed notions of blockage and sacrifice. This last observation ties in with Taylor's later statement on the terror of 1994, that political and historical analysis cannot explain everything, since "something cultural happened as well" (1999: 101). In effect, he argues that in a reversal of the former practices of ritual sacrifice in Rwanda, "it was overwhelmingly Tutsi who were the sacrificial victims in what in many respects was a massive ritual of purification, a ritual intended to purge the nation of obstructing beings" (ibid.). If so, we would have to explain how the former symbolic order, which depended on Tutsi as the agents of fertility and flow, came to be reversed. We would also have to ask if the same form of explanation will apply to Burundi, where Tutsi mostly killed Hutu. The earlier rituals fix "blockage" on post-menstrual Twa women from outside the kingdom in Rwanda, not on Hutu males inside it.

Taylor is surely right in insisting that cultural elements, albeit transformed and manipulated, are at work in ethnocidal circumstances. Malkki's study shows, without fully following it through, how the culturally refashioned mythico-history of the Hutu at Mishamo, could feed immediately into a collective enactment of justified revenge. It seems important here to keep our own emphasis on reciprocal revenge in play while exploring Taylor's delineation of cultural elements in the domains of sacrifice and terror. Taylor himself also disavows any attempt to explain away genocide as "caused by culture" (p. 102). But he quotes with approval Malkki's statement that "historical actors mete out death and perpetrate violence mythically" (Taylor 1999: 104, quoting Malkki 1995: 94). This also resonates with our point that history as it is inscribed cannot be separated from history as it is experienced. Since history is sometimes inscribed by experience on the body itself and the body then becomes a repository of memory (Taylor, p. 105, quoting Clastres), we can see that specific forms of bodily atrocities are ways of recording history, the history of terror itself.

Recognizing the partly military character of the Rwandan kingdom, Taylor notes that it was an expansive one and that "it was through obstruction, impoverishment, strangulation, murder, and sorcery that the Rwandan king manifested the coercive aspect of his power over subjects and adversaries" (p. 126). Rwandan warriors carried curved knives used to cut off the genitalia of slain enemies. Women were also sometimes victims. Victors might "cut off the breasts of women" of a defeated group (ibid.). Kings themselves were sometimes sacrificed in order to ensure the continuing fertility of the land and its people.

Taylor's argument is that Hutu extremists also participated in the ideological framework of ideas about flow and blockage and turned these back on the Tutsi. He quotes (p. 131) a speech in which a Hutu politician said they would throw Tutsi bodies into a river that flows northwards, so that the bodies would flow back towards Ethiopia, where the Tutsi supposedly came from. An image of flow is certainly involved here. Another element also appears when we are told that ordinary Hutu at roadblocks were ordered to save their own lives by killing Tutsi, thus spreading the responsibility for these killings and granting them some legitimacy, a move in accordance with the element of contested legitimacy in violent acts.

With regard to the theme of impaling victims, Taylor notes that in pre-colonial times Rwandans inserted wooden stakes into the anus of cattle thieves "and then pushed it through the body, causing it to exit at the neck or mouth" (p. 139). Cattle theft blocked the path of social relations, and there was considered to be some symbolic appropriateness in punishing it by obstructing the conduits of the body itself with a pole or spear (p. 139).

These examples do show relevant connections with past practices. And we could argue that either Hutu or Tutsi could employ them as means of purifying the nation, appropriating a symbolism that previously had belonged to monarchy. The problem is, rather, to explain the scale of the killings. These were not selected, representational sacrifices but large-scale massacres. It is the efficacy of violence, in David Riches's (1986) terms, that we need to think about here. Was it an effective, pre-emptive way of dealing with conflict to kill so many? Hardly, we may comment, because of the huge aftermath of bitterness and feelings of revenge that must have flowed from such acts of collective punishment of "the others," not to speak of the protracted international trials for genocide which were held later.

There is a final element of significance here, which Taylor calls "the dialectics of hate and desire" (p. 151). It is a theme that emerges clearly also in the Mishamo camp refugees' mythico-history. It has to do with sexual relations that cross Hutu–Tutsi identities. First, Taylor notes that women played active military roles in the conflict, both as fighters and as informants. They could be targeted for pragmatic reasons. But he suggests that the 1994 genocide aimed to do more – to reassert the cosmic order of the Hutu state, seen in patriarchal terms (p. 154). A part of this drive was in opposition to intermarriage between Tutsi women and Hutu men, which produced children who were officially Hutu but with Tutsi connections. Taylor goes on: "during the genocide itself Hutu men with Tutsi wives were often forced to kill their spouses themselves in order to prevent their own deaths and a more gruesome death for the wives" (p. 156). In counterpoint to this, Hutu male vigilantes raped Tutsi women as a way of violating and humiliating them (p. 158). The regime of President Habyarimana instituted a campaign against single young urban women, charging them with vagabondage and prostitution (p. 161). Many of these women were educated Tutsi. They were seen as having the capability of exercising power through both their minds and their bodies. In 1990 a Hutu magazine published a set of rules for behavior. Of ten rules, three concerned sexual relations. The first rule declared that all Tutsi women work for their own ethnic group, so that any Hutu who marries a Tutsi is a traitor. The second rule declared that Hutu women were better than Tutsi. And the third adjured Hutu women to be vigilant and curb their men's sexual tendencies. At one point a communication from the Hutu army told young Hutu women to put on good dresses in order to meet incoming French allies, because "the Tutsi girls are all dead, so now you have your chance" (p. 175).

"The Tutsi girls are all dead." The statement raises again the question of ethnocide and the purposes of violence. Taylor notes that when the Rwandan Patriotic Front soldiers, led by Tutsi ex-refugees, regained control in Rwanda, 1,500,000 Hutu had been driven out, "but 80% of Rwanda's Tutsi population was now dead" (1999: 51). Was the violence instrumental? Was it rational? Was it regarded by its perpetrators as fully legitimate? Was its core purpose pre-emption? The scale of these killing events transcends any rationality model of explanation. Perhaps a part of their further explanation lies in the idea of winning a war at all costs. Another lies in the kinds of emotionally saturated symbolism, including sexual symbolism, which Taylor explores. Other dimensions point to the complex but discernible patterns built up piece by piece in pre-colonial and colonial history, each process adding to the potential for a lethal result, but none in itself determining such a result.

In the next chapter we examine some further cases and also consider them from the point of view of contested legitimacies.

CHAPTER 3

The Domain of Contested Legitimacy: Riches's Triangle

David Riches's (1986) model of violence as an act entails the kind of divergence in narratives that we have followed in the case of the conflicts in Rwanda and Burundi in the preceding chapter. In particular he notes that while victim and witness may condemn an act of violence, the performer may see the matter in a very different light. There is a triangle consisting of performer, victim, and witness. The apparent simplicity of this triangular representation hides a large number of complexities. For example, there may or may not be a direct relationship between all three parties, and this circumstance affects their narratives. Witnesses may be multiple and themselves have divergent views, depending on whether they identify with the performer or the victim, and their disagreements may lead to further violence. All parties, however, maintain their own narratives, regardless of agreement or disagreement with others, and it is from the genesis and divergence of these narratives that the history of a violent act or a series of such acts is built up. Again, it is in the divergence of the narratives that the contest for legitimacy takes place. An event, seen in this light, is not simply a record of a parti cular attack or harmful act, although sometimes the facts may be disputed at this level also. Indeed, this latter situation is precisely the case in most narratives regarding hidden violence, such as assassination, sorcery or witchcraft (to which we will pay attention here and elsewhere in the book, as appropriate). Apart from these cases, the event itself must be seen as characterized by its moral standing. What is a vile terrorist attack to some is seen as a heroic defense of a cause by others, while both sides may agree that a certain number of people were killed. Disagreements of this kind are most poignant within political boundaries defined by nationality and state structure, as when a lone bomber destroys a large part of a government building in protest against state power or when schoolchildren kill their schoolmates. (The bombing of the federal building in Oklahoma City and the shooting at Columbine High School in America in 1996 and 1999 stand as examples.) In such cases the disapproval and dismay of witnesses at the event may influence shifts in government policy itself; but hidden, dissident factions may have quite a different opinion, even if it is not publicly expressed.

More obvious circumstances of divergence arise in contexts of attacks and intrusions across political boundaries, which have become a major preoccupation of the metropolitan powers in post-Cold War years. Hijackings and suicide missions provide compelling examples here, and correspond to schemes of coercive reciprocity. Hijackers usually demand the release of persons held by a state power as political prisoners, on pain of the death of innocent hostages. Lives are bargained for with lives, leading to harsh dilemmas and variant outcomes, as happens also in systems of blood-feud. While the actualities of the exchanges involved may be brutally clear, the narratives may be unclear or may waver from one moment to another. Hijackers may kill a single victim to demonstrate their willingness to kill and so to capture serious attention, but otherwise they may not elaborately justify their acts. Almost always the context is one that involves at least two opposed nations or states, as in the case of the Air India plane that was hijacked by Kashmiri separatists in late 1999. The narrative of the hijacking thus becomes the larger narrative of competing recriminations between the nation-states or state splinters involved. Since nation-state ideology lends itself potentially to exploitation by any given entity whose members wish to claim nationhood, it is evident that an endless set of possibilities for contested claims of legitimacy of action is thereby created. The legitimacy claimed is based on perceptions of identity, but is pursued in pragmatic terms through negotiations, or, where this is considered preferable, justified, or necessary, violence. These patterns of hijacking were further altered with the hijacking of four US commercial flights on September 11, 2001, on a combined mission of suicide and murder in which the hijackers succeeded in crashing into and destroying the World Trade Center in New York City and damaging the Pentagon building in Washington, causing over three thousand civilian deaths.

In Riches's propositions a characteristic of violence is that it is performed in contexts of contested legitimacy and itself provokes such contests. Reading this in a different way, we can also say that contexts of contested legitimacy themselves conduce towards acts of violence. Such acts may take the form of protests as an attempt to gain legitimacy, or of coercive force to put down such protests and reassert legitimate government control. Violence in these contexts, as in many others, is a gamble. It may pay off or it may backfire. The history of conflicts in Northern Ireland provides examples of violence used as a means of argument in this way, and in this chapter we will use case history material from this area to illustrate the discursive domain of contested legitimacy sketched here. We will draw on Allen Feldman's study *Formations of Violence* (1991) for some theoretical underpinning and ethnography in this regard, with particular reference to the theme of torture and its place in the political process of conflict between the British authorities and IRA fighters, but also as a mechanism of control within political factions themselves. Torture may depend on the suppression of one corner of Riches's triangle, that of the witness; although in another sense it may also depend for its effectiveness on rumors that are spread through either fictitious stories or actual experiences.

How the contest of legitimacy is settled greatly affects the outcome of conflicts. If ethnocide is greeted with widespread condemnation, it is perhaps less likely to be repeated, particularly if the condemnation is backed up by sanctions. The role of the witness is crucial and complex. For example Russia's war against Islamic rebel forces in Chechnya in 1999–2000 was viewed by the Russian government of the day as a necessary act of retaliation against terrorists, but by international witnesses as involving acts of violence against civilians that violated human rights and could possibly destabilize the wider region, although direct intervention was not seen as feasible. As long as there is no direct contest between these divergent witnesses the question of legitimacy will be left unresolved, making it more possible for the conflict to continue. The role of the Russian people as themselves witnesses of the conflict is also important. As with blood-feuds again, the tally of military deaths, and the interpretation of the meanings of these deaths, are important factors in influencing opinions.

Similar considerations apply in Northern Ireland, where the contexts of struggle are different, but the various witnesses of violence are not just passive spectators of it, in large part because when violent acts are common and diffused through the populace, all witnesses are also potential victims and everyone may be suspected of being in some sense a performer, causing Riches's triangle to implode on itself.

The historical conflict in Northern Ireland over the future of the province offers an opportunity to consider the question of violence and contested legitimacy in a sharp form, for here we have two entrenched political sides, appealing to different sets of identities in relation to the same historical events, and each claiming legitimacy for their viewpoint in terms of their relations to those events. Moreover, both sides proverbially see themselves as victims of history, while accusing the others of being in a sense its perpetrators. Conflict situations of this sort, which are found also in the Middle East between Israelis and Palestinians, and in the Balkans between Albanians and Serbs, are notoriously hard to mediate or bring to an agreed resolution. They also raise for the analyst the question of the purpose of violence. Since both sides have political aims that are clearly articulated, it might seem that violence has as its core purpose the achievement of those aims, through the intimidation of opponents and the pre-emption of force. However, if the aims of violence are political, they can be sought by other means, which are constantly at the disposal of those involved in the conflict. Second, severe sanctions are brought to bear, wherever possible, on those who commit illegal acts of violence, impairing their abilities to pursue their aims. Third, political aims can be achieved in democratic contexts only with the support of the populace at large, and violent acts tend to be regarded by people in general as problematic, partly because they fear that they themselves may be harmed. Such acts also provoke extreme reactions of a punitive or revengeful character from the other side and therefore may prove costly to their perpetrators. All of these considerations show us that rational action models of violence do not explain everything about violence in Northern Ireland, or anywhere else where similar political conditions hold. McFarlane, for example, writing in the mid-1980s, pointed out that rural people considered violent behavior to be aberrant, and an intrusion into their way of life from the urban context of Belfast (McFarlane 1986, drawing on work by anthropologists). Severe damage to property and the loss of human life that tends to occur after the explosion of car bombs generally mean that those who claim responsibility for these acts are at risk of losing legitimacy in the eyes of the public, particularly if the damage is done in their home areas and not far away, for instance in London. Since much of this kind of violence is committed by, or is attributed to, the IRA, the question of the motivation and intentions of the members of this organization does require an answer.

This answer, however, is unlikely to be found in terms of folk or analytical attributions of essences. Rather, it has to be looked for in the symbolic frameworks of action which people bring to their political convictions. The actual name of the organization we have cited, the Irish Republican Army, gives a clue here. The organization calls itself not a movement or a political party, but an army, meaning that it sees itself as conducting a war; and in wars ambiguous violence is converted in many instances into the legitimate use of force to attain one's ends, provided those it is used against are labeled as the active enemy. From this point of view, setting off a bomb in London would constitute an act of war and the ensuing "collateral damage" would be an inevitable consequence of the state of war itself. That this appears to be the ideological justification involved is supported by the historical reluctance of the IRA to decommission arms, even though this refusal has imperilled the overall "peace process" and the power-sharing between parties in the Northern Ireland Assembly, leading the British government to threaten the reimposition of direct rule. The IRA's putative reason for this refusal is that disarming would amount to admitting defeat in the "war" when they have never in fact been "defeated." The semantics involved here might appear to be tortuous; but given the historical fact that the British government's major form of visible presence in Northern Ireland has since the inception of the "Troubles" in the 1960s been the British Army, the ideas involved are not surprising. Direct rule from Westminster is the mark of a military and imperial presence and all it stands for. Writing of the situation up to the early 1980s, the historian John O'Beirne Ranelagh (1983: 269) noted that "the year 1972, following direct rule, was the most violent in Northern Ireland's history with 467 killed (103 soldiers) and 4867 injured." He goes on to note the correlate of this: "during the 1970s the IRA and their 'loyalist' counterparts seem to have become dedicated to violence as an end in itself." Can this be so? The answer must depend once more on aims. If the aim of the IRA is to achieve a complete break from the United Kingdom, such as was achieved earlier for the Republic of Ireland, then devolution as such does not meet this aim, and they could logically refuse to disarm because they were still at war. It becomes difficult, however, to wage a war when the public at large, even among those with whom the IRA ostensibly identifies, no longer supports it. The balance of claims in the contest of legitimacy accordingly shifts, and it is the category of witnesses that is crucial to this process of shifts. A struggle is therefore bound to set in between adherence to a diehard ideological framework and accession to the realities of political consensus.

However, matters are again not so clear. A refusal to disarm is not the same as the continued exercise of violent acts, hence it cannot attract the same level of either praise or opprobrium. And it can, on the other hand, act as a political catalyst, influencing the state of politics not just on the IRA's own avowed side of the conflict but among its opponents also, who have been split by the impasse over arms control, one faction declaring that this shows power-sharing is unworkable and untenable, the other attempting to save the process of reconciliation necessary for a democratically devolved internal government to come into being. In this way, a muted threat of the capacity for violence, signaled by a refusal to disarm, achieves more than the exercise of violence itself could do. And the refusal to disarm can be claimed by its supporters to be an act of sovereign principle whereas its detractors will declare that it shows the other side to be "in league with terrorists." The aim of refueling conflict and re-energizing opposition between people is thereby also achieved through the return of the semantics of polarization. And as long as the conflict continues it can be labeled as war, and victory in the war can continue to be pursued. Perhaps it is in this light that we have to interpret acts of intransigence of this kind, rather than as simply proof of dedication to violence "as an end in itself."

Ranelagh's remark, delivered at the end of his book, cannot, however, be simply dismissed in favor of a reconstructed model of rationality directed unambiguously to public and political aims. There is first the point that even a state of war requires a form of consensus. In the shared framework of political ideology in Western Europe, armies are drawn from and represent nation-states. Sets of fighters who do not have this legitimate role cannot be regarded as armies in this sense of the term. Such groups can claim that they are fighting on behalf of a nation-state that is yet to come into being and that they therefore do have legitimacy, at least in their own eyes. Still, they cannot declare war on behalf of such a notional nation unless the majority of the people who constitute it (or would constitute it if it existed) mandate this. Since the IRA has no official status, no such mandate exists, although its analogue in popular sectarian support may do so. Further, the British government does not recognize any sovereignty on the IRA's part and therefore cannot grant it the right to wage war. Instead, it labels its acts of violence as terrorism, and uses this label as a justification for acts of suppression. On the other hand, the "loyalist" opponents of the IRA who espouse armed action do, in a sense, grant the IRA a greater legitimacy than the British government does, seeing themselves also as an army, fighting their opponents as an army. The field of contested legitimacy is therefore complex and confusing. In the peace process itself the aim is to remove legitimacy from violence as such and to grant it only to an elected parliamentary form of political action in a devolved assembly. We may suggest here that opposition to this aim stems from the idea that violence is effective as a political tool and that it is easily accessible and its effects visible – all elements that are found in Riches's model. But opposition also stems from the entrenched behavior patterns and the internal, self-defining rewards and values that characterize the organization of tight-knit, secret groups that are not accountable for their actions to outsiders. We may be reminded here of Riches's remark about British football hooligans, another enclave group and one with few claims to wider legitimacy in their society: the hooligan is engaged primarily in offering to his group a statement about his own worth as an associate, but also in a statement of power to rivals/enemies, and of defiance to others (Riches 1986: 25). Exactly this same roster of internal rewards would apply in organizations such as the IRA, in addition to their own "mythico-history" or their belief in their historical role within such a narrative. All of these elements, then, could enter into a continuing adherence to violent activity. Finally, it needs also to be recognized that any pattern of behavior can be reproduced if there are coercive patterns at work to make it do so, and no doubt such coercive patterns are often generated by leaders who have most to gain from them and most to lose from any deviation from them. "Violence in itself" therefore here subtends a whole organization and the norms developed within it.

These issues need to be borne in mind when we consider a work dating from the mid-1980s which gives an anthropological account of violence in Belfast between 1969 and 1986, using a number of testimonies and oral histories, and setting them into a framework of theory derived partly from Michel Foucault and his concept of discourse (Feldman 1991). Feldman focuses on bodily practices and the use of space as territory, taking into account both cultural constructions and practices that constitute political agency. The approach has affinities with that used by Christopher Taylor in his study of the Rwandan genocide of 1994. Feldman is particularly interested in the ways in which antagonism is reproduced over time, and he points to "the growing autonomy of violence as a self-legitimating sphere of social discourse" (1991: 5), a process that surely makes the pursuit of peace more difficult. A further focus of his study of space is its categorization as "eulogized, purifying, or defiling spaces that mobilize spectacles of historical transformations" (p. 9).

Feldman gives origin stories entertained by some nationalists, specifically "imprisoned Republican paramilitaries in the late 1970s" (p. 17). These men were conducting political education classes while in prison. Their situation was comparable to that of Hutu elders in the refugee camp at Mishamo, Tanzania, studied by Malkki. They began with a myth of geological division, the division of the island of Ireland from the continental land mass of Europe. This division was presented as a charter for the separate identity of Ireland and for the presentation of the British as interlopers, "undoing what geography had created" (p. 18). Feldman refers briefly also to a Loyalist myth that traces the origins of the Ulster Protestants back to the lost tribes of Israel, thus giving them also a separate identity of their own. (This seems curious, given that Protestants of Scots origin have such a separate identity on their own terms.) He does not present these stories in detail, or say how widespread they were, nor does he comment on the obvious antithesis between "Israel" and "Catholics" implied in the Protestant myth. We catch a glimpse here, at any rate, of processes of mythologizing narratives of origin that we saw documented in detail by Malkki. And Feldman points to an effect of myth we also saw in Rwanda and Burundi. Through origin myth "violence is treated as a psychological artifact and surface effect of the origin," and it is therefore legitimized "by endowing social actors with a predetermined, normative character" (p. 20) in spite of the fact that an outside observer might say that this legitimization is fabricated, and a way of denying personal responsibility for action.

Belfast has been a center of violence in Northern Ireland because of its volatile mix of Catholic and Protestant working-class areas. In these areas, from which Feldman draws many of his examples, something of a specialized subculture has developed with its own categories and terms that index situations of violence and the players in them (for example, the Royal Ulster Constabulary (RUC), who wear black uniforms, are referred to by some Republicans as "black bastards," and prison officers, who wear white shirts are called "polar bears," p. 271). Feldman's ethnography becomes, then, an exploration of this subculture. We will give some examples from this ethnography.

One theme is that of partitions. After severe rioting in Belfast in 1969, sectarian violence increased, and there were large-scale relocations of Catholic and Protestant working-class populations. The effect was to further polarize these populations from one another. In one account, a "Protestant male community activist" told Feldman that they would wire up abandoned houses in streets so that when the Catholics invaded them and turned on the lights the houses would blow up. An example of violence as pre-emption, this instance also illustrates violence as counteraction and as an attempt to make "conquest" difficult. Contexts like this, and almost all of Feldman's categories, are reminiscent not of single acts of violence but of the strategies and tactics associated with war, as when a defeated force blows up bridges and train lines on the route of its retreat.

The resegregation brought about issues of interface between Catholics and Protestants. Clashes occurred along the new boundaries. Such clashes classically occur in conjunction with Orange Order marches in which Protestant marchers attempt to pass through areas that are Catholic. The British Army erects barriers to prevent this. Often, rocks, stones, and firebombs are hurled across the boundary at the army personnel. Since these Protestant marches are triumphalist in character, commemorating the historic military victory by the Protestant William of Orange (William III) against the Catholic King James II at the battle of the Boyne in 1690, a Protestant march along Catholic boundaries "transforms the adjacent community into an involuntary audience and an object of defilement through the aggressive display of political symbols and music" (Feldman, p. 29). (In fact, it is particularly the songs and the imposition on listeners that may spark off violent responses.) Such displays at boundaries are common between antagonists. They are epideictic in character, containing threats and warnings. A triumphalist note certainly adds to their ability to insult the other side. Music and singing carry strongly over space, forcing people to hear them. This political use of music in space is comparable to the practice in some New Guinea societies of staging celebratory dances in conjunction with information that they have just succeeded in killing an enemy leader by sorcery. Where possible, the marchers physically transgress the boundaries as well as projecting their voices across them. Feldman points out that these marches often provoke violence because they transfer political symbols from the center of a community to its edges, where they act as provocations (p. 30). A particularly well-known boundary that repeatedly figures in such outbreaks of violence is between the Catholic Falls Road and the Protestant Shankill area in Belfast. The erection of barriers by the British Army in spaces like these prevents outright clashes but increases the "attraction of violence to this type of space" (p. 31). The same may be said of barriers, roadblocks, and boundaries set up between Israelis and Arabs in contested urban spaces in Jerusalem and elsewhere. The barriers visually enhance the sense of a division and increase paranoid apprehensions, which in turn feeds into attempts at "pre-emptive" violence. Behind the barriers, the community becomes a "sanctuary", which is "pure," while the other side becomes loaded with a sense of impurity as the "outside source of danger" (p. 35). The idea of sanctuary itself is deeply tied in with violence and the fear of violence, because paramilitary operators use community centers as their bases of operation and themselves terrorize people within them (p. 39). Feldman stresses the aspect of this which relates to Protestant state organization, saying that the state, pursuing a counterinsurgency policy, used both the Royal Ulster Constabulary, a largely Protestant force, and citizens' militias to dominate communities and to encourage populist Protestant sentiment. If this is correct, it would help to explain why the Sinn Fein leadership, pressed on the question of disarmament in mid-2001, countered by arguing that "the real issue" was the reform of the

RUC by ensuring Catholic membership of it. This must surely be modified by the presence of the British Army, which is required to, and does, protect Catholic as well as Protestant communities from attacks. Feldman, however, stresses the overall erosion of ideas of sanctuary by the incursions of paramilitaries, which produced maps of another spatial category, the *runbacks*, networks of pathways permitting evasion of the police. These exist in conjunction with *safe houses*, where people can hide, and *wash houses*, where paramilitaries clean up after killing people. Invoking the idea of sacrifice as Taylor does for Rwanda, Feldman writes that "entry into the space of sacrifice [i.e. killing] and exit from it are qualified by contact with impurity and by decontamination rites" (p. 45). How seriously we are to take this idea of sacrifice is not entirely clear. In another sense, Feldman notes that the "confessional community," that is, the world of ordinary people, itself becomes sacrificed to paramilitary imperatives. Surely the same could also be said of Rwanda, where the Interahamwe youth groups also functioned as paramilitaries. We may note here that the paramilitaries perhaps regarded their cause as sacred and therefore as justifying killings, but a sense of impurity, i.e. of the illegitimacy of their acts of violence, remained with them, as with others. McFarlane (1986: 193) notes that this ambiguity leads to exculpation. Significantly, such exculpatory remarks take the form of a discourse of revenge. "Sure it would sicken you ... but d'ye remember what some of that crowd did to that fellah in ... ". The citation of revenge makes a claim to legitimacy here which stands in opposition both to "senseless violence" and to state authority.

Feldman provides a roster of stereotypes of characters involved in violence, which explains how these are seen as emergent cultural stereotypes to which experience is adjusted. These stereotypes represent the steps by which acts of violence are institutionalized and come to be seen as the perquisites of roles and statuses of people. Feldman lists "hardmen, gunmen, butchers, doctors, stiffs, ghosts, and black men" here (p. 47). *Hardmen* were a previous category of tough men who fought with their fists within their areas and represented the claims to autonomy of their communities through the immediate physical risking of their bodies in fights. *Gunmen*, who came later, transgressed this pattern. An extreme manifestation of this transgression was found, Feldman says, in the Shankill *Butchers*, who killed so many people that they often included Protestants among their victims by mistaking them for Catholics, and became a sign of random violence. On the whole, however, they contributed to the idea of deliberate genocide, Feldman declares (p. 64); and he notes that each death contributes to the narrative of "ethnicity," using "ethnicity" as a way of labeling Catholics and Protestants. He does not elaborately explain this usage, but simply adopts it. It clearly declares a set of affinities with narratives of ethnic violence elsewhere. For example, from Rwanda and Burundi, we learned of the ways in which ethnic types were said to be distinct, and of the "necrographic maps" of horror which were constructed accordingly. Here, Feldman remarks on the phenomenon of "telling," "knowing" by bodily signs whether a person is Catholic or Protestant. Clearly there are parallels, though we might hesitate before using the language of ethnicity here, because the term itself might contribute to the hardening of lines of division.

Whether we employ the term ethnicity or not, Feldman's substantive point holds. Genealogies of the dead build up the narrative of the community and its losses, and these genealogies are linked to places, times, and events. They are "calendrical markers that anchor overarching events ... in local temporalities and representations" (p. 65). Here we see an important mechanism by which acts of violence enter history, are given a sacrificial significance, and can also involve notions of unquiet *ghosts* walking the streets (p. 67), as a result of their assassinations. Persons killed in this way for political reasons are called *stiffs* (p. 68). Killers who specialize in attacking people could also be called *doctors*; they called their bullets *pills* or *medicine*. Sometimes *stiffs* were deposited on doorsteps, violating domestic "sanctuary." The victims were reduced from being persons to detached parts or objects, and Feldman again compares this process to the process of sacrifice, in which a whole creature is transformed into parts in order to purify another whole body, the body of society itself (p. 78). Accepting that there is a possible analogy here, we may perhaps demur. To call these killings acts of sacrifices may in a sense be making the error of dignifying them by giving them a religious aura. That people themselves do think in ritualized terms is attested by the category of the *blackman*, a figure of terror who was said to wear a black hood and an upside-down cross, and to sacrifice dogs in acts of black magic, before killing people. This category is a Catholic fantasy, and was associated with the entry of government paratroopers into the Ardoyne, a militantly Republican area of Belfast (p. 81). Here the figure is clearly demonic, satanic, but belongs by the same token to an overall religious picture which provides a framework of interpretation of events. What we would like to know about the use of the idea of sacrifice in relation to paramilitary killings is whether this also was a folk model, or was a piece of interpretation by the anthropologist.

Feldman applies ritual concepts to the context of arrest, pointing out that arrests are part of the apparatus of what he calls the counterinsurgency state and its endocolonization of the populace. He sees arrest itself "as a *ritual* form for the constitution of power" (p. 86), and also as a kind of "information taxation" imposed on the people. In his examples, this ritual policy is enacted mainly on the Catholic population and against the IRA, characteristically by pre-dawn house raids supported by army Landrovers (p. 89). He argues that, in what is also a battle for the legitimacy of the state, arrests that result in "arbitrary victimage" in fact reduce the state authorities to the same level as the paramilitaries themselves. Narratives paint a picture of violence on the part of the paratroopers in smashing homes and property, and beating those arrested. Feldman's informants applied the expression "being done" to the process of arrest, interrogation and beating of suspects in a political culture defined in terms of categories of the body and categories of performance, with the ever-present possibility of imminent death, followed by a paramilitary funeral procession. The objective of techniques of interrogation is to "soften" those who are considered "suspects" and so to break them down. From an analytical viewpoint, however, Feldman, following Scarry (1985) argues that interrogation marked by torture is a performance which manufactures power and "truth" from the materials of the tortured person's body and its surface (p. 115). At one point in his account Feldman takes note of the element of retaliatory revenge that enters into the violence of interrogation: "The narrative depicts a scene of violence in which the soldiers exchange the mutilation of their comrade for the attempted mutilation of the PIRA (Provisional Irish Republican Army) captive" (p. 121). We may comment here that this is not an incidental feature – it is intrinsic to the *emotional* context in which ritualized forms of behavior are produced.

Questions of identity also emerge. One captive described how the interrogators break down those who share cultural features with them. "You see guys come in for interrogation and they're as English as the English, except they claim to be Irish. They have a lot in common with the police; they break down and become informers. If they had the culture and the Gaelic stronger, they could hold out" (p. 132). The beatings also socialize both the torturer and the tortured into a common culture of violence. If the tortured survives and eventually is released, his political "rite of passage" is completed. In Chapters 5 and 6 Feldman explores procedures in prison ("the breaker's yard") and the struggles over hunger strikes by Republican prisoners ("eschatology"). The processes he describes in these chapters fall within his general purview: "the structuration of each enactment of sacrificial violence into a binary iconography of mastery and victimage" (p. 263).

Here lies another point at which we can consider the relevance of these materials for David Riches's propositions about violence. The social and emotional contexts here entirely outrun a rational action model based on individual encounters. The collectivization of violent interactions is what pushes Feldman, searching for an understanding of them, to invoke the ritual ideas of sacrifice and rites of passage. Another element is present. Sacrifice may enact mastery but the sacrificial victim may also become a martyr and his memory be used to hit back at the sacrificers. This is the political meaning of funeral processions and their connection with the fundamental drive for revenge. Further, the struggle for mastery means that in each encounter both sides can be either perpetrators or victims, and the chain of retaliation and revenge links their roles over time, transcending the initial triangle of perpetrator, victim, and witness. Feldman's account is focused on the paramilitaries; there is little about the views of the ordinary public other than as people whose lives are interrupted and ruined. We therefore learn little about the broader context in which processes of making peace might have a chance, although we learn much about why those processes have been continually devalued by violence. We learn also how we can reformulate Ranelagh's remark about violence as an end in itself, since the negative relationships between the British authorities and the paramilitaries defined, in Feldman's view, a shared cultural arena of violence which ensured its own reproduction over time. Curiously, we do not learn so much about the conflicts between the Republicans and Loyalists themselves that are presumably at the heart of the wider confrontations involved. Rather we see the British authorities and the paramilitaries both completely denying legitimacy to each other and in another sense granting it by their mutual adoption of codes of violence. This feature corresponds to a context of war, in which mutual mimesis takes place.

Outside of the paramilitary context there is much, of course, that occurs in the broader arena of sectarian activity, an arena that is characterized by protests, disputes, and disagreements but is not entirely taken up with violence as a preferred mode of action.

Two studies are of particular relevance here. David Cairns has published a paper analysing the place of material culture and of everyday behavioral practices in the continuous production of sectarianism in contemporary Northern Ireland (Cairns 2000). Cairns links sectarianism in Northern Ireland to the expression of identities that are exclusionary and oppositional. He also argues that such identities, although labeled with terms such as "Catholic" and "Protestant," should not be seen as primarily based in religion, since "there is no religious conflict ... Religion is clearly only the colouring, not the essence, of sectarianisms" (Cairns 2000: 438). In his view religion in this context has "a more sinister role, that of providing a mask for sectarian exercises of power." His formulation here draws on Michel Foucault's concepts of discourse and discursive formations as the loci of power distributed over the various roles and contexts of social action (Foucault 1972). Cairns sees "sectarianism as *using* religion" rather than being "intrinsically religious in itself" (p. 439). This position might itself by seen as somewhat essentialistic, in that it appears to set up an (undefined) idea of an "essence" of religion, in order to contrast it with "sectarianism."

We can understand Cairns's position, however, as applying in general to the situation in Northern Ireland, where the primary contexts in which sectarian designations are employed are ones whose tone is oppositional and conflictual. Cairns's focus is on the Orange Order Lodges in Northern Ireland, their marches held on the Twelfth of July in celebration of the victory at the Battle of the Boyne in 1690, and the patterns of everyday behavior that pervasively underpin the occasional outbursts of violence.

As Cairns notes, Orange Order followers do not regard themselves as violent sectarians, but "prefer to regard their culture as a freedom-upholding tradition, to be respected and acquiesced in by all" (p. 441). Commemorating the Battle of the Boyne signifies not just the victory over "Catholicism" (seen in the person of James II, William of Orange's adversary) but also the creation of a renewed form of allegiance to the British Crown as a sovereign entity with domain over Northern Ireland. This is the meaning of the term Loyalist, a meaning that has become somewhat paradoxical as the British Government tries to persuade the Loyalists to participate in a government of their own in Northern Ireland along with their adversaries of Sinn Fein, and thus in some ways to decrease their effective attachment to the British state.

Cairns discusses a number of cultural markers that operate in informal contexts to signal sectarian identity. One is linguistic classification: the casual use of the term "Fenians" for people suspected also from their accents to be "southerners" from "across the border" (p. 442). Another is residential segregation, reinforced by the construction of wall-barriers at boundaries. Walls may be decorated with Loyalist paintings, and arches constructed with pictures of the present Queen along with "King Billy" from the past. Flags are hung on flag-poles along streets and also inside people's homes. Football (soccer) identifications are common: adherence to Glasgow Rangers as opposed to Glasgow Celtic marks a Loyalist, Protestant identity as against a Republican Catholic one. The Orange Order itself sponsors social events such as discos and barbecues at local halls, in addition to the marches. Participants may become drunk and at a certain point break out into sectarian songs. Cairns refers to all these activities and markers as the "materialization" of sectarianism, which in some instances is imposed by Loyalists on others in their community areas. It would have been useful in this context to know what, if anything, corresponds to this situation on the "opposite side of the fence." Presumably it is not practical to try to study both sides in a severely polarized context of this kind. Cairns's fieldwork is recent, carried out during four successive marching seasons of 1993-6. (His data can be compared with those of Cecil 1993, who does not, however, give us a date for the fieldwork.)

Cairns's study reflects the continuing processes of polarization that seem to run in contrapuntal fashion to attempts at peace-making and agreeing on a form of devolved government in Northern Ireland. A study by Anthony D. Buckley, and Mary Catherine Kenney (1995) attempts to take a nuanced look at questions of identity in the same context, with materials dating from the mid-1970s through to the present in both Protestant and Catholic areas. Kenney's fieldwork dates from 1984–6 in "a particularly troubled Catholic area" (Buckley and Kenney 1995: ix); Buckley's first work in Ulster was carried out in 1975 and he has worked mostly since then among Protestants away from the more troubled areas. The focus of their book, as its title, *Negotiating Identity*, indicates, is on "how specific individuals construct their own identities in concrete and immediate circumstances." The main impact of this approach is to break down the impression of holistic, enduring, unbending antagonisms between people based on categorical oppositions. In order to explain how hostility nevertheless is maintained, they focus on boundary maintenance mechanisms in the way that the anthropologist Fredrik Barth (1969) did in his studies of ethnic groups. They also stress the use of rhetoric and metaphor in the process of creating and maintaining boundaries. Of course, the complementary emphasis in Barth's own work was on the flow of social transactions *across* boundaries (see also the studies in Donnan and Wilson 1994). The potential for conflict is increased when such flows are reduced. Obviously, the everyday patterns Cairns describes can be seen as ways of creating and maintaining boundaries through social stereotyping including self-stereotyping. Other mechanisms correspond to those delineated in Rosemary Harris's classic rural study of Ballybeg (Harris 1972). Buckley and Kenney note, for example, that Protestant-Catholic intermarriage is discouraged and that fears of intimidation and murder accompany it. Language usages also function as markers. In deciding whether they would beat up passers-by gangs of youths may say "tell us your alphabet," purporting to discern from forms of pronunciation whether people are Catholic or Protestant. To what extent this is tied in with Ulster Scots pronunciation is not clear from the examples Buckley and Kenney give. Another important phenomenon is that of "intellectual property," the idea that particular parts of history or tradition belong to either Protestants or Catholics. Traces of these phenomena can be found in both urban and rural contexts. Buckley and Kenney express their discontent with the idea that urban and rural locales are quite different, and also with what they call an anthropological obsession with place in the sense of discrete local communities.

In particular they maintain that as individuals in either rural or urban locales move from one social situation to another they consciously construct their identities. This is a good point, but we must wonder whether urban-rural differences and the existence of communities can be waved away, since there are certainly social pressures on individuals and these vary from place to place. Why otherwise would there be variations in patterns of conflict and violence?

For example, in the urban area of Ardoyne in Belfast which Kenney studied, the metaphor of the siege which is predominant in Northern Ireland was applied strongly to ideas of territory, marked by metal and concrete fences. The British Army maintained a continuous presence there also in the time of Kenney's fieldwork. Demonstrations and marches by members of the Ancient Order of Hibernians were a part of life. Ardoyne is also a poor area and Sinn Fein ran an Advice Center in it, providing community services. "The community" is thus defined politically.

On the other side of things, in Buckley's study, his observations of the Protestant Pentecostal churches and their impact on identity-constructions led him to conclude that the Pentecostalist themes of sin and the need for redemption can readily enough be "translated into the long-standing Bible-based religious traditions that identify the Antichrist with the Pope" (p 124). Thus, religion again becomes intertwined with politics. In other contexts around the world (for example in Papua New Guinea), this Protestant motif of the Pope as Antichrist is also found, but it does not lead to quite the same patterns of sectarian conflict (see e.g. Stewart and Strathern 1997a). In Northern Ireland an overdetermined set of factors bears on cultural details of this kind, engulfing them in the direction of conflict, even while some seize on Christian ideology in general as a possible focus of peace-making, or perhaps as a means of escape from the tribulations of the world and as an expression of hope for otherworldly rewards. Liam Murphy has stressed the aims of reconciliation among charismatic Christians he has studied in fellowship or "restoration" churches in which Protestants and Catholics may come together, through the ideology that the Holy Spirit moves them to overcome their differences (Murphy 2000: 6). This movement is sometimes referred to as the Northern Irish Renewal, whose members see the progress of the peace process as a test of the involvement of the Holy Spirit in history and healing as something for the whole social order (p. 8). Prayer is seen as the means whereby this healing may be achieved, since prayer is regarded as the power to bind Satan, and in the absence of effective prayer "this present world is in the hands of the evil one" (p. 9). The emotional rituals of prayer enact the desire for salvation from evil, the possibility of reconciliation, and the feelings of belonging to a single divine community. Practitioners look to Jesus to produce miracles, citing cases where gunmen have missed their target because of the influence of Jesus on behalf of believers. Speakers at meetings distance themselves from the established churches, saying that these have quelled the spirit of God rather than encouraging it, a classic kind of statement made in new religious movements in many places. The participants also look to events for signs of who is winning the spiritual "war," the Devil or Jesus. Murphy notes that the signing of the Good Friday Agreement in April 1998 is "often cited by Charismatics as evidence for the increasingly assertive action of the Holy Spirit across Northern Ireland" (p. 14). (For parallel materials on healing relating to Catholic Charismatics in Donegal, see L. Taylor 1995.) Similar pronouncements, in situations of political and economic difficulty and disarray and in the face of violence, are found in contemporary Papua New Guinea. There, too, the violence and the attempts at peace are dialectically related, standing in stark contrast to each other, yet in some ways existing in a relationship of symbiotic opposition. In the next chapter we turn to colonial and post-colonial contexts in the Highlands of Papua New Guinea in order to trace contrasting narratives of peace through exchange and of conflict through the expression of physical and "mystical" violence.

CHAPTER 4

Colonial and Post-colonial Contexts: Papua New Guinea

The narratives pursued by colonial powers that create empires often have to do with the supposed benefits of civilization and the associated suppression of internecine conflicts, considered as a necessary precursor to the creation of a rule of law. These narratives amount to a rationale, from the point of view of the colonizing power, for actions that may be seen as instances of hostile violence by those colonized. In addition, there may be a narrative of the intrinsic superiority of centralized state authority as a foundation for society by contrast with the supposed anarchy of societies without state institutions.

These narrative themes conceal great complexities. First, while the colonial power tends to see itself as possessing in advance a mandate to use physical force in pursuit of imperial aims, in practice a whole range of negotiations may be set in hand in order to establish a colonial presence. Ferguson and Whitehead have neatly summarized this point in their distinction between coercion and seduction as colonial strategies (1992: 7). Seduction itself may be regarded from some analytical viewpoints as a kind of "symbolic violence" in Pierre Bourdieu's terms (Bourdieu 1977: 191). Bourdieu rightly argues that there is a relationship between overt, physical violence and socially coercive mechanisms that conceal domination under bonds of kinship or patronage which he calls symbolic violence. However, for our purposes it is worthwhile to make an initial distinction between coercion and seduction as Ferguson and Whitehead do, in order to point out that seduction may sometimes be a more effective strategy than coercion for a colonial power to pursue, especially when it is operating in what Ferguson and Whitehead have also aptly called "the tribal zone," the zone at the edges of expanding states in which state powers engage with peoples outside their immediate territorial control but within their sphere of influence, though not exclusively so (1992: 8). Coercion may be most effective when it can be unequivocally exercised; but seduction may work better where the state cannot or is not prepared to bring overwhelming force to bear. In such cases state agents tend to operate in Bourdieu's modality of symbolic violence. To quote, "they cannot appropriate the labour, services, goods, homage, and respect of others without 'winning' them personally, 'tying' them – in short, creating a bond between persons" (1977: 190). This observation applies equally to the concept of seduction. This is clearly also related to the idea of hegemony; and at a certain point along the line between coercion and seduction, it becomes doubtful whether we can continue to speak of "violence."

The context of colonialism in the Highlands of Papua New Guinea from the 1930s onwards provides an excellent illustration of this theme. Equally this case shows that seduction tends not to work alone but in tandem with coercion as its guarantor. Elements of both continually appear. The two strategies do not appear separately but together, although one may predominate over the other at a particular phase of history. In the context we are looking at here, this interplay between seduction and coercion takes the form of an alternating stress on the lethal power of the gun vis à vis the "life-giving" (from the viewpoint of the indigenous people) powers of shell valuables which the early colonial explorers brought with them. Our account is organized around the local systems of exchange and how these were affected by and in turn affected the colonial presence, tracing the narrative into post-colonial times when these systems of exchange have themselves been greatly transformed and severe problems of intergroup conflict and interpersonal violence have emerged. One reason for this is that the systems of exchange were themselves historically underpinned by threats of force: when exchange breaks down, there is a possibility for violence. Some analysts argue that these two, exchange and violence, are intrinsically in fact linked. This argument depends on a number of considerations. One of these is that exchanges that encode intergroup competition also express hostility which may later break out into violence. Another is that exchanges which fail to reach a desired level of satisfaction between the parties can also lead to violence. At one stage in the history of post-pacification conflicts in the Highlands of Papua New Guinea it appeared that the traditions of speech-making about past fighting and killings in the Mount Hagen area had become vehicles for a local sense of history that could express an ongoing sense of grievance against other groups and so could extend the possibilities of violence into the future. By comparison, in the

Eastern Highlands, where such post-pacification exchanges and speech-making were less stressed, hostilities were also fewer. This was in the 1970s (A. Strathern 1977). Later, episodes of renewed fighting also broke out in the Eastern Highlands over a range of contemporary issues, indicating that fighting can have many causes that are independent of the effects of rhetorical traditions.

"Exchange" has been taken by many writers as a defining principle or characteristic of Highlands societies in Papua New Guinea, and more widely in the Pacific region. Whether this characteristic is especially true of the region or not, it is certainly pervasive. But as a characteristic it is both fluid and historically flexible. In this chapter we look at the ways in which the European explorers, government officers, and businessmen entered into a series of exchanges with Highlanders, how these exchanges were perceived on both sides, and how the local patterns of exchange were altered over time. We also look at a particular span of history in which changes took place – from the flowering of ceremonial exchange activities in the 1960s in Hagen to the decline and transformation of these ceremonial exchanges in the late 1990s. This period coincides with the time span of direct field observations in Hagen from 1964 through to 1999 (see Strathern and Stewart 2000a).

The history presented is largely "internalist," in the sense that it depicts the ideas and actions of the Hageners themselves, but these ideas and actions have always been directed by perceptions of the outside world also. We look at the continuous interaction between government and mission pronouncements, and the local peoples' interpretations of these. For example, the shell valuables currency in Hagen was replaced with introduced money during the 1970s, largely because the Hageners realized that Europeans did not value shells in their own economic worlds and that shells therefore enclaved them away from those worlds (Strathern and Stewart 1999a). However, they also used money in contexts similar to those for which shells had been used, making a double step of abandonment and reappropriation. This in turn geared their own exchanges to the worlds of cash-cropping and marketing, and set in motion a particular dynamic of escalation in factors of change. Competition for land and competition for money both led to killings and to the need for more money to pay compensation for the killings. By 1995 some leaders were calling for the abolition of compensation and the exclusive use of jail punishment as a way of settling conflicts, while at the same time bemoaning the growing selfishness and "individualism" of a younger generation. Contradictions of attitude of this kind all have their roots in the span of history since 1964 and earlier in which forces of change elicited one another dialectically: "pacification" led to the flowering of exchange, shells were replaced by money, the exchange system was made dependent on the market, it went out of control and led to calls for its abolition. Yet in 1998 we found that compensation payments were being used as a vehicle for new political statements and purposes in an expanded arena of multi-ethnic relationships, geared to the symbols of the nation, the province and modernity. Modernity as a local construction became the focus, as it had done before in different guises. In 1999 we found that there was talk of reinstituting some further exchange activities as a part of a build up to the next national elections. Social change and history are a matter of flows of experience. Elements from the past are captured and reshaped as a means of building the future. Equally important to consider are the ongoing changes and struggles connected with gender relations. Women are active agents in politics, even though men claim a monopoly over public power, and they participate strongly in debates regarding exchange, compensation, social control, and the narratives of modernity, especially those developed within the rubrics of Christianity (see Stewart and Strathern 1998a, 2001a).

This synopsis of changes since the 1930s needs to be set alongside another part of the picture, the continuing history of violence. Exchanges of wealth never fully extinguished violence, and the interaction of local with national politics has meant that violence is now often associated with the cycle of elections for national political office. Considerations of this kind turn original colonial "wisdom" on its head. State structures themselves generate violence, and acephalous political systems have in the past been better vehicles for the resolution of conflicts than have state institutions in post-colonial circumstances. Indeed, this point was anticipated by the colonial-era British social anthropologists who worked in African contexts (e.g. *Tribes Without Rulers*, edited by Middleton and Tait 1958).

Exchange in Mount Hagen

The literature on continuity versus change in the Highlands of Papua New Guinea is by now quite extensive. Most observers are agreed that the problems involved are complex and are not to be solved by deciding in favor of either continuity or change as an exclusive point of emphasis (e.g. Brown 1995; Knauft 1999). Rather we have to examine how these two elements are intertwined and how they merge into each other, blurring the boundaries of separation. This debate regarding Highlands historical processes goes back to the questions of longer-term prehistoric developments (Feil 1987; Wiessner and Tumu 1998), but it has mostly to do with the rapid changes set in hand by events from the 1930s onward, when Australian explorers first entered the Central Highlands of what later became Papua New Guinea, bringing with them not just change in terms of material aspects of life but an entirely new psychology toward life which influenced the way the local people saw themselves, their transactions, and their place in the cosmos.

Theories regarding the persistence of exchange practices tended in early anthropological writings of the 1960s to be balanced against accounts of the alacrity with which Highlands entrepreneurs took up the possibilities of business and economic profit (e.g. Finney 1973). These studies were challenged by writers with a Marxist orientation in the 1970s, who discerned developing class structures, conflict, and the emergence of "big peasants" (Amarshi *et al.*, 1979), processes they sought to use to explain the outbreaks of group violence in the Highlands from the 1970s onwards. Such approaches in turn have given way to more nuanced analyses that emphasize both cultural, political, and economic factors as necessary for a rounded standpoint on change. In the last decade, the residual elements of an incomplete picture of the Highlanders as simply secular pragmatists have been abandoned as we have come to better understand the rich ritual life that the Highlanders had, and which entered into their day-to-day transactional practices and expressed itself across the gender divide. In addition, the very early impact of Christianity on these Highlands societies had from the first years of missionary influence in the areas begun to be incorporated into and blended with indigenous patterns of thought and action (see Stewart and Strathern 2001a; Strathern 1984). The subsequent spread of evangelical Christianity further altered the ways in which transactions were conducted under the influence of new sets of moral codes.

In this context we are provided with our newest opportunity to consider the basic wellsprings of action in these societies and the extent to which people within them are still motivated by ideologies of exchange. At the outset it is important not to accept in a simple way any empirical opposition between gift and commodity as constitutive of the field of debate. This is because there is a long history of intertwinement of gift and commodity transactions in these societies, making it possible for gifts to be commoditized and commodity transactions to acquire gift-like aspects (compare Carrier 1992, and see Strathern and Stewart 2000a, b). What we have to discern, instead, is the pattern of shifting strategies and meanings captured in exchanges and the major trends of history over the last 70 years.

A mixed background of notions that combines together "secular" and "sacral" dimensions has more recently fed into the contemporary scene of discussions about change among the Highlanders themselves; and it is this scene that we propose to examine with some examples in order to pursue the point further.

Starting from these viewpoints assists in the interpretation of data from the outset since it avoids the imposition of typological schemes. However, a set of analytical ideas is needed to replace the typifications that have earlier been employed. We use here a range of ideas – substitution, transformation, and the long-term trajectories of practices. These are concepts similar to those which the people employ in their own reflections on their histories. We focus on a familiar theme, that of historical changes in the items used in exchanges, as seen in indigenous commentary (see also Stewart and Strathern in press; Strathern and Stewart 1999a). The commentary was given to us by two of our research collaborators in the Hagen (Melpa-speaking) area of the Western Highlands Province in 1999. Both men were old enough to have seen many of the changes they described, although not to have witnessed the first arrival of the Australians in the early 1930s. We asked them to explain how the use of different items in the Hagen system had changed over time. These objects had been used in brideprice and in the system of exchange known as *moka*. *Moka* is a general term for the delayed exchange of wealth items such as shell valuables and pigs or pork between individual partners or groups, marked by a principle of giving more than one has received in a previous phase from one's partner (A.J. Strathern 1971, see also Strathern and Stewart 2000a; Stewart and Strathern 1998b). This system of exchange has been on the decline in the 1990s and is considerably altered in tone from its earlier form. The items used have also shifted somewhat, according to a logic of indigenous perceptions that have been modified, or perhaps even produced in some instances, through transactions with outsiders, as the narratives will show.

For the Hageners, the pearl shell (*kokla kin*) (also described in Tok Pisin as "kina," a Gazelle Peninsula word from the northern coast of New Guinea) was the most admired and sought-after valuable from at least the 1930s until its demise in the 1970s. Many other shell types were given up as currency earlier than the pearl shells, while still used variously as forms of bodily adornment. These included the baler (*raem*), cowrie ropes (*ranggel*), nassa shells (*nuin, pikti*) sewn into mats (*pela öi*) with a central diamond called a navel (*uklimb*) from which the shells radiated outward in a design, and green snail (*kötö, örpi*), used largely as ornaments, attached to the ears and ringlets of hair, primarily by women (A. Strathern 1971: 102).

These shell items had been dropped from *moka* exchanges prior to 1964, perhaps in the late 1950s.

Pearl shells began to lose their place in *moka* after the mid-1960s. For the Kawelka people of the Dei Council area, the first beginnings of the use of state money in *moka* were observed in July and August of 1964, at a new kind of event known as a "tobacco *moka*," indicating its initial lack of importance in the order of things. In 1999, seeking to elicit some retrospective reflections on the historical passage of shells, we asked two senior Kawelka tribesmen of the Kurupmbo sub-clan, R. and P., to outline their views on this general topic of changes in the use of valuables. R. spoke, checking from time to time with P., who also prompted him on occasion. It is important, though, to note that R. was in fact casting around to put his thoughts in order about a topic which to him clearly appeared antiquarian by this time. Nevertheless, the events and processes he described had played a significant part in his own life. It is evident that in his account he was producing a meditation on the character of historical change and on discourses of modernity.

The account

"Pearl shells were the most important. After them in importance came cowries, nassa shells, balers, and finally green snail. Pearl shells continued to be used after the cowries and nassa shells were given up. The White people did not bring many of the cowrie and nassa shells with them, so we dropped them because we saw the Whites did not see them as important and we decided not to consider them as valuables any longer. When paper and coin money came we stopped using these smaller shells. We saw that we could use money to buy pearl shells [these were sold at tradestores during the colonial years alongside sacks of rice, tins of fish, and packets of cracker biscuits].

"At first we thought that money was just a means to obtain pearl shells. So during the 1950s and early 1960s we used both money and pearl shells. Subsequently, we got Local Government Councils – we became members of the Dei Council. The Kiaps [Australian government officers, placed as Council Advisors at this time] said that money would make the Council work efficiently. So the people began to think that shells were unimportant and they gradually gave up the use of them. It was not as though some one person made a speech and said, 'Let us give these shells up,' – it just happened gradually as money was used more frequently. The people saw by then that pearl shells did not produce anything [they could not be used to purchase the same sort of things that money could] and only money produced things. Previously it was true that pearl shells had work in brideprice payments and other payments, but from that time forward they did not think that they had work anymore. In the past there were hundreds and hundreds of pearl shells with resin boards, but where are they now? They are not to be seen at all!

"As for the shape of the pearl shell, the top is the 'head' (*peng*) and that is what bore the shell. This 'head' was broken off. It is not shiny, so it was removed when the shell was processed for use. They took the part with the good yellow color and fixed it on a board with tree resin, but if they wanted the shell as a neck decoration then they would cut it smaller. The edge of this colored part that is used is called the 'tongue' (*anmbil*). [See Strathern and Stewart 1999a for a full description of this manufacturing process.]

"We had stopped using the small shells (cowrie and nassa) in the 1960s. We remember this because this was around the time that there was a big sickness and people were using money instead of shells at this time [for small transactions; the date should probably be the 1950s]. Early in the 1970s we gave up using pearl shells because at that time there was plenty of money and we saw that the money could be easily carried to other places and used to purchase food and things that we needed. We did not complain about giving up the use of shells. We are not sorry for these shells or nostalgic about them. Now we have money and we can use it to buy pigs or as brideprice."

Discussion of the account

R. is a man who was well into his fifties in 1999. In 1965 he was engaged along with his father in partnerships involving pearl shells and pigs that belonged to an elaborate sequence of *moka* prestations between the Kawelka and their neighbors the Tipuka people (A. Strathern 1971). At this time R. was in his very early manhood and newly married to his first wife. He therefore recalls the whole sequence of events at least from the 1960s onwards. Overall, it is clear that he sees the transcendence of pearl shells and their replacement by money as a mark of historical progress. In their views of history the Hageners have until recently seen themselves as reaching out to the external world, grasping it, and incorporating or "pulling" it into their own spheres of action. This is how in fact an older generation of male leaders saw the expansion of the *moka* system itself and the later influx of shells brought by the Australians. R. continues in this broad tradition of thought, with a discourse about change having to do with the media of exchange, at each stage of which something new is taken in, substitutes for an earlier item, and is transformed while itself becoming an agent of internal transformation. Since wealth items continue to be central to identity, the past in a sense repeats itself; and since each historical situation is different the past is also in another sense always left behind while the imagination incorporates the present into the future. The types of shell valuables are historical markers of these transitions in people's narratives of change.

In organizing his account R., with P.'s help, systematizes the different shells in terms of their remembered importance. In fact, in the earliest phases of direct contact with the Australians, Hageners were keen on all types of these shells and manufactured them into impressive valuables. Cowries, however, were used in the colonial context for smaller transactions between the outsiders and the Hageners, and so came to be identified as of "less importance."

His account makes it clear that the Hageners from the 1960s onward saw state money as having more expansive power than shells. The perception coincided with, or closely followed, the opening up of the Highlands for travel and labor migration, and the new senses of identity that came with this process. Money was an efficient medium for interethnic exchange. It could be used to obtain food. Just as the first White explorers had used shells to break into the Hageners' world by offering them these wealth items in return for food and labor, so the Hageners could use money to break across their own social horizons. In Tok Pisin, R. said that shells did not "bear food," *ino karim kaikai*, with the wider sense that there was no further profit to be gained from using them at this time. Mimetic appropriation of the "white-men's" ways thus took over, coupled with a feeling of overcoming what, again retrospectively, was seen as the trickery of the Whites in at first withholding their own "true" money. But it is also true that the Australian government itself had a program to switch the people to state money over time, as its own means of incorporating the Hageners into the state structure through local government council taxes and cash-cropping, mostly the planting of coffee bushes by indigenous smallholders. Both sides, therefore, in fact participated (for quite different purposes) in the same transition, each feeling that they were taking the initiative either to grasp at new opportunities or to impose a new economic order. R.'s rejection of any notion of nostalgia for the past is interesting, and stems from his views of progress and the changing objectifications of self and culture that go with such a view, also enunciated by other senior men such as Ongka-Kaepa (Strathern and Stewart 1999b). Shells were first identified with the new order of colonial life in the 1930s, then were themselves seen as transcended by a further new order in the 1970s (see also Merlan and Rumsey

1991: 229). The narrative of shells and money thus becomes a means of self-reconceptualization over time, a gathering of perceptions of change into a form of shifting historical consciousness.

R. omits from his account any stress on the fact that state money was introduced into *moka*, displacing shells (Strathern and Stewart 1999a). This move of "involution" runs counter to his own narrative of change as "evolution," but it has been an important part of the overall history of change, begun, as we have noted, in mid-1964 with a *moka* event among the Kawelka people. Accounts of this kind are not common and we now describe this event in further detail.

A tobacco-moka

The genesis and execution of this *moka* show the incremental and improvisatory steps by which money entered these exchanges. Various reasons were given for the event, which was dubbed a *rok moka*, a *moka* for tobacco, i.e. by meiosis something unimportant or trivial, having to do with the casual exchanges of younger men and comparable to their sharing of tobacco for smoking while playing at card games. Another version was that the two groups involved, neighbors and closely intermarried, had stolen pigs from each other and the *moka* was to put an end to this. One middle-aged man declared that he had paved the way for the *moka* by tying up a pig belonging to a clansman of the other side which had given the first sum of money, and had returned the pig to its owner, establishing a pact of good behavior. The groups were the Minembi Yelipi and Kawelka Kundmbo clans in the Dei Council area, and the Yelipi Councillor, the son of a traditional "big-man," had initiated the sequence by giving money to the Kundmbo. Ndamba, a senior and respected Kundmbo "big-man," said that the money *moka* was also to forestall any sorcery being made on the young men of his clan who were going around playing cards (gambling for money) with their Yelipi peers. Young men at this time spent much time gambling and on chasing the winners in a particular game from place to place in an attempt to play again and win back their stakes plus a profit. Older men such as Ndamba saw the conversion of all this money back into *moka* as a device for stabilizing the younger generation's activities and for reasserting some of their own control as leaders in the group, an interpretation that older leaders made once again in later years explaining why in the 1970s they encouraged women to contribute money to the purchase of large commercially reared pigs for *moka* occasions (A. J. Strathern 1979).

Not only young men were involved. The older men, including the leaders, had joined in also, and all combined in providing a small feast of cooked food, including new items such as chickens, cabbages, tinned fish, dripping, and rice for the visitors. The Kundmbo were the donors for the event, which was staged on August 4, 1964 at the Möimanga ceremonial ground where later in 1973 the Kundmbo performed the Female Spirit fertility cult (Strathern and Stewart 1999c). They attempted to divide up both contributions and recipients according to clan subdivisions known as men's house groups, but found the arithmetic and accounting complex. At this time the Australian currency was still in pounds and shillings. Each men's house group or sub-clan was supposed to add an extra amount to the sum the Yelipi had given earlier. The chief Kundmbo recipients had divided out what they previously had received to their sub-clansmen and now these were expected to provide a return plus increment to bring about the *moka*. For example, in Ndamba's sub-clan, the Kiklpuklimbo, a total of 12 men out of 20 in the group had received £51 and now added £36 in order to make a total of £87 to give back (according to one set of accounts). Older "big-men" tried to direct the proceedings, but younger men crowded round the money, engrossed in the actual work of counting it. The amounts of money were tied up in handkerchiefs and presented as bundles to Yelipi recipients. One young man shouted out that all this was the fruit of business and coffee-growing. The Yelipi Councillor was prominent among the recipients, and he attempted to get some of the totals down on paper, while the Kundmbo laid out the money in three rows, the first row to acquit the debt, the second row to add something to this (referred to both as "profit" and as "*poroman*," that is, "companion," money), and the third "new money" (*ku kont*) to stimulate the Yelipi to make returns. This performative act of laying out rows of money as though they were shells indicates the transfer of the people's mind-set between one cultural schema and another, and shows how money truly was slotted into the place "vacated" by shells – on later occasions money was laid out in rosette formations that resembled in size and shape pearl shells mounted on resin boards (see Strathern and Stewart 1999a, for photographs). At the same time the introduction of a written record indicated the mimetic context, in which the accounting practices and techniques of the Whites were being followed by a new generation of leaders within the council system, set up in 1962 only two years earlier. Meanwhile older leaders such as Ndamba either quietly supervised the practical arrangements, trying to fix them in their own cognition, or made overarching remarks. A., for example, a leader in a sub-clan different from Ndamba's, declared that the "big-men" were not involved in the event since only the young men were giving, but everyone needed money to pay their council taxes before the year's end, so the Yelipi should make returns quickly. (In fact, A. himself had received earlier but is not recorded as contributing to the returns, which may explain why he found it difficult to get a hearing for his remarks.) The overall total recorded as presented was 317 pounds and ten shillings, a very considerable sum for that time.

Presenting saucepans of food along with the gifts was a part of the new style of this *moka*, and K., a Lutheran mission evangelist (*miti-man*) who came from A.'s sub-clan the Kumbambo, said a Christian prayer to bless the food, adding: "Money is strong and comes from Jesus, who is our big-man (*wuö nuim*) up above, so you can make *moka* with it. Later, when the Yelipi make returns, you Kundmbo can use this money to build a church here. This money is being given to end the stealing between the Yelipi and the Kundmbo. We do not have much business in our place, we are short of money, so you Yelipi must make returns to us quickly."

The whole event shows the complex performative ways in which money was socialized into an existing order and how this order was itself changed to accommodate and to express something that was new. The participants' horizons of consciousness included the demands of the new council system, so that the nexus between an old institution and a new one was made quite explicit. Finally, the Lutheran evangelist spoke of funneling the returns into a further new institutional investment with God, legitimizing money itself as the blessing given by Jesus and implying that a return gift to the church was needed for this. At the very start of the entry of state money into the *moka* we see an instance of the sacralization of money in a context of gift-giving and also an early foreshadowing of developments in the late 1990s, when the *moka* system overall was in decline and further transformations had taken place, so that in 1998, 35 years after the prayers at the event detailed here, a new sort of *moka* was planned in which money was sought through local relational ties in order to build a new Assemblies of God church at R.'s settlement place (Stewart and Strathern 2000a; Strathern and Stewart 2000c). The church was to be of permanent materials with a metal roof, replacing the first building with its thatched roof and woven cane walls. In return God would, it was hoped, increase his blessings to the community, returning the gift of the building "with interest."

Commentary

This observation regarding the sacralization of state money in the context of a local political event also enables us to elucidate further our analytical scheme of substitution, transformation, and long-term trajectories of change as objects of analysis. First, outsiders bring a greatly increased supply of pearl shells. These shells carry established aesthetic and ritual values, and their increased availability is seen as an enrichment of cultural life. They substitute for all the other types of shells used before. The perceptions that they arouse in people are also transformed, because of their new association with the outsiders who have now brought them and the fact that they are obtained through transactions with vegetable foodstuffs and pigs, and in return for labor. The pearl shells are commodified items but they also belong to the world of the gift. They are seen as items whose power depends, at least in part, on a new magico-religious link with powerful incomers who themselves introduce the people to new forms of transaction that are an extension of earlier patterns of external trade between Hageners and others at the edges of their social world. As the outsiders become the sole new source of these shells, so the shells come to express (again, in part) a dependency on these outsiders and a transformation of the outsiders partially into insiders – extending the network of what we have termed relational-individuality (see Stewart and Strathern 2000b). The Hageners' notion was that shells were "Whitemen's wealth," and that these new incomers' ideas were miraculously coincident with their own idea about shells as valuable items. But this transformation contained within it the seeds of a longer term trajectory of further change. When Hageners realized that shells simply enclaved them in their own world rather than truly allowing them to tap into the world of the outsiders, they were disillusioned. Hence, at the instigation of the colonial administration, they substituted again and adopted state money, in turn transforming it into a valuable by employing it in *moka* and using it in brideprice payments. Pearl shells were in the past sacred to the Female Spirit (Strathern and Stewart 1998a), who was also seen as an exogenous power, coming to the Hagen area from Tambul in the south-west, roughly the same direction as that from which pearl shells came in trade networks. When money was adopted, it was quite predictably regarded as something that came from the new Deity (the Christian God of the outsiders) as well as the new government (which had also emanated from the southern coastal city of Port Moresby). By this logic of substitution and transformation, the society as a whole was set on a pathway of further change, since if money was to be used in ritual contexts for exchanges it had first to be obtained in new economic ways. The gift exchange system was therefore harnessed to the labor market and to the smallholder production of cash crops. It was precisely, therefore, the intertwining of gift and commodity in a nexus of values and conative aspirations that drove the ongoing trajectory of change. Furthermore the presence of commodity exchanges in pre-colonial contexts of external trade had played an initial part in the transformational processes set in hand by the arrival of the first colonial explorers. But equally important was the ritual or sacred linkage of wealth with the powers of ancestors and the spirits. This facilitated the eventual absorption of money into the *moka* system, revealing the enduring links between "economic" exchanges and "ritual power." These two are not fully separate categories but are closely inter-related. In addition, brideprice payments, which reaffirm cosmological links with powers of renewal and fertility, incorporate into themselves money as *moka* exchanges did. In 1998 one of our Hagen field collaborators explained to us while we were attending a brideprice occasion that, although *moka* exchanges were not held as they had been previously, brideprice occasions were still considered to be an enduring aspect of local life. But this practice too has altered significantly over time, as has *moka* (Stewart and Strathern 1998a). For example, brideprice occasions now incorporate separate gifts of money to the bride, contributed as a kind of "tax" or generalized donation by men and women kinsfolk of the groom.

Anthropological categories of commodities and gifts, "bigmanship" and "greatmanship" are best seen as elements in an inter-related series of historical processes over time and space. These distinctions were never completely firm and the movement of change carries these elements along with it in a complex set of inter-relations which the Hageners, as their words suggest, understand quite well.

The various changes that time has brought to the Hagen area carry with them also a disjointed set of problems and dilemmas, and to these we now turn.

Contemporary dilemmas

The revalorizing of money in the context of *moka* exchanges has over time caused these exchanges themselves to undergo historical shifts. First, people must be involved in the cash economy in order to obtain money. This in turn exposes them to the buying power of money itself, a point that R. makes clearly in his account. As new desires for consumption enter, and as forms of socialization into the values of group solidarity and communal ceremony loosen their grip on succeeding generations, the linkage point between money and local ritual enterprises is threatened. Renewing it by diverting it in the direction of a novel prestigious activity such as church building represents an attempt to strengthen the link again. But the very "strength" of money – its association with outside powers – that led people to want it in the first place imperils that link.

Older leaders, perceiving these trends clearly, work to reharness money for church purposes which are also intimately linked to political functions within the communities. These leaders also try to get people to invest another kind of valuable in feasting activities for the opening of new churches. This is the pig, which has maintained its fundamental place as a store of prestigious value throughout all the fluctuations in the use of shells and state money. However, pigs require a considerable investment of food and labor, and in Hagen women have traditionally supplied a great deal of that labor. Within the context of the old *moka* activities, their efforts were harnessed to a relatively unitary system of values. The decline of *moka* has meant that women are no longer as keen to undertake all the work of rearing pigs and men are even less inclined to pick up the jobs themselves. Women are also more able to earn money by doing other kinds of work. This money in many instances is more highly valued because of the immediacy with which it can be transformed into other goods or enter into various transactions.

In future, there may emerge a system that is based entirely on money, in which money alone is used to purchase goods for feasting purposes. For many years, since at least the early 1970s, the purchase of "freezer meat," mostly sides of beef but also "lamb flaps," and tins of corned meat or canned mackerel pike, has formed a part of feasting occasions. If the rearing of pigs becomes less popular, feasts will become more expensive affairs in terms of immediate cash needed to obtain goods. This will represent another remote point on the long trajectory of unanticipated changes initiated by the relatively smooth substitutions and transformations of earlier years.

Hageners perceive these processes as creating dilemmas for them, centering on money itself. They adopted money in order to mimetically appropriate the world of outside powers and have since learned that this world is full of problems of its own. Two parallel and contradictory discourses about money coexist uneasily, the one condemning it as bad, a cause of strife and dissolute behavior, linked to alcohol consumption, criminal activity, prostitution, and the corruption and violence that goes with political bribery, as well as most recently a realization that AIDS has made its way into a number of Hagen communities. People relate the entry of AIDS into their lives on the one hand with the wrongdoings of individuals (rich persons and sportsmen, who travel outside Papua New Guinea and come into contact with the disease) and on the other hand with fears that this disease may be a sign that God is punishing people because of their failure to observe proper rules of behavior. These fears reflect deep concerns about the ways in which people should be organizing and leading their lives. The discourse on money reflects the dilemmas of deciding how money should be used: for longer term communal ends or for more immediate personal and group consumption. The dialogue on this issue extends and reverberates between men and women, and between members of different generations. Some of the older male leaders criticize younger people for their unwillingness to work to produce wealth that can then be put into community enterprises. Younger people declare that the older people are perhaps too interested in controlling things and keeping wealth for themselves. Exchanging the world of proper participation in events for the world of personal consumption is seen as potentially leading to a dissolution of social bonds as such. These concerns become most evident when stressful events occur such as in the following story.

Early in the year 2000, in the first days of January, two middle-aged men died among the Kawelka Kundmbo clanspeople at Kuk, raising questions about the present and future in a sharp way. First, the deaths were taken by some as possible omens of the feared impending world's end because of the fact that they happened at the turning of the new millennium. Second, the men died of severe disease conditions that were apparently not well understood by the doctors but which caused the wasting away of their bodies over a relatively short time. And third, their deaths at about the same time produced a strain on people's organizational capacities to stage and manage the contributions of food and money to the funeral feasts that form an integral part of cycles of exchange and in the past have been tied in with *moka*. During the speeches made at the funeral feast there were complaints that people were not contributing enough to the event. There were expressions of factional divisions between sub-groups. There were also expressions of conflicts of interest between clansfolk living at Kuk as against those living in the more remote Kawelka territory at Nggolke (Strathern and Stewart n.d.). There were also complaints about the people at Kuk having to deal with the corpses of men who died in urban centers away from home and whose bodies were always brought from the nearby airport at Kagamuga to Kuk rather than being taken on the longer and more difficult journey straight to Nggolke. Meanwhile some older speakers protested their loyalty and commitment to the funeral prestations themselves. Finally, in a remarkable series of discussions, great confusion arose as to how exactly leadership was to operate on the occasion itself. The major division was between church leaders and those seen as outside of the church. The church leaders were also at odds with one another because of the divisions between the Catholic, Seventh Day Adventist, Lutheran, and Assemblies of God churches in the community, and they debated with each other on how best to conduct the funeral proceedings. Gendered issues arose when some of the male church members suggested that perhaps female leadership should also be recognized. Leaders outside of the churches wondered how church affiliations would fit with the old-established system of division into clans and sub-clans seen as "men's house groups" (*manga rapa*). A debate about what the local social structure actually is or should be took place on this occasion in the public speeches. Partial resolutions were declared so as to move the event forward without too many people becoming disgruntled and leaving.

Such a debate is part of a process in which people are coming to terms with the confusing circumstances of change. Comparable organizational discussions were foreshadowed in the 1964 arguments about how to make a money *moka*. There the problem was seen in substitutive terms; in 2000 it had to do with long-term trajectories, brought fully into people's consciousness. And the underlying dilemmas which the debates reflected, and reflected upon, were those we have delineated here: how to make people contribute to events once the overall frameworks of society have begun to alter; and how to decide who is to be in charge of and responsible for events. The church leaders represented a new version of sacralized control but without the old knowledge of how to organize and motivate people; whereas the leaders outside the church knew how to organize matters in accordance with the old social structure but lacked now the element of sacralization. The result was an attempt to combine both, in search of a new hybrid form not yet developed: a form that combines sacred and secular, and binds commodity and gift together again, as happened previously in recursive processes of history. Pearl shells and state money were at successive historical moments introduced and incorporated into an ongoing holistic matrix of activities, which was underpinned also by the ritual complex of fertility expressed in pig sacrifices and other ways. Money and Christianity have since brought with them further dilemmas of choice, leaving the Hageners to consider how to achieve a form of social structure that can resolve these difficulties and reinstate a balanced cosmos.

Conflict in Mount Hagen

This account of changing exchange practices in Hagen might suggest a gradual and graded set of peaceful, if problematic, transformations away from patterns of violent activities. However, we have presented only one side of the picture. The other side is that the potential for violence was never eradicated, and that new circumstances have in fact aggravated its scope. The history of this process has been given in a number other publications (e.g. A. Strathern 1974, 1977, 1992, 1993a, 1993b; Strathern and Stewart 2000a). Here, therefore, we give a selection of points that bear on our main themes for this book.

First, there is the context of earlier colonial practices in the Highlands, from the 1930s to the 1950s. The colonial intruders brought with them the two basic tools of "empire," coercion and seduction, in the form of guns and valuable shells. They used the guns to defend themselves against attacks, and to shoot their way out of threatened attacks. These attacks were sometimes aimed at gaining access to the supplies of trade goods, including axes and shells, which the incomers brought with them. At other times they were generated by earlier occasions when the intruders had shot people. Because of the tremendous appeal that both axes and shells had for the local people, recourse to shooting was needed less than it might otherwise have been. In this regard we might argue that the Hageners, and other Highlanders, pacified themselves rather than simply being pacified, because of their own desires for the goods the incomers brought with them. Clearly, both coercion and seduction were involved. In the 1960s older Hagen men remembered keenly how administration officers had brought in their native police and had put people in "jail" for wrongdoing. A vivid account of these happenings is given by the Kawelka leader Ongka in his life-story (Strathern and Stewart 1999b). Ongka's account is valuable also because it details how leaders such as himself, who were young adults at the time, seized on the trappings of power (afforded them by being appointed as minor colonial officials) to establish new forms of domination for themselves in their own communities (Strathern and Stewart 1999b: 7–9). It was in this context of coercion, exercised by the colonial field officers and aided by local officials, that fighting among groups, and also isolated killings, declined and the indigenous emphasis on *moka* exchanges developed and thrived to the mid-1960s.

Pacification, self-induced or coerced, did not, however, mean the end of conflict. Fights between sets of persons, escalating into the involvement of others of their groups, continued in the 1950s, and field officers regularly intervened and jailed participants in these. However, such conflicts were encompasssed by the widening remit of the circuits of exchange of wealth that preoccupied the new generation of leaders who grew up in the shadows of colonial control. People were also kept busy with compulsory labor on road-building and the construction of "rest-houses" for visiting colonial officers, and with the introduction of coffee trees as a source of monetary income.

These patterns of change and development were interrupted by some unforeseen consequences. The administration sponsored the introduction of local government councils, joining together several large groups into single deliberative bodies with powers of local taxation and disbursement of funds for projects. Councillors and their associated committee-men became an important new part of the political and administrative apparatus in the 1960s. From the mid-1960s onward, also, political electorates were constituted for elections of members of a House of Representatives, the forerunner of the national Parliament which was set up a decade later when Papua New Guinea gained its independence from the colonial power, Australia. These electorates often, though not always, coincided with council areas. In such cases, the effect was to create new political bodies, composed of an uneasy amalgam of differing groups, some with long-standing enmities toward one another, which stood potentially opposed to other such units in a political configuration much larger in scale than the clans and tribes that had operated in the political domain in pre-colonial times. Further, people from different groups and electorates traveled more into one another's areas, for example to buy coffee, or on government service, or to visit kin, or to campaign for political causes. The net result of these changes of scale and content in social and political relations was an increased potential for conflict and violence, one that was hard for the expanding exchange system to keep pace with. The introduction of vehicles and roads, with their potential for accidents, and the opening of taverns at which local people could consume alcohol, made the situation more explosive. Settlers from other provinces short of land for coffee-growing were also brought into the broad expanses of the flat Wahgi valley around Hagen. Laborers were imported to work on expatriate-owned plantations. Goods became available for purchase in towns, leading to desires for the money needed to buy them, and possibilities for quarrels and fights in the urban centers themselves. The introduction of Village Courts in the 1970s was intended to give back to local leaders the powers to settle disputes, including those involving violence, in communities which had over time been eroded by colonial control. These courts had some success; but they were plagued by their inability to enforce their decisions, by corruption, and by a rising tide of indifference to the authority of the magistrates. In more serious cases of assaults or actual killings, "trouble committees" were appointed, consisting of local notables, to arbitrate disputes and decide on compensation payments.

By the mid-1980s the relatively benign surface of affairs that held in the 1960s was broken. In the Dei Council area of Hagen, the killing of a young Kawelka Kundmbo clansman in a drinking spree with some contemporaries of his among the Minembi tribesmen (who included ancient enemies of the Kawelka as a whole) escalated, through the non-payment of compensation, into a major series of collective hostile encounters, fueled for the first time by the use of guns. The numbers of those killed in conflict accordingly increased, and a wide area of group territories was embroiled in fear, distrust, ambushes, and open armed engagements for a period of two years, leading to partial devastation of coffee crops, tradestores, and dwelling houses as well as direct killings by gunfire and the rape of women in enemy territories. The establishment of peace was uneasy and difficult, abetted by the erection of a memorial including a Christian cross at an interchange point between the territories of the Kawelka and the Minembi at a place called Ekit Kuk near to Nggolke in the Dei Council area. Many of the Kawelka left their territories and dispersed to other places. Since then, however, major fighting on this scale has not broken out again (up to 2001).

Parliamentary politics themselves contributed to these and subsequent patterns of conflict. Members of Parliament were granted large sums of money to spend on projects in their own electorates, and this stock of money made the position of parliamentarian highly valuable, increasing the competition and animosities between candidates for elections. National politics began to be a causative factor in local conflicts, just as earlier colonial administrative decisions to set up councils and electorates had been (Ketan 1998; A. Strathern 1992, 1993b). In the 1990s, politics also began to be re-entwined in the networks of exchange themselves, since the sponsorship by politicians of particular payments of compensation for killings between groups can be seen as ways of seeking political support in elections. Violence before and after elections reflected the high stakes.

These effects of the nation-state on the Highlands have been matched also by the effects of large-scale commercial enterprises, especially mining, which have brought huge, uneven, rapidly spent influxes of cash into certain areas as a result of royalty and compensation payments to groups. Conflict over the division of these monies is endemic. Groups whose members feel aggrieved at being left out hijack vehicles and block highways. Since the 1990s the blocking of highways by criminals who threaten and sometimes kill travelers has been commonplace. These phenomena are frustrating, upsetting, worrying and expensive for the local populations themselves. What is known as the "raskol" problem has become endemic to the Highlands. Declining coffee prices have worsened things further. Small wonder that millenarian movements and ideas regarding end times circulated widely in the Highlands around the year 2000 (Strathern and Stewart 1997a; Robbins et al. 2001). The elaborate *moka* chains of the 1960s have finally disappeared. They have been replaced by isolated large-scale compensation payments for killings. Among the Kawelka one such payment was made in 2001 amounting to some K26,000. A newspaper report named another payment of more than K100,000 in the same year, made by one Central Hagen group to another. The principle of compensation, and the fear of revenge killing, goes on in the midst of a hugely transformed world; but it is a far cry from the expansive *moka* of the 1960s, inspired by the colonially-induced lull in fighting and the emergence of leaders under the colonial aegis.

These two narratives, of exchange and of conflict, seem hard to fit together. Yet they both belong to the historical experience of the same people and their region. The overall narrative is one of the dialectical engagement of forces for non-violent change and forces that induce violent action. At a systemic level, these forces can be seen as uneasily counterbalanced. In other ways they have produced each other. The growth of the coffee business, for example, has fueled local animosities between people over land and led to violent altercations between them. Christian churches preach against violence, but the division between churches and sects can exacerbate local tensions. And parliamentarians promote "law" and "development," but their distributions of funds cause jealousy, distrust, and severe local competition.

Three arenas of conflict and their interpretations

A number of the themes we have touched on here have been debated extensively by anthropologists, historians, and political scientists working in the Highlands. In particular there has been much discussion on three areas: *raskol*, parliamentary competition and electoral violence, and state violence. The phenomenon of the *raskol*, or community members turned criminals who associate loosely together to rob, rape, and terrorize others in mostly urban contexts; the phenomenon of parliamentary competition and the electoral violence that accompanies it; and the question of state violence expressed putatively in actions by the police against both criminals and the communities said to harbor them. All of these themes contribute in turn to a fourth, the arguments regarding "weak states" and their problems in ensuring "law and order" within their borders (see Dinnen 2001; Strathern and Stewart 2000d).

Raskol

Debates about *raskol* center on historical causation, meanings, and consequences. Prominent in ideas about causation has been the observation that the confluence of partly educated but unemployed and therefore frustrated and resentful youths in urban centers leads easily to the formation of loosely knit sets of such youths bent on specific projects of robbery (Hart Nibbrig 1992). The "school leaver problem," that is, the difficulty of creating jobs for all those who have been educated with the expectation of finding prosperity, is in this view at the root of the matter, and the ultimate causes have to do with the difficulties of creating sufficient levels of industrial employment in a country that can attract only certain forms of outside investment. These are important background factors. Youths in towns also link up with members of both their own language areas and those from other places, rapidly sharing experiences and knowledge of crimes and how to commit them. Shifting networks of kin and allies are thus formed and these networks spread along roads between rural and urban areas, providing pathways for criminals to move from place to place and work together while seeking to elude the attentions of the police. The criminals can vanish back into their own natal communities or take refuge in others via their links or they can even set up communities predominantly composed of criminals themselves in peri-urban locations. Owning guns and the willingness to use them inhibit the process of informing on them and can often intimidate the police themselves, who become reluctant to enter community arenas that reputedly contain *raskol*, for fear of ambush.

Guns are obtained in various ways. Some are stolen from police armories, from private citizens, or from security officers who are overwhelmed and killed. Some are reputedly introduced by ex-soldiers of the PNG Defense Force into contexts of intergroup fighting and then find their way into the hands of criminals, who may also act as clan fighters when at home. Many are bought illegally with large sums of money or in exchange for marijuana in trading networks that surreptitiously cross provincial and national boundaries. In one narrative, the son of a missionary in the Southern Highlands was declared to have secretly imported guns in packing crates surrounding sawmill machinery parts that the mission had purchased. AK47 assault rifles are a favorite item and there is a quest for weapons that are superior to those the police carry. Finally, large numbers of guns, especially those used by fighters in intergroup contexts, are home-made weapons, shotguns with metal barrels, hand-made wooden stocks and simple but unreliable firing mechanisms which occasionally backfire and injure their users. The multiple ways in which guns can be obtained illegally both facilitate the activities of *raskol* and constitute a temptation to youths who are drawn into crime as a part of fantasies of empowerment. The experience of urban life with its overt disparities of wealth and the visible availability of goods in stores feed into such patterns of behavior.

The urban-based class system is therefore another obviously significant background factor in generating criminal activity. In relatively small towns, such as Mount Hagen Township in the Western Highlands Province, the physical layout of the town also makes certain kinds of crime relatively easy to perform. The town's central shopping center is small and is surrounded by steep gullies which lead into squatter settlements and then into clan territories with tree cover and small concealed pathways. *Raskol* from these peripheral areas can quickly seize goods and disappear. Stores attempt to combat this pattern with steel mesh and armed guards, and the police conduct frequent foot patrols; but with the press of large numbers of people on the streets, spilling out of the produce market at the eastern end of the town with small amounts of money to spend, effective surveillance is difficult. Youths specialize in breaking car locks and swiftly stealing any possessions incautiously left, even for a few minutes. In larger cities, such as Port Moresby and Lae, the battles between police and criminals may have higher stakes, involving helicopters, high-speed chases, and shoot-outs, in which the police are empowered to kill fleeing criminals. The peri-urban back roads around Port Moresby have for many years been unsafe for outsiders to drive on, although during the 1970s they were relatively safe.

It is sometimes argued that the background factors of emerging class differences and shortages of employment opportunities (familiar from many other contexts), would not necessarily have produced the *raskol* phenomenon, without the co-presence of certain cultural factors. Foremost among these is what we might call the aftereffects of the "warrior" ethos. Youths who formerly would have been trained as clan fighters found themselves at a loose end in a pacified polity and some then turned to violent crime as a form of self-expression. In a sense, the argument represents another version of the "unemployment" thesis. For the Mount Hagen area we can observe that while *raskol* do see themselves as being in an ongoing violent struggle with the police, they do not see themselves as fighting for a cause or restating a clan ethos of political relationships. Such restatements do occur in intergroup conflicts and *raskol* may take part in these as clan fighters, seeking some prestige in that way; but there is no systematic linkage between clan fighting and criminal activities, except in contexts where whole clans become embroiled in wider scale processes such as disputes along the Highlands Highway west of Mount Hagen leading to the Porgera gold mine. In this context clans whose members felt they had been left out of distributions from payouts made by the mining company ambushed company supply vehicles in bids to extort money. This is a special circumstance but obviously one that could easily be replicated elsewhere.

Related to this argument is a more general one that points to a kind of "culture of violence" interpretation, particularly with reference to Highlands society. The argument is that general attitudes to the acceptability of the use of force in interpersonal and intergroup affairs lead easily to the place of violence in *raskol* activities. These general attitudes are in turn related to traditions of warfare. Again, such an argument cannot be discounted. Nor on the other hand can it be accepted as the only factor at work. At least some influence must be attributed to film and cartoon representations of gang-related criminal actions that have entered Papua New Guinea from the outside world, especially video and television images. In towns such images are freely seen in cinemas, bars, and hotels. They feed into folk narratives about *raskol* who have magically powerful cars, or who can fight and defeat the police, or at least use their powers of escape from them. Such narratives do not exactly depict *raskol* as "heroes." They do indicate a certain mystique or glamor that surrounds them; and these stories flourish in the communities of origin of the *raskol* themselves, providing motivations for mimetic actions by aspirant new *raskol*.

The overall consequences of *raskol* activity are relatively clear. They are costly to private individuals, businesses and the state. They inhibit business investment and reduce profits. They are intimidating to individuals and result in loss of life. They restrict tourism and the money it brings. They produce anxiety and discomfort among ordinary citizens who are held up and robbed on highways by thieves who have more money than they themselves do. Stated in this way, the consequences appear obviously negative, as they are in the experience of all those who are victims of these activities. Karen Sykes (2000) has given a more abstract version of such consequences in terms of ongoing state–criminal interactions. Sykes sees what she calls "raskolling" as a form of "contestatory sociality," referring also to the "fundamental reflexivity of youth violence" and arguing that "Raskolling is a form of sociality in which Papua New Guineans overtly consider the nature of political order" (p. 175). The background to this argument is her work on the school-leaver problem which we have mentioned above. By calling *raskol* violence "contestatory sociality" she means also to argue against a view she attributes to others to the effect that *raskol* behavior is "asocial." Sykes's formulation falls within social constructionist approaches to meanings in social life. She suggests that "*Raskols* do challenge the legitimacy of the State with acts that declare, implicitly or explicitly, that their own natural interests are thwarted by nationalist politicians, yet they would not overthrow the State" (p. 176). In other words, she is arguing that *raskolism* is a political practice, directed toward the state and constituting a political demand. It is therefore a kind of social action, centering on a contest over resources. She goes on to suggest that, in terms of its secondary consequences, *raskol* activity contributes to defining the shape of state-based laws and practices, and that therefore the state and *raskols* come mutually to define each other. (A similar argument might be constructed for the case of terrorists.)

There is some truth in this approach, seen from the point of view of history or of processual analysis. However, there are drawbacks and difficulties in it also. The viewpoint involved tends to anaesthetize the reader from the character of the activities themselves. Taken to an extreme, such a viewpoint could be applied also, as we have noted, to destructive acts of terrorism, for example, with the proviso that the terrorists' acts of "contestatory sociality" would have the aim of overthrowing a specific governing party. By calling *raskols*' activities forms of "sociality" Sykes is saying that they are not "asocial." What, then, would be an act of "assault?" From the point of view of the victims of violent actions by *raskol*, these actions are not "social" or "asocial," but are "anti-social" in the sense that they inflict harm on people and conflict with certain social norms. Calling them "social" in some analytical sense cannot remove from them their "anti-social" character from the point of victims, and of the state as an interested and responsible "witness" of these acts in David Riches's sense of this term. Sykes's relabeling of *raskol* activities then is unlikely to impress those who suffer from them.

In analytical terms also it is not evident that *raskol* activities are such clear political statements as Sykes declares them to be. She modifies her claim by writing that these activities are "explicitly *or implicitly*" (our emphasis) designed to challenge the legitimacy of the state. How would we adjudge an "implicit element" of this sort? The difficulty arises from the fact that *raskol* activity has other overt aims, for example the acquisition of property and wealth, or of a particular "name" among a set of peers. Attributing to it a further aim of "implicit" political protest may not be plausible. Further, even if *raskol* actions constitute or imply a protest against national politicians, these could be seen in terms of local factional politics rather than of any challenge to the legitimacy of the state as such.

Sykes carries her argument further with an appeal to "Melanesian" forms of sociality in general, assimilating the actions of *raskol* to these imputed norms. Here there are two problems. First, can we generalize about Melanesian forms of sociality in this global way? In our view this cannot be done on any empirical basis. And second, can we interpret *raskol* activity simply under this rubric? Again, the answer from the literature on the topic appears to be no. Sykes quotes Simon Harrison's argument that an alternation between peaceful and violent relations *constitutes* sociality in non-state Melanesia and that in this alternation there is no goal of hegemony or domination (Harrison 1993: 149). Hence sociality is always contestatory in this sense. The argument here reduces processes to essences. While we can say that in empirical terms an alternation between friendly and hostile patterns often occurs, and that there are many reasons for this, we cannot necessarily project this as a Melanesian explanatory model to be applied to all contexts. This is especially true for the case of *raskol*, whose actions are influenced by inputs from the contemporary outside world as much as by any indigenous cultural forms.

In Sykes's discussion, the fluid and temporary character of the sets of people who may coalesce for *raskol* activity is stressed. She speaks of *raskolling* as a form of action rather than of *raskol* gangs, and stresses that in some cases the activities are temporary and limited to particular places outside of the actors' home areas. This pattern may certainly be true in some cases. In others, however, something more like gangs does emerge. Stressing the temporary or partial aspect of *raskolling* may also tend to underestimate the serious character of the problem for society at large.

In one respect Sykes's account meshes clearly with other discussions. This has to do with the pattern by which "the *raskol* leader conducts a campaign of violence and theft until he turns himself in as a repentant criminal" (p. 181). This syndrome has been recognized also by Sinclair Dinnen (2000b) and is found in the life-history narrative that appears in Strathern and Stewart 1998b, centered on the life of N.S. (pseudonym initials). The switch from violence to peace and penitence, expressed in a Christian idiom, also gives limited support to the idea of a contestatory sociality defined by such switches; but the specific Christian elements involved must also be noted (see also Strathern and Stewart 1998c). Dinnen traces the history of the rise of *raskol* activity from the mid-1970s onward, in a context of swift urban growth and the removal of colonial restrictions on the movements of indigenous people. Settlements such as Morata in Waigani grew up containing makeshift houses sheltering large numbers of people, many without jobs, which both gave refuge to criminals and encouraged criminal activity itself. These have since become no-go places or ghettos of violence, wedged in between middle-class suburbs, and as such form a persistent reservoir of potential threats to these suburbs. Dinnen points out that "many of today's urban youth retain only tenuous links with rural villages" (Dinnen 2000b: 54). Such an observation must weaken any notion that there is anything especially "Melanesian" in urban patterns of activity. He also points out that, in 1990, 62 percent of the population in Port Moresby was under 25 (p. 55). Young people in urban settings are much less socialized into "indigenous" cultural ideas than are older people in rural conditions. But Dinnen also notes that *raskol* themselves have developed strategies of exit from crime. He found in a search of local newspapers between 1991 and 1994 accounts of 13 surrenders staged by a total of 913 criminals from 8 of the 19 PNG provinces. The youths involved usually announced their conversion to a branch of the Christian church and asked also for resources to help them set up businesses and lead non-criminal lives. These surrenders can thus be seen as peaceful forms of political action involving demands or pleas for help; and their preceding violent acts can be interpreted as having a latent political component also, although such a proposition, as we have seen, raises problems of evidence. Depending on how assistance is offered and used, Dinnen suggests that these forms of surrender and the appropriation of a Christian identity constitute more hopeful ways of meeting the problems than the forcefully suppressive actions of police (Dinnen 2000b: 70). He also suggests that civilian "brokers," who are skilled at dealing with sets of criminals who wish to surrender and make requests for help, in return may be an important element in bringing such surrenders to useful fruition. In his book-length study of problems of law and order in Papua New Guinea today Dinnen (2001) also puts this suggestion forward. He notes the successful intervention of church workers in some instances, such as that by Pastor Charles Lapa, who was given K50,000 by the Minister for Home Affairs and Youth in 1992 for his mediatory work in which Christian crusades can be led by born-again former criminals (p. 97). Here he also introduces a "culturalist" perspective to his analysis in the manner proposed by Banks (2000), suggesting that *raskol* leaders are generally involved in redistributing stolen wealth among their followers in the style of a traditional "big-man" (see Goddard 1992). In this scenario, violent theft becomes comparable to the entrepreneurship of business leaders. As with all culturalist approaches of this sort, there is a risk here of mistaking analytical similarities for equivalences. *Raskol* leaders themselves are not identical to "big-men" or "entrepreneurs," but in publicly announcing changes of heart they are appealing to the moral sense of the community to give them the opportunity to make a switch from one domain of life to another. They first have to make a moral "gift" of themselves in order to claim back a "gift" of government help. Christian rhetorical concepts mediate this proposal for an exchange, providing the possibility for forgiveness and trust. The gang surrender is thus an amalgam of indigenous ideas about gifts and Christian ideas of moral transformation projected onto the context of relations with the state.

Parliamentary competition

Similar considerations may be applied to the contentious issues that surround parliamentary competition, corruption, and violence. Dinnen (2000b and 2001) notes that *raskol* leaders often express their distrust of politicians and their feelings that they have been abandoned by them. If *raskol* are demanding legitimate forms of "gift exchange" with politicians, these politicians themselves have become enmeshed over time in sets of exchanges with factions of followers which may also be looked on as "gifts" but also make them vulnerable to charges of corruption (A. Strathern 1992, 1993b). We are referring here to the sectoral allowances or funds made available personally to national parliamentarians for direct distribution in their electorates, a program that was initially designed as a quick start mechanism to get development going in local areas without bureaucratic delays. Placing these funds in the hands of MPs has politicized their use and caused considerable jealousy and unrest among the groups and factions left out of the distributions. MPs have almost perforce used these monies to shore up their political support, to reward followers, and to secure votes for their own re-election. In the Highlands, political support is often influenced by considerations of group membership and ongoing patterns of alliance or hostility associated with such membership. This means that an MP is likely to be perceived as spending the money within his own group and its allies. Those left out may see themselves as being treated like "enemies." Indeed in some cases indigenous forms of group enmity have not just survived but have been sharpened by the processes of parliamentary competition for office. Since the office of

MP carries with it not only great prestige but also monetary resources, it is a prize worth competing for. Pre-election forms of forceful intimidation and post-election violent disturbances are to be expected. Some MPs, recognizing the dangers inherent in these processes, including their own assassination, try to find projects that will demonstrably benefit all sections of their electorate. Thus in the Dei electorate in Hagen in the Western Highlands the candidate elected in the 1997 election, Puri-Ruing, who came from a relatively small group in central Dei and also declared himself to be a born-again Christian of the Assemblies of God Church, proposed to use a major part of this allowance for the rebuilding of the Dei Council Chambers as the seat of local government for his area. The Council's site had long fallen into disrepair after the last government advisers or *kiaps* had been withdrawn and council taxes were no longer collected.

Elections in the Highlands are played out as political dramas in which elements of social structure and processes of conflict are put on public display. The police are called in to pre-empt or to quell disturbances that surround these displays. Inevitably in this and in other contexts, such as those of intergroup fighting, the police appear in the guise of the repressive agents of the state, at least in the eyes of the fighters or of those who are producing the disturbances; to others they appear as the defenders and legitimate upholders of law and order.

State violence and the "weak state" argument

Sinclair Dinnen (2000a,b; 2001) has been a major contributor to this debate. From the point of view of those trying to run businesses, large-scale enterprises such as mines, or those who are holding government and public service positions, the rising tide of crime and the *raskol* problem is seen as a threat to "society" at large. Social scientists may see this situation as one marker of the weak hold the state as such has within the wider society. All such views are relative and depend on the interests of those who hold them and on their own structural positions. There is little doubt, however, that an overall set of stereotypes about "government" has grown up in many rural areas; these stereotypes tend in general to be negative. The distrust of politicians stems in part from the suspicions that politicians favor their own kin and also pocket large amounts of money themselves. Rural people see an overall decline in government-run services, for example agriculture, health, education, and road construction and maintenance, this in spite of active government planning and policy

in all of these fields. What counts ultimately is the effective local
delivery of services. This depends on efficient, reliable and safe
communications, and on good working conditions and good motivation for public servants. Throughout the 1990s in rural government centers such as Lake Kopiago in the Southern Highlands
Province it was apparent that no such circumstances held. In areas
such as this the majority of the people are bound to point out that
"the government is not strong" and "government has forgotten us"
(Stewart and Strathern 1999a). Whether this equates overall with a
"weak state" as a whole is another matter (Strathern and Stewart
2000d). The Papua New Guinea Westminster-style democracy set up
in 1975 has proved quite resilient and all the major parliamentary
institutions and the division of government into its executive, legis-
lative and judicial branches have successfully endured to date. Where
difficulties have arisen, they have had to do with overall national
economic problems on the one hand and political faction-fighting on
the other. The country has been heavily dependent on large-scale
revenues from mining enterprises, which have themselves touched off
political conflicts especially over environmental issues. Particular
governments have been put together from small parties, and frag-
ments of parties, and have lacked cohesiveness and a single vision.
Parliamentary politics have survived, but particular governments
have been weakened by these processes of political fragmentation.
The police have been called on more than once to contain the forces
of protest and dissidence in cities, as well as to combat individual
acts of crime. In rural areas their forceful actions in search of stolen
property have sometimes led to accusations of brutality, heavy-
handedness and corruption. The "Operation Mekim Save" (operation "We'll teach them") which the police conducted in rural parts of
the Highlands quite often met with subsequent protests of this sort in
the 1980s. Recently, a rural village group made a successful claim
against the police for damages in connection with such an incident.
In 2001 there was a confrontation between student protesters at the
University of Papua New Guinea over a purported issue concerning
plans for the individual registration of land ownership. During the
confrontation three students were shot dead and the police were
accused of needless killing. The subsequent inquiry highlighted both
resentments against the police and the difficulties of establishing
exactly what had happened. Regardless, such a dramatic event and
the deaths associated with it was bound to raise again the question of
police brutality as well as the ambiguous involvement of politicians
in the background. Two of the students killed were from the Western
Highlands Province, a province which has often been centrally
involved in national political issues since Paias Wingti from Mount

Hagen became the PNG Prime Minister in 1992. Wingti himself was involved in a set of controversial issues involving the creation of a Rapid Deployment Unit to protect the mining operations at Porgera from 1993 onward. The Unit's controversial actions, credibly blamed for worsening rather than ameliorating riotous conditions in the peri-mining area, caused the government later to withdraw support from it (Dinnen 2001: 125–34). Possibly some of these more recent patterns of activity and problems arise at least partly out of the traditions of colonial service among the police in which police might be implicated in revenge actions and sanctions were not always taken against them for the unauthorized use of force (see Kituai 1998).

Conclusion

In this chapter we have moved a long way from a discussion of the relatively benign and adaptive processes whereby Hageners altered some of their exchange practices to an ever-widening set of themes indicating the causes of conflict and violence in a post-colonial world marked by both small-scale criminal actions, intergroup fighting and the conflicts that large-scale economic enterprises such as mining bring with them. Historical changes and experiences of this kind have deeply affected people's senses of themselves in their world. In the next chapter we discuss this further.

CHAPTER 5

Subjectivities: Papua New Guinea

Violent and uncertain conditions in life lead to an alteration in the ways people see their world. In the rhetorics of change that held in Mount Hagen in the 1960s the relatively new projects of road-building were seen by the local people, responding to colonial instigation, as the visible marks of progress and as a part of a march to modernity. The whole world view which the colonial adminis-tration attempted to institute had to do with the "opening out" of previously enclaved communities into a wider world of opportunities and exchanges. Ultimately this opening out was to emerge into the creation of a nation-state at some undefined point in time. Many of the Highlands leaders of the day embraced this vision (to the extent that it came their way) with enthusiasm, and at the time they saw no necessary conflict between the new worlds of business and parlia-mentary politics, and their old worlds of pig-rearing and competitive exchanges. They, and everyone else, thought that the new world brought to them by the incomers would be one in which they would be prosperous and life would be safer than it had been in the times of pre-colonial fighting. By the mid-1980s this vision of safety and prosperity for communities as a whole had been lost. By the mid to late 1990s the growing problems of criminal activity on the highways and in towns had made people afraid to go on journeys. The adventure of traveling on the main Highlands Highway to the coastal city of Lae had turned into a source of anxiety over *raskol* attacks. Instead of life opening up, it began to close down.

These conditions have generated a particular kind of con-temporary consciousness in the Highlands. We will illustrate this with an account of a journey we ourselves took on the Highlands Highway in 1997; and then by a more general look at how ideas about sorcery and witchcraft have burgeoned in these modern contexts.

Roads of violence

In 1997 we collected a set of narratives of violence while driving along the Highlands Highway from Mount Hagen to Lae on the Coast (Stewart and Strathern 1999b). As we drove toward the town of Kerowagi, leaving the Western Highlands behind us, we crossed over a small wooden bridge that marked the entrance into Chimbu Province and T. (one of the Hagen companions accompanying us) leaned forward from his position in the back seat and told us that we were now leaving his home territory. He announced that we were now to be extremely careful to watch for any signs of trouble because the people here were different. We were told to slow down because people often pushed their chickens or piglets onto the road so that vehicles would hit them, which allowed compensation payments to be demanded. T. said, "Watch out for these people, they will jump out at you on the road! They'll attack you and demand compensation! These people don't care about anyone, they don't think about law!"

Then we entered a long stretch of road with rough unsealed edges, to one side of which stood a row of large ramshackle, partly boarded-up and iron-gridded tradestores with gaping doors and dark interiors. T. wanted to buy some cigarettes, so we stopped at the far end of the row while he went back to do so. We did not feel comfortable. As we drove on the car suddenly lurched into a particularly rutted area right at a sharp corner. T. urged us to speed up again and just as he did so a bandit jumped onto the road with a handkerchief covering his face and a rifle pointed at our vehicle. We had no option but to continue to drive, having heard various stories of what can happen to women and men who stop. At the last moment, the bandit jumped out of the way without firing a shot.

After the attack T. began to relate stories to us, extending the confines of the car into the lives of many people far beyond. The journey became a mapping of ritual violence as in the commemorative narrativizing of headhunting exploits in Sulawesi, Indonesia (George 1996). We were journeying through areas which we knew from studies made earlier by visiting anthropologists. Now they were to take on for us a different kind of reality.

As we approached a particularly steep drop-off on the left-hand side of the road in the craggy Sina-Sina area (where Robin Hide

(1980) studied pig production levels for traditional festivals cele-
brating group solidarity in the 1970s), T. told us the following story:

> K. N.'s son, who was traveling with his wife, went over the edge of the
> road here. They were killed. Sorcery had been made on them by the
> woman's previous husband who was a Madang man [a coastal pro-
> vince north of Hagen]. She was from Madang also. Her husband was
> jealous of the new marriage and made this sorcery which caused the
> car to have the accident and kill the two passengers.

From this story we hear echoed the fear of the "other." This had
begun when we crossed into the Chimbu area and been warned
about how different the Chimbu people are from the Hageners. Here
we were being warned about the powerful sorcery knowledge that
other groups can use against Hageners. Both of these reflect worries
arising from the increasing multi-ethnic interactions between peoples
that often lead to conflict and violence – the same interactions that
were originally envisioned as a part of the positive "opening up" of
the Highlanders' world.

Up into the Chuave District, the road grew even steeper and
narrower. Houses built of planks, wire, and iron sheets lined the
roadside, perched on little platforms of land. The dry, burnt-looking,
dusty hills beyond attested to the effects of an El Niño-caused
drought that were later recognized as devastating throughout many
parts of the Highlands, South-East Asia, and the USA. Troops of
small white goats ran skittishly out in front of us prompting careful
evasion tactics. For a moment it seemed as though we were in the
mountains of Greece. But we were not about to stop to buy any of
the honey of Hymettus. T. began a discourse of sociological explanation, stimulated by the "rural slum" appearance of the place.
"These people attack travelers on the highway because they are so
poor. Their land is not fertile and good like ours in Hagen. They
cannot grow coffee and sell it. So they have to turn to robbery, hold-
ups, thieving, and tricks. That's why they do it."

Looking around, we could see no coffee plots. Wayne Warry
(1987: 110), an anthropologist who worked in the area, gives us a
contrary clue, however, when he writes that individual men all plant
small plots, mostly less than a quarter of a hectare, so that "coffee
ownership serves as a universal resource for all men and offers only
slight advantage to the most industrious planters." Perhaps Chuave
egalitarianism has restrained the growth of local inequalities, but in
lean times it makes many desperate for cash. El Niño certainly
destroyed the subsistence base temporarily in many places and
Chuave might have been feeling its worst effects a little ahead of
Hagen. T.'s discourse had that curious combination of verisimilitude

and open-endedness that accompanies much anthropological explanation.

As we drove on T. began to discuss other hold-ups along the road. He said that this was the third time that he had been involved in a hold-up. The first time was when he had been working for a security firm in Port Moresby. After he had been working there for some time he had the job of checking in the cars at night and locking them in behind a fence. As he was coming out of the gate one night he saw someone stretched out on the ground moaning. T. thought that perhaps the man was drunk or hurt and went over to see if he could help him, but the man jumped up and forced T. to go back and get one of the cars. At this point the *raskol* was joined by another man who made T. go with them to the hideout place where they drove the car. T. was shut into a house but he was saved by a stroke of luck. It happened that a friend of his, with whom he had done weight-lifting as a hobby, came onto the scene, and recognized T. He beat up the kidnappers and forced them to release T.

The second time that T. was held up was while traveling from Lae to Hagen. He was with a friend who was driving. The driver was stopped when a *raskol* jumped out at the vehicle at exactly the same spot where the attack had been made on us. This was why T. had warned us to speed up as we approached the place even though the road was badly rutted. The *raskol* threatened T. with a knife, saying that he would plunge it into T.'s side, so T. told him to take his money, 30 Kina (the Papua New Guinea currency). They were allowed to go after their money was taken.

Going through the Chuave area we encountered an example of one of the things T. had warned us of as we first entered Chimbu: a young man jumped out onto the road and shouted at the vehicle. Exiting the area, we looked forward to stopping at the police post on the provincial border that T. had told us was supposed to be ahead so that we could report the incident with the gunman. We drove up a steep hill and at the top found only a flimsy metal-bar gate swung to the side of the road and a cleared space on the other side. There was no police post or any government presence, just an empty sense of abandonment.

We hastened on to the high Daulo Pass. On leaving the pass, T. mentioned how a clansman of his had been driving a PMV (Passenger Motor Vehicle) truck when it went over the edge, but he survived. The car had fallen several hundred feet. This was the only narrative of disaster in which a death or robbery did not figure.

After Daulo there is a sharp descent from the summit of about 8000 feet above sea level to about 5000. We were passing into Asaro, the "high valley" written about by the anthropologist Kenneth Read

(Read 1965, 1986). In his second book, Read refers to the event in which his friend Makis had been killed in an automobile accident, generating stories like those T. told us, and of this he wrote: "Automobiles may be characterized as potentially lethal weapons in our culture, but this 'potentially' means more to the Gahuku, by whom automobiles may be perceived as a ... kind of weapon in accidents involving people from groups who are traditional enemies." He goes on to detail a conflict arising from one such case in which eight people were killed on the Highlands Highway near the village of Susuroka where he worked, and opposing factions had to be kept apart by police using tear gas (1986: 63). A comparative ethnography of Highway-related violence in the Highlands remains to be written, but the picture is similar from Hagen to Goroka, and indeed to the west and south of Hagen also.

We left Goroka and as we approached the place Kombri T. said a terrible thing happened there:

> A man was driving with his pregnant wife along the road when she began to feel the pangs of childbirth. The husband stopped and took her down to the river's edge to let her give birth, which she did. They were resting there with the child when along came some thieves and *raskols* who saw them and killed their child, cutting it into pieces. Then they told the parents to eat the butchered bits of the newborn. In fear and terror the mother was about to eat a piece of the child when the father said he would rather die than do such a thing. He sprang upon them, taking out a bush knife which he had been concealing under his jacket, and killed two of them. The third attacker escaped. The couple reported what had happened to them to the police, who went and burnt down the houses of the group of the people who had done this thing.

T. went on to say that the people living in the Kombri area are famous for holding up cars, shooting people, and kidnapping PMV drivers and passengers who are taken far out into wooded areas where they may not be found for weeks. This area is one in which people from various ethnic groups (including Hagen and Chimbu) have settled, living together in an unstable and improvised way which no doubt contributes to the high criminal activity in the place. Fascinating, perhaps, but it would be a tough choice as a field area. Such places are extreme examples of the dislocations and perturbations that have produced problems throughout the Highlands.

The Highway is a major artery for the movement of goods from Lae to the interior, and as we drove on T. pointed to a spot where a large Coca-Cola delivery truck had tipped over, spilling all of its cargo onto the road and roadside. He said that the local people came up and took away the cargo from the driver, putting it in their tradestores, drinking it, and sharing it with others. When T. came along in his PMV vehicle, slowing to drive around the spill, he was given two cans of Coca-Cola to drink himself. Not far from this spot, slightly further along, we came to a deserted area with a debris of houses which T. remarked represented the scars of a great bout of fighting that had occurred in 1996 when all the houses in the area were burnt down in a payback counter-attack against the community by a rival group. Although we were still driving through apparently empty, stony, low-growing grasslands T. rejected place after place for a possible rest and photo-taking. *Ples nogut*, he said, meaning *raskols* could be nearby.

Finally, we reached the Kassem Pass and descended towards Yonki, approximately 212 km from Lae, which is the support town for the Upper Ramu hydro-electric project. Eventually we entered the dry expanse of the Markham Valley and reached Lae by mid-afternoon, before darkness fell.

A Papua New Guinea newspaper, the *National* (16 March 1998) reported that, "The Highlands Highway, the lifeline to the five Highlands provinces, has been declared by police as being too dangerous for travelers at night. Police Commander, Chief Inspector Barclay Larume, pointed out that rape and armed robberies have increased . . . individuals and the communities at all levels must know who was responsible for various crimes committed around their own areas." The report went on to say that many people felt that reporting to the police incidents along the Highway would eventuate in no action and that, "they feared reprisals from the criminals . . . and [they] have come to accept them [these attacks] as a part of life in Papua New Guinea." The communities along the Highway are also suspected of condoning these crimes because they serve as outlets and markets for the goods stolen in these hold-ups.

Not unlike these stories of violence along the Highlands Highway are narratives of witchcraft and sorcery attacks. These too reflect historical changes as well as recurrent cultural motifs, blending memory and the imaginary together.

Histories of violence and the imaginary

Violence in the Highlands of New Guinea is often seen through the two categories of the imaginary: assault sorcery and cannibalistic witchcraft. The ethnographic and historical locus for our discussion here concentrates on three ethnographic cases where we have conducted fieldwork – Hagen, Pangia, and the Duna speakers of Lake

Kopiago. The time period we are chiefly interested in is from the mid-1960s to 1999, coinciding with events of colonial and post-colonial changes in this region of the world. With colonial pacification and post-colonial transformations in political economy many alterations have occurred in indigenous perceptions with regard to violent conflict generally and with regard to the political values attached to social space. These changes have been reflected in changing notions about sorcery and witchcraft, two sorts of "mystical violence" that have tended to flourish in contexts where open fighting between groups or open interpersonal violence are suppressed or restrained. Sorcery involves the conscious manipulation of magic in order to cause harm to others. Witchcraft involves the use of magical powers to attack and consume the substance of victims in the spirit world, resulting also in bodily death.

We direct our attention to both sorcery and witchcraft because we see these as two overlapping conceptualizations of the kinds of hidden violence that transgress boundaries of the human body and the body politic, as argued by Mary Douglas and others (Douglas 1966; Lock and Scheper-Hughes 1987; Stewart and Strathern 1997b; Strathern 1996). Such forms of violence can clearly be seen as alternatives to fighting, or as forms of supernatural combat themselves. Sorcery and witchcraft accusations and ideas can also be precipitates of patterns of disease, and the sickness and death caused by disease (Stewart and Strathern 1999c).

The New Guinea Highlands is an opportune area in which to examine these themes because the history of colonial contact and post-colonial change is relatively recent (since the 1930s) and ethnohistorical accounts by the people themselves are an important part of the narrative as a whole. Furthermore, this was a region in which fighting flourished in pre-colonial times and has readily re-emerged subsequently as a part of alternating patterns of hostility, revenge, and peace-making. Exchanges of wealth goods are made in order to make and remake alliances and to pay for killings, but these are counterbalanced against perceived continuing, if covert, acts of hostility by sorcery/witchcraft. The imagery of cannibalism is used in some groups (Hagen, Duna) to express aspects of aggressive hostility and the transcendence of these aspects by "proper" forms of consumption and exchange. Assault sorcery depends on magical notions of bodily invasion and destruction which parallel those of witchcraft, but without cannibalistic images. We argue that the common theme linking these two phenomena is that of bodily invasion, resulting either in the destruction or the consumption of body parts. Legitimate exchange is then seen as substituting the "consumption" of wealth for the consumption or destruction of bodies.

Alterations in perceptions of space over time in these societies can further be related to changes in political economy. The integration of previously autonomous local polities into administrative areas in colonial time had complex results, causing forms of interdependency that have also been accompanied by latent intergroup hostilities. Changes in patterns of production, consumption, and exchange that have resulted from cash cropping in certain areas (Hagen) have also led to new patterns of fears of witchcraft, while alterations in the conditions of communication between local and ethnic groups have led to increased fears of assault sorcery (Pangia, Duna). Finally, gender relations have been affected by both economic and political changes, leading in certain instances to intensified or renewed fears of female witchcraft (Duna).

The framework we use here involves the idea of political space or the fields of power that are created and altered in colonial and post-colonial conditions. The power of the state, seen most broadly, has altered political space in the societies we will consider here, not simply by colonial "pacification," i.e. the removal of organized fighting and the creation of "peace" between groups, but rather by setting up new forms and categories of space within which political power was both denied and exercised (i.e. indigenous forms of power were denied and colonial power was exercised). The removal of organized fighting did not mean the removal of animosities, or the pre-emption of future hostilities. Rather it provided a basis for the elaboration of these, with permutations of scale, setting up new conditions for fears of both sorcery and witchcraft to operate within.

We begin our discussion by a brief review of theories of hostile sorcery and witchcraft in contexts from Africa and New Guinea, partly because it is our impression that our New Guinea-based arguments probably apply also to the materials on change in patterns of witchcraft/sorcery ideas in colonial and post-colonial Africa.

Sorcery, witchcraft, and conflict

Images of bodily invasion clearly go with perceptions of conflict between persons, the penetration and permeability of boundaries of the body, personhood, and groups, as stressed in the work of Mary Douglas (1966, 1970, 1991, 1996) and others (e.g. Lewis 1970, 1989; Purkiss 1996: 120). In the earlier literature on sorcery and witchcraft, arising to a fair extent from Africanist ethnography, stress tended to be laid on the basis of such practices in conflict, tension, and strain between persons in positions of competition, jealousy, or incompatibility (e.g. Max Marwick's theory of sorcery as a social "strain-gauge" and the notion that sorcery provided an avenue of redress for perceived wrongdoings, Marwick 1952, 1970). It is clear that such a theme has empirical applicability to the contexts we will be discussing, where the images in terms of which notions of conflict are expressed take the human body and by analogy the bounded community as the chief site for their symbolic work. We are also primarily interested in contexts of historical change rather than in synchronic typologies of systems.

At the outset it is also necessary to remark that we are interested generally in comparing processes (social and historical) rather than in setting up definitional typologies. Therefore, in discussing assault sorcery and cannibalistic witchcraft, we do not lay stress on the distinction between the terms "sorcery" and "witchcraft" as such, but rather use these terms for convenience in order to refer to symbolic syndromes of mystical violence that are partly distinct and partly overlapping. Several authors, in reviewing the question of definitional distinctions between sorcery and witchcraft in general, have concluded that hard and fast distinctions can be made in hypothetical terms but then fail to fit the complexities of ethnographic fact.

In Africanist studies of the historical contexts involved in changing patterns of witchcraft accusations one point that is made very clear is that the societies concerned had been subjected on the whole to severe political and economic dislocations, through wage labor, missionization, and the growing dissolution of social bonds resulting from the movements of people and challenges to moral codes and patterns of local authority. Douglas (1991: 727) notes that in Zambia, Malawi, Zimbabwe, and Zaire where many ethnographic studies were done, "the old political systems were not functioning" and witchcraft accusations between rivals for village power therefore arose in contexts where other ways of obtaining redress against an unpopular leader or of contesting succession to an office of leadership were no longer available. Although in an earlier work Douglas (1970: xx) points out that propositions about "social breakdown" and "increase in frequency of accusation" are usually empirically untestable, we are on safer ground in pointing out the demographic, spatial, and structural changes themselves. Thus, in situations of increased movements of people it is likely that arenas of ambiguity and distrust in social relations, cited as those in which witchcraft accusations are made, will also increase (referred to by Douglas 1970: xvii). And the developmental cycle of competition for local power in villages will also be exacerbated by wider processes of social instability and so give rise to witchcraft accusations, such as Middleton notes for the Lugbara of the Sudan (1987: 137, 153). The

91

same holds for sorcery and witchcraft in other parts of the world (see Ellen 1993: 16 on South-East Asia). It is not simply a matter of arguing for an increased frequency of types of action, but rather of studying the changing loci of accusations and ways of handling them over time, and of relating these changes to wider processes. In this regard the conclusions from African studies certainly apply, *mutatis mutandis*, to some of the cases we will consider here (e.g. the Duna). Stephen (1987: 277–88), in a section on social change in her survey on sorcery and witchcraft in New Guinea, argues that in the pre-colonial past some sorcery roles may have been seen as legitimate, but that this was altered by colonial changes. This may well be true for certain cases, but we need not suppose that the structures in place prior to colonialism were necessarily stable rather than fluid and changing. However, where changes are recent and documented we can make some headway in delineating structural transformations as, for example, when sorcery, like wealth, is no longer restricted to an elite of specialists but is attributed to the populace at large.

Douglas, in one of her surveys of different patterns of boundary-maintaining/redefining behavior, points out that a witch may be seen either as an outsider, or as an internal enemy (a member of a rival faction or having outside liaisons, or as a dangerous deviant) (1970: xxvi–xxvii). These patterns may change over time, but in one of our categories, the assault sorcerer, the predominant assertion is that the perpetrator is an outsider, a classic version of a terrifying enemy. We discuss this image of the assault sorcerer next.

Assault sorcery and images of violence

Assault sorcery is generally correlated with distance and hostility. The sorcerer is seen as an outsider who penetrates a community area or isolates a victim on the periphery of such an area (in a garden or a secluded pathway) and makes a physically aggressive attack by stunning the victim, butchering the internal organs and removing them, sewing the person up again and sending him or her home to die later. Often, if not usually, the image is that assault sorcerers operate in squads trained by adepts. Assault sorcery is closely cognate with notions of organized fighting and is therefore likely to flourish as an idea when community spaces defined by organized fighting have lost their definition owing to pacification and colonial restructuring and there is a struggle to define new spaces and exercise power within them.

In assault sorcery, further, the sorcerer directly confronts and overcomes the victim by minatory force. R. M. Berndt, in a classic examination of types of sorcery and violence among the Usurufa, Jate, Kamano, and Fore of the Eastern Highlands Province in Papua New Guinea, explicitly notes that in performing this kind of sorcery "the sorcerers have two main intentions in mind. They have received an injury which demands retaliatory action ... [and] they want to avoid open warfare" (Berndt 1962: 224). An assault sorcerer who is caught will also be shot and his corpse dishonored and abused before being returned to its home village, in the same way as might happen to a casualty in fighting. Fears of such sorcery may rise after the forcible ending of open intergroup conflict. In this case sorcery can be regarded as a form of feuding between groups. Nevertheless it is a special kind of feuding, thought to depend on the exercise of magical powers, and therefore contributes to a higher level of terror between groups, making "pacification" less "peaceful" than it might otherwise be.

G. W. Trompf, in his wide-ranging survey of types of "payback" activities in Melanesia, makes a similar point when he notes that an attribution of deaths to sorcerers or witches "is actually a common post-contact development in many areas of Papua and one consequent upon the fact that indiscriminate payback killings or tribal wars have been debarred" (Trompf 1994: 64). Trompf goes on to discuss several cases where sorcery accusations have in general altered with social changes, for example overcrowding and population pressure in Kalauna (Trompf 1994: 67 citing Young 1971), disease patterns, intergroup mobility, and altered political configurations as among the Mekeo where the colonial power congregated people in large villages and kept chiefs under tight control so that sorcerers "now being highly mobile and bent on freely negotiating with each other in côteries ... emerged as a fearful power bloc, accumulating real local political power as steadily as chiefly authority was sucked away under expatriate control" (ca. 1880–1940) (Trompf 1994: 77). Sorcerers had previously acted to inflict punishment/retribution on people at the behest of chiefs. Now they began to act for themselves. Sorcery thus became more than a way of pursuing a feud or punishing wrongdoers: it became a mode of politics in itself.

To pursue our own exposition of these themes we now give composite ethnographic accounts pertaining primarily to three areas of the Papua New Guinea Highlands, Pangia, Hagen, and the Duna area, specifically Duna speakers who live near the Strickland River in the Aluni Valley. We begin with the Pangia case.

Pangia: assault sorcery and change

The Pangia District in the Southern Highlands Province of Papua New Guinea was first brought under administrative control by Australian patrol officers in the 1950s. It contains some 20,000 speakers of the Wiru language, horticulturalists and pig-rearers, who were engaged in classic patterns of organized fighting and exchange between local groups until the time of pacification and missionization after 1960. In this area there were in the 1960s some 20 partly colonially created, named "villages," containing various groups and group-segments, whose members saw themselves in certain contexts as "communities." At the far southern part of the whole area, eight hours walk from the next village, lay Tangupane, a place with fewer than 100 residents, a high proportion of unmarried men, situated at a low altitude, and with an immense reputation for being the home of feared assault sorcerers, called *mãua* or *uro* (these names themselves would be pronounced only furtively by informants). (In some parts of the area a distinction was made between *mãua* and *uro*, but for others the two terms were practically synonymous.) People were thought to be greatly at risk from these sorcerers if they traveled to Tangupane and especially if they slept there. Visits to the outside latrine at night could not be made alone. One person had to stand guard at the latrine's entrance to watch for a sorcerer's approach while another watched from the house door. But the *uro* supposedly did not venture far beyond Tangupane itself and its environs. By the 1980s it was held that the number of these sorcerers had greatly multiplied and they also were now ranging over the whole Wiru area, even besetting people near the government station. Why this marked change in perceptions? We suggest that colonial power had drained the villages of some of their indigenous powers of setting boundaries and had set up a space in which invisible, uncontrollable powers that previously were held into local spaces by structures of organized fighting and restrictions of movement, were now seen as able to move more swiftly and widely. The space seen as that of pacification and development by administrators was seen by the people as the space of these invisible powers, let loose from their previous local contexts.

In more detailed terms, the colonially created villages were material concentrations of more dispersed forms of sociality than had existed previously. The villages, which were themselves beset by internal factionalism, became bounded arenas of social relations outside of which space was seen as less positively social. Pigs were no longer allowed to be kept in village houses, and were fed and stalled in small huts in garden areas defined as in some way "wild." The creation of these "wild" areas set the stage for fears of sorcerers threatening the boundaries of the new village settlements. Internal conflicts in the villages made people nervous and apprehensive of hostility. The previous solutions of social spacing were for the time being no longer available.

This example shows that in restructuring community spaces the colonial power in Papua New Guinea both set up new sorts of local units and produced problems of how to define community contexts. Forces of sorcery in Pangia, seen as threatening the integrity of local places, were also seen as forms of bodily invasions. The assault sorcerer lurking on the edge of the village exactly expresses this dual imagery.

There was no known counteraction against *mãua*, hence the great fear it inspired. *Mãua* sorcerers presented an extra threat to women, since they were said to rape them before killing them. The sorcerer's presence was marked by heat that suffocated the victim. On sending the victim home the sorcerer first asked "Where does the sun rise/set?" and if the victim reversed the proper answer, he was satisfied and sent the victim off, with his/her own kidney in the mouth. Upon arrival at home, the victim began to roast and eat the kidney in an auto-cannibalistic act and was then recognized by kin as doomed to die. Here we see an image of the victim in a state of disorientation, being no longer aware of what is inside or outside, or how to relate himself/herself temporally or spatially relative to the surroundings. This is similar to the type of confusion experienced by persons who are placed in particularly terrifying situations. For example, a soldier who does not realize that his arm or a leg has been blown off during a battle until there is a lull in the fighting and the immediate terror has lessened so that he can take note of his own body.

Among the Daribi, neighbors of the Wiru to the south-east, assault sorcery was known as *kebidibidi*, and there were apparently methods of divination to determine who had caused a death by it, as well as statements that counter-raiding parties would be organized in revenge (Wagner 1967: 52). Wagner points out that a larger number of deaths was attributed to this kind of sorcery than could in practice be feasible (1967: 53). Assault sorcery thus played a special part in the Daribi imaginary economy of death. It would be particularly interesting to know if this situation had recently emerged, i.e. since "pacification," as Wagner notes that most of the adult deaths which took place during his first fieldwork period were attributed to assault sorcery. This was during 1963–65, ten years after the beginnings of Australian colonial administration. Possibly this represented a shift in consciousness of senses of agency resulting from "pacification," as we have suggested for the Wiru. The sense of control of boundaries that collapsed inward during colonial times may have driven communities such as those among the Daribi and Wiru to attempt to re-establish new ways of explaining what was occurring around them and differentiating themselves from the potentially hostile "others" who were around them, and increasingly among them, and whom they were not allowed to kill in open fighting. The inability to express collective group agency through organized fighting may thus have increased rumors of assault sorcery attacks in both these areas.

Witchcraft among the Melpa

Melpa-speakers of Mount Hagen in the Western Highlands Province of Papua New Guinea number some 80,000 people, divided into tribes and clans, intensively linked by exchanges and by intergroup hostilities belonging both to the past and to contemporary contexts (discussed in Chapter 4).

The Melpa, who have an elaborate array of ideas about the causation of sickness and death, do not appear to have the idea of assault sorcery in quite the way the Daribi and Wiru do. On the other hand, they have notions about *kum*, a kind of witchcraft that is held to operate in a terrifying way reminiscent of assault sorcery, since the *kum* may eat the inner parts of a person, also causing its host to become a cannibal seeking out corpses to consume. The technology of death that eventuates from either assault sorcery or witchcraft is quite similar. It is pertinent, therefore, to compare the Melpa ideas of *kum* with those of assault sorcery in Pangia, since both destroy the inner parts of a person that are emblematic of life-force and human feelings.

The core idea in notions of witchcraft among the Melpa is greed (Strathern 1982; Stewart and Strathern 1997b; cf. Kahn 1986 on Wamiran ideas). In 1964–5 such notions were attached to the supposition that one or two women in each clan were cannibals who could turn themselves into dogs in order to rob new graves of their corpses and consume the flesh. The propensity was held to pass from mother to daughter. Historically, there was a greater emphasis on such notions in the Northern Melpa area close to the Jimi Valley, and in many ethnohistorical representations of witchcraft the Jimi is cited as its origin place. The Melpa who live in the Jimi are bordered on the north by the Karam, among whom witchcraft ideas are common and are called by the term *koyb* which is the same as the Melpa *koimb* (Riebe 1987). *Kum koimb* is the Melpa term for "cannibal witchcraft," so that the concept may be a fusion of ideas of *kum*, shared with the Wahgi and Simbu peoples to the east of the

Melpa area, and *koyb* from the Jimi area to the north. This may help to explain why *kum* is sometimes spoken of as a category of spirits that live beside watercourses or in bush areas separate from people, and sometimes as the force of witchcraft inside people. The witches of the Jimi Valley are held to be able to enter people's bodies through their anus and to eat their way through their intestines, exiting through their upper orifices, and leaving their victims as good as dead. The image here is one of "assault witchcraft." These ideas represent the Melpa people's fears of their very different northern neighbors in the Jimi Valley.

Michael O'Hanlon describes *kum* witchcraft among the Wahgi as intangible malevolent powers which certain individuals of both sexes have that allow them to cause illness and death in others. Descriptions of witch attacks may stress the intense gaze of the witch or the harboring of small familiars (e.g., cat, marsupial rat or snake) that a witch unleashes against his/her victim. This familiar is often said to emerge through the anus of the witch and to devour the inner organs of its victim. Accusations of *kum* witchcraft among the Wahgi also tend to occur after an epidemic outbreak, illness, or deaths in an area (O'Hanlon 1989: 57–8). O'Hanlon also has reported for the Wahgi a heightened number of *kum* sorcery accusations at the time of funeral feasts when dysentery epidemics may spread through the attendees. The Wahgi people at these funeral feasts said that the people practicing *kum* should be sent back to the Jimi Valley, indicating that they share the same ethnohistorical traditions as the Melpa. There are traces here of a pre-colonial history of intergroup relations and fantasies, but these are hard to follow up. We turn therefore to more recent times.

In 1978 (three years after Papua New Guinea became an independent nation-state) a rumour spread throughout the Northern and Central Melpa areas that more people were becoming cannibal witches. Instead of just a few women in particular kin-lines, now it was feared that many people of both sexes were turning into cannibals, and that this was because the previously existing witches were secretly placing pieces of human flesh into the headwaters of streams from which people drew their drinking water. The "grease" or "fat" from the human meat was tasted and experienced as "sweet," therefore people would become cannibals. People were enjoined never to drink water outside of their own clan areas and even within these to be very circumspect (Strathern 1982). We see here a prime idea of the spread of danger through the pollution of water and the need to control consumption in order to avert the new danger flowing through the clan areas. We suggest this was an expression of the collapse of the "properly" bounded clan area as perceived in the post-colonial imagination. The connections with fears of greed and excessive consumption associated with the advent of cash through the growing of coffee for sale and the beginnings of the decline in the exchange ethos in Hagen also seem clear here. The solution suggested was that everyone should control consumption of the medium held to carry danger, the water supply, a solution that mimicked epidemiological hygiene. Water is seen in Hagen curative rituals as a healing, purifying substance. Yet it was also held to harbor *kum* stones. As an element flowing between categories in a landscape it could take on either healing or harming capacities. Persons who have greedily consumed pork at a feast and go to slake their thirst at a stream give an opportunity to these little *kum* stones in the water to jump into their throats and sit there. In one image these are seen as *namb* and *pilamb* ("let me eat, let me experience"). They would scrape at their host's throat and make the host insatiable for pork to feed them.

We may compare this now with the rumors of 1995 (Stewart and Strathern 1997b). Previously, witches had been reported to eat only the dead; they patrolled around burial sites and fed on corpses. In 1995 the idea emerged that there were not enough corpses for the witches to feed on and that they needed an alternative source of food (i.e. living people). R., the male Kawelka leader who gave this account, noted: "We're afraid because we think the witches may eat all of us living people and finish us off. *Kum koimb* is the name for these witches." R. also described the practices of a traditional healer, Toa, an expert in all kinds of magic spells, who had developed a new technique for removing witchcraft familiars from people.

Three differences can be seen between the 1978 and the 1995 narratives. First, the cannibal witches had become more aggressive by 1995. Second, R. declared that they were said to be controlled by a Queen who lived in the Simbu [Chimbu] area east of Hagen, seen as the home of dangerous people belonging to a different province (another image of post-colonial political space, which we have already seen at work in the narrative of our Highlands Highway journey). And third, the situation was so serious that it now supported the entrepreneurial rituals of a witch-finder (who acted like a pest exterminator by coaxing out and trapping the witches' animal familiars).

Comparing the 1978 and 1995 rumors directly, we see that in both cases there was a fear of an outbreak of excessive desires for consumption. In 1978 this was to be controlled by "hygienic" taboos. In 1995 these were not adequate: the cannibals were turning into direct murderers and curative magic was invented to restore them to normality.

In 1997 a further development of ideas took place. We found the Melpa people to be experiencing a wave of millenarian notions concerning "world's end," in which witchcraft activity was now seen to be on the rise because Satan had instilled *kum* into his followers, and this in turn was taken as a sign that the world would shortly end (Stewart and Strathern 1998c). The domination within the world of greed and desire would consume everything and bring about retribution from God and Jesus, since curative rituals could not control the situation any longer.

The increased passage in colonial times of notions of *koimb* (*koyb*) from the Jimi into Central Melpa coincided with travel by Melpa people on colonial government patrols into the Jimi area in the 1950s and later. The later epidemics of witchcraft fear among the Melpa are also correlated with historical perceptions of growing tension over inequalities between people, marked by capitalist-style consumerism and, as we have suggested, further compounded in 1997 by millenarian notions (Stewart and Strathern 1997a, 2000a).

Duna witchcraft and assault sorcery

Witchcraft can be an idiom for gender politics, as materials from the Duna-speakers of Lake Kopiago in the Southern Highlands Province will show. Our fieldwork was conducted with some 1000 Duna-speakers belonging to five distinct parishes in what we call the Aluni Valley. Like the people of Pangia and Hagen, they cultivate gardens and rear pigs, but they have little cash cropping. These people classify what we have labeled assault sorcery in the same general category as female witchcraft. Both are described as *tsuwake*, assault sorcery being *tsuwake tene* (the base of *tsuwake*) and witchcraft *tsuwake kono* (the *tsuwake* of the mind). Since pacification and missionization in the 1960s, almost all other forms of sorcery practiced by males as a part of interparish hostilities have been abandoned and are not an object of fear (up to 1999), but, in this political space that has been cleared of other kinds of mystical violence, ideas about both types of *tsuwake* have flourished and perhaps intensified. Assault sorcerers were considered to be crossing the Strickland River between the Duna and the culturally different Oksapmin areas to the west and menacing the outskirts of Duna settlements in the Aluni Valley during 1991 and 1994; and internal fears of female witches (often with Oksapmin origins in their genealogies) led to suspicions and occasionally accusations. These two kinds of attack by unseen "others," internal-female and external-male, had effloresced in people's imaginations again precisely

99

because of post-pacification conditions. Cultural bricolage was also at work. One informant who declared that he had trained squads of youths to be *tsuwake tene* said that instead of the traditional sago-spine dart employed to pierce a victim's breast he was able to use syringes from his trade as an aid post health orderly. In 1998 we were told that the assault sorcerers had mostly themselves been shot with guns in retaliation for their raids, but that the few that were left were now improvising methods to lure victims into their power by persuading women to act as sexual decoys and then closing in for the kill. The sorcerers were always described as being from the Oksap-min area, i.e. as prime examples of "the immediate other" to the Duna themselves.

Gender politics were at work here in two ways. First, outside male assault sorcerers were thought to be threatening local women, making them nervous outside of their village areas, and requiring men to stand guard over them as they formerly did in warfare, so as to take revenge for any attacks on them. Women were thus made to feel dependent on male protection. Second, female witches were thought to be threatening villagers internally as a result of their desire for "meat." This idea was used to discourage women from meeting to talk together or to complain about pork distribution, and so to reassert male control and surveillance. Both processes may therefore be seen as post-pacification responses by males in an attempt to reinforce their authority over females. Another detail is significant here. In pre-colonial times female witches were said to have been sent as agents by male leaders to kill and consume males in enemy areas. With pacification they ceased to be used in this way and instead acquired an independent will, allegedly turning against victims in their own communities. This historical narrative parallels in muted form the narrative of Mekeo sorcerers given by Trompf (see p. 93).

The underlying issue here is the perception of appetitive desire just as with the Melpa. Pork is highly prized, and in pre-colonial times men excluded women from consumption of cuts of pork that they themselves consumed in the course of a roster of religious cult per-formances. With the demise of these cults, the introduction of Christianity, and the loss of communal men's houses, men found it harder to deny pork to women, and correspondingly, we suggest, began to accuse them more vigorously of witchcraft. In a further twist, by 1994 certain prominent men whose wives were rumored to be witches would specialize in turning up at pig-kills expecting to be given meat to share with their wives. Their hosts, afraid of the witchcraft of these women, would give especially generous portions to the husbands. The conflict of the sexes over consumption was thus resolved by these men in terms of an alliance coalition consisting of male leader and witch–spouse. In 1994, in the village Hagu, men also rebuilt their communal men's house, and these itinerant pork-seekers would stay overnight in this so as to share at least a portion of their meat with its regular male residents and establish ties of male sociality and solidarity.

By 1998 the situation had developed in further and more complicated ways. These have to be understood in terms of the dynamics of historical change since the time just prior to the first regular administration patrols in the 1950s and the 1960s. Epidemic outbreaks of disease that were spread through the intrusion of European outsiders and their workers from other parts of the country caused widespread dislocation and depletion of groups among the Duna. In the low-lying areas immediately near the large Strickland River which marks the boundary between the Duna and the Oksapmin peoples of a number of small intermarrying groups fought among themselves, both prior to this time and during it. Many of their members migrated up-valley to the mountainside parishes where they had ties through cognatic kinship or marriage. The composition of these parishes thus became more heterogeneous than before.

Furthermore, these immigrants were coming from areas that were identified with the perceived primordial origins of witchcraft itself. Indeed the conflicts between the Strickland groups were partly, according to the ethnohistorical accounts, about accusations of witchcraft. In 1991 and 1998 informants in the parishes of Aluni and Hagu indicated that witchcraft had originated from the actions of a male earth-demon, who had emerged out of a rock in the Strickland area and had proceeded, according to the origin myth, to seize people and consume them. He was persuaded by a woman of one of the local groups, the Makalan, to have sex with her instead of killing and eating her, and she then became the host to his cannibalistic propensities which were passed down in turn to her children and descendants (emphasis was placed on the transmission through females). The women carrying witchcraft powers married into further local groups and their descendants carried these powers with them in the pre-colonial shift from the environs of the Strickland grasslands to the forested mountain parish areas. Among the Duna it was a male spirit who brought the knowledge of witchcraft to women; but it is a female spirit, the Payame Ima, who brings the knowledge of how to divine who is a witch to men (Strathern and Stewart 1999d). The Payame Ima was not the spirit who brought witchcraft to humans. Rather, she is said to enter into and possess the men to whom she grants ritual power to divine for witches.

Duna parishes are local collocations of kin, affines, and associates, conceptually organized around a core of co-resident males descended agnatically from a parish founder. This core is known as the *anoagaro*, the paternal line, distinguished primarily from those who are *imagaro*, belonging to the parish through maternal ties. The effect of parish incursions by immigrants was to make the *anoagaro* a minority in their own parishes and therefore to make the exercise of their leadership more difficult. They are supposed, for example, to control the disposition of land, and this task would be made harder with the absorption of newcomers, including ones thought to be witches. At the same time a good proportion of these *anoagaro* leaders were themselves polygynists with at least one wife thought to be a witch.

In 1991 and 1994 fears of the actions of these witches appeared to be on the increase, but the local Christian churches (Baptists, Apostolic) forbade the use of traditional methods of divination to seek out and punish witches thought to have killed and eaten people. In 1996 this prohibition was broken after the dramatic deaths by fire of two young men from Aluni parish who had taken part in a hunting expedition to the Strickland and had lit fires in the grasslands (to burn out wild pigs) which then consumed the men themselves. A diviner was hired and he pinpointed four local women as the witches responsible, who were said then to have confessed to their acts. The women were driven out of the community and their kin paid compensation to the relatives of the two dead men. In 1998 this kind of sequence was repeated in Hagu, with two twists. The deaths that triggered accusations were a result of an epidemic (of malaria, typhoid, and pneumonia) following an unusual period of drought and food shortages (the El Niño events of 1997, mentioned earlier); and the son of a female witch who had "confessed" to her actions himself killed his mother, causing the original accusers to pay compensation for the death. Those who had died were two small children of the only *anoagaro* leader in Hagu; one of them was his youngest child and only son, the sole successor to the *anoagaro* line. The witches included people from a family with whom he had been in a dispute over land use (see Strathern and Stewart 1999d for fuller ethnographic details). The witches all left Hagu, but at a later point they were said to have returned and we were told that the leader and his wife, who now had a young son to replace the one who had died, were concerned for the safety of their new child and so shifted their residence downhill to a new location.

These dramatic and troubling events brought to the fore the results of some 50 years of change: alterations in village composition and the dynamics of village leadership as well as the prior alterations in the gendered consumption of valued foods and the latest ecological stresses of famine and sickness. Furthermore, another dimension was revealed – accusations about witchcraft can be a part of arguments about legitimate control within the parish by *anoagaro* leaders. These leaders may accuse others of subverting their control on their line of reproductive descent. But the leaders in different parishes also harbor resentments against one another as a result of the idea that they themselves have witches as wives. While a leader may use this attribution to coerce others into giving him pork, he is also vulnerable to accusations by rival leaders and others that his wife has killed and eaten someone within his parish or of a different parish. Accusations of witchcraft, like those of sorcery, can thus become a mode of politics, entwining together issues of gender and interparish as well as intraparish conflict. The control exercised by *anoagaro* leaders was in the past heavily buttressed by their prominence in rituals. Nowadays it appears that their position has been weakened to some extent.

Cannibalism, consumption, and change

We have seen that in the Duna narrative of the origins of witchcraft a male earth-demon (*tama*) emerges from a hole and immediately begins to seize people and eat them. This direct form of cannibalistic consumption is then mediated by his sexual relations with a human woman and witches emerge, born from their congress. The same myth goes on to explain that, in those early times, the people at the Strickland ate people instead of pigs. When a pig died it was placed on a burial platform and mourned, and a human person might be taken as a captive to be killed and eaten as a funeral sacrifice for the pig's death. A wandering hero from a different area comes upon a woman about to be sacrificed in this way, and he saves her by cooking the pig instead, offering to the mourners its flesh sprinkled with salt which he has brought as a gift from his own area. The people are thereby persuaded to abandon cannibalism and eat pork instead.

The image of cannibalism here is cognate with witchcraft, as we have seen, since it belongs to the same myth as the story of how witchcraft first developed. Both witchcraft and cannibalism generally, therefore, are to be seen as forms of inappropriate consumption, and social progress is marked by their abandonment. The problem for the Duna is that while straightforward cannibalism is seen as having been transcended by the gift of salt, witchcraft is still thought to be passed on within the community (Strathern and Stewart 2000e).

Narratives of an implicit shift away from cannibalism and its ritual transcendence in other forms of behavior belong in turn to a wider class of origin stories in which "civilization" is presented as a mode of evolution in sacrificial practices. Michael Young's (1983) discussion of victimage in Kalauna fits in here. Victimage in Kalauna (Goodenough Island, Milne Bay Province, Papua New Guinea) is institutionalized in two principal modes: a projective system of vengeance, homicide, and sorcery, and an introjective system of self-castigation. "Although these types of victimage may sometimes appear in pure form as vicarious sacrifice and self-sacrifice respectively, they are often found in combination" (p. 29). The legend of the cannibal warrior, Malaveyoyo, culminates in his sacrificial death which serves as a marker of the beginning of the colonial period when *abutu*, competitive food exchange, altered the previous pattern of vengeance and violence, serving as a surrogate for killing and eating one's enemies. *Abutu* retained the idiom of oral aggression but displaced the object of consumption from the flesh of one's enemy to food such as pigs that one had reared (pp. 92–109).

Exactly the same logical structure is shown in the conventional Hagen statement by relatives of a victim to the killers: "You killed our man but you did not eat him or taste anything sweet, so we give you back pork as his 'bone', and you can give us back pigs for this 'head' later." Here, the figurative phraseology does not rely on a trope of past versus present but on a notional cannibalism juxtaposed against a real non-cannibalism. The message, however, is the same as in Kalauna: the exchange of pork transmutes oral aggression into sociality; or, put otherwise, it is the conversion of "feasting *on* my enemy" into "feasting *with* my enemy." Images of cannibalistic witchcraft show that transition arrested or denied, or nowadays a "regression" to a wild state that threatens contemporary life when the life of order through exchange no longer can control the disordered spatial forces of post-colonial turbulence.

Ideas of the spread of assault sorcery also reflect these alterations in spatial relations, since assault sorcerers, like witches among the Melpa, are thought in Pangia and the Duna area to be spreading more widely than before, reflecting the facts of greater movements of people and continuing distrust among them. The assault sorcerer destroys the community by marauding it from the outside, while the witch destroys it by eating victims within the community. Both images reflect the complex changes in the meanings of "the outside" and "the inside" in an altered world of spatial relations.

Conclusions

Our arguments here have been presented *seriatim* in our review of historical changes in three different areas of the Highlands of Papua New Guinea – the Pangia, Hagen (Melpa), and Duna areas. The materials from these areas differ somewhat in their scope and focus. The Pangia area does not appear to have notions exactly corresponding to those of cannibalistic witchcraft such as are found in Hagen and Duna, therefore for this area we discussed only the case of assault sorcery. Hagen lacks the exact notion of assault sorcery, but *kum koimb* witchcraft partly includes images comparable to those found in Pangia. The Duna have both assault sorcery and witchcraft ideas.

This disparity of ideas, combined with areas of overlap, does not affect our main argument. Indeed we have been concerned to show that the wider field of assault sorcery plus witchcraft can be examined to reveal alterations in scale and intensity of the kind we have been exploring. These alterations have involved some shifts and innovations in cultural tropes or images, for example the 1978 Hagen idea that witches hid pieces of human flesh in streams or that in 1995 witches were now attacking living people not just corpses, or the Duna idea of the substitution of syringes for sago-spines and the use of women as decoys to attract male victims. These alterations in images can themselves be traced to various changes in the life-worlds of the people. Our main focus, however, has been on changes in the contexts of operation of these "mystical" ideas and the ways in which they go with wider patterns of change. Our findings are that several factors have combined to produce the alterations observed: the movements of people, the mixing of linguistically or socially different groups, the effects of disease, alterations in group composition and the condition of leadership, changes in patterns of inequality arising from patterns of cash cropping and the consumption of goods purchased with money, and shifts in the balance of power between the sexes and between local leaders themselves. Finally, in all instances we have argued that colonial "pacification" and post-colonial instabilities have combined to produce perceptions of political space in which notions of sorcery and witchcraft, far from disappearing, have mutated and spread.

Ideas about sorcery also enter into the processes of contemporary parliamentary politics. A case history from 1999 in the Southern Highlands Province illustrates this point.

In mid-1999 an issue arose in the Southern Highlands Province of Papua New Guinea whose ramifications widely disrupted social and economic activities throughout the province and continued to do so for some months. Dick Mune, a politician who had been ousted as governor of the province in the 1997 national parliamentary elections by Anderson Agiru, had challenged the validity of the election result. The Supreme Court was about to begin the process of deciding on his challenge, and Mr. Mune set out by car to travel to the town of Mount Hagen in order to catch a plane for the capital city, Port Moresby and attend the court hearing. On the drive to Mount Hagen his vehicle left the road and tumbled over a hillside. Mr. Mune was a passenger in the car, and he jumped out to save himself but struck a rock and died from the blow. The driver of the vehicle survived and declared that the brakes had failed. Mune's relatives and supporters declared that this apparent accident was in fact caused by sorcery or by tampering with the car, engineered by supporters of Agiru in the expectation that the court was about to rule in Mune's favor. A revenge attack was mounted on a relative of Mr. Agiru, who was manager of a major store in the provincial capital Mendi. After this killing, Tari people from Mr. Agiru's electoral area seized police vehicles in Tari township and killed several people from Mr. Mune's home area in retaliation. The whole province was convulsed by this conflict, since Mune and Agiru had contested the regional seat for the entire province and had divided the province between them. Supporters of Mune's cause set up road blocks on major roads. People were afraid to travel. Business transactions were widely disrupted. There was much criticism of the Southern Highlands MPs as a whole who like every other politician in the country were embroiled in the faction fights to replace the government led by Prime Minister Bill Skate. The new government led by Sir Mekere Morauta, elected in mid-July by a vote in Parliament for the prime ministership, inherited the problem and set about resolving it with a province-wide committee.

This case showed the enduring, and still urgent, significance of modes of thinking about the causation of events in places such as the Papua New Guinea Highlands. It also clearly indicated the pervasive power of politics. A single car crash led to province-wide conflict, further loss of life, polarization of different areas, and considerable economic loss. Of course, this was linked to the fact that an important politician was killed in the crash and to the interest of his constituents, but the results would have been different in a different cultural context. Both notions of sorcery and of the political imperative of revenge were important in this "modern" context. Both factors entered into the "violent imaginary" of those involved and caused a protracted set of disturbances in provincial and national politics. Ideas such as the suspicion of sorcery, generated out of the tensions and competition for money and power in politics, but drawing also on an available repertoire of cultural patterns, blended with the reaction of seeking revenge for a death to produce a major crisis and brought travel almost to a standstill in the province, greatly impeding the operations of business firms and mining operations. Certain subjectivities, then, may have massive material consequences, as well as themselves reflecting the consequences of change.

In the next chapter we pursue the issue of revenge further.

CHAPTER 6

Revenge

In considering a part of the history of violence in the Papua New Guinea Highlands we have seen how an aim of exacting revenge may enter into people's interactions. It is a part of our overall argument in this book that revenge is a persistent and significant theme which must be taken into account in building up a theoretical understanding of violence generally. This is so because revenge is a major motivation in the replication or reproduction of violent relations over time. Treating revenge as a contingency, secondary to other factors such as political expediency, tends to push it into the background in favor of arguments based on political economy or the general psychology of aggression. It is important, however, to keep revenge in mind as a central not a peripheral factor, since it provides a link between psychology, culture, and politics. It is also important to keep in mind the ways in which some peoples have replaced immediate physical revenge practices through accepting compensation payments for killings. Further, the question of revenge poses for us once more the issue of contested legitimacy. Revenge killings may be a legitimate basis for political interaction, accepted by both sides. But this situation can change over time. Further, witnesses of one kind or another may not grant the act the same legitimacy that immediate participants do. Colonial governments sought to suppress revenge activities by redefining concepts of law and justice as belonging only to centralized authorities. Difficulties in supporting that claim have been inherited by post-colonial governments, whose inability to check patterns of fighting and killing between people over time leads analysts to speak of "weak states" (see Dinnen 2001; Strathern and Stewart 2000d). In the Highlands of Papua New Guinea, where earlier elaborate patterns of exchanges have been attenuated, Christian forms of prayer and attempts at reconciliation between groups have been inserted into practices as ways of criticizing and controlling violent responses by people to what they see as the wrongdoings of others. In Hagen, for example, these forms of prayer are aimed at reducing or removing the anger (*popokl*) which people feel and inducing them to accept material atonement for killings. It should not be thought, however, that revenge is an issue only for "newly emergent" ex-tribal societies, of interest to a few anthropologists but not to the bulk of sociologists, historians, and political scientists. It is rather an underlying tendency in human behavior that is always capable of emerging in social relationships of whatever scale, interpersonal or international. And this is so because, in spite of long-standing historical attempts by local or state authorities to discourage it, the idea of revenge is closely tied to ideas of justice.

A centralized system of justice allows people to engage in mediated combat with each other via words and representations in court contexts. Essential to this appropriation of control over disputes is the imperative to separate the forceful actions of individuals or small collectivities from the concept of justice. "Taking the law into their own hands" is precisely forbidden; although the phrase itself betrays its own partial negation in the recognition that it is in a sense "the law" that people may be taking into their hands rather than "senseless violence." From the viewpoint of centralized law enforcement, however, all exercise of physical force without the sanction of "the law," i.e. central authority, becomes violence: assault, homicide, murder, unlawful killing, physical harm. Fighting between people is unlawful and is classified as a public disturbance. Obstructing others, which also has a bodily referent, is seen in the same way. On the other hand, forceful action by authorities is seen as legitimate, up to a point. This point itself may be ambiguous and contested. "Reasonable force," "unnecessary force," and the like are adduced as concepts to demarcate the licit from the excessive use of force, the latter in all cases now being labeled as violence. The upshot is that violence becomes associated as a term with the realm of illegitimate action. "Police violence," "mob violence," and "youth violence" all in the end come to be placed in the same category.

The effect of these transformations of the concept of legitimate force in social relations is to render difficult many of the principles or patterns in terms of which acephalous societies studied by anthropologists are organized, all the more so when these societies are incorporated into colonial or post-colonial states. Automatically these societies, which had their own complex and nuanced systems of dispute settlement as well as standard recourse to feuding and intergroup fighting in specific circumstances, became vulnerable to being labeled as "violent societies." Concomitantly, the bifurcated classification of societies into those which had "law and justice," as against those in which "tribal blood-feuds" were practiced, sprang into being. As anthropologists were at pains to point out, these classifications are ethnocentric; but they are persistent, and they explain why accounts of blood-feuding applied to European societies are viewed as belonging only to the past, and incapable of being applied to contemporary events. The mistake here has been to equate "revenge" as a general principle with "blood-feud" as a particular institution, and to see that institution as signifying "violence;" and finally to see violence in this sense as opposed to law. The possibility of seeing either revenge or feud as law is therefore pre-empted. Law, like so many things, is in the eye of the beholder or witness, of course, and it is not our purpose here to justify any particular set of practices by exempting them from the category of violence. It is our purpose, however, to situate forms of activity into their appropriate analytical contexts. Acts of physical force or harm can be situated on a sliding scale of perceived legitimacy. They are also perceived differently by different witnesses. "Revenge" is a category that is particularly subject to negative evaluation in societies with centralized law; yet, in a broader sense, it is an enduring pattern of action in these societies also, expressed in modalities other than physical action itself. And in a deeper sense the execution of criminals who have committed murder or treason surely represents the sublimation of revenge, much as state authorities and the relatives of those murdered may dissociate themselves from such a notion with phrases like "This is not about revenge, it's about justice." For other societies, as we have seen, revenge *is* justice, in the sense of "getting even." This is one of the meanings of the Hagen word *kapokla*, applied to appropriate forms of counteraction against aggression. And that sense of "getting even" is pervasive in social relations in many centralized societies also, as is shown in the maxim: "Don't get mad, get even." This, too hides the fact that the reason why many people do work hard to "get even" is precisely that they have "got mad." The further problem lies here in the definition of what constitutes "being even" and what might be "overdoing it" or might provoke further untoward consequences.

With these provisos in mind we turn to some historical contexts in which revenge actions have played an important part.

Christopher Boehm's book on the blood-feud in Montenegro greatly broadened the scope of social anthropological analyses of revenge by placing them in a complex diachronic context of relationships between groups and between Montenegro as a whole and the Ottoman Empire, up to the mid-nineteenth century and beyond (Boehm 1984). Boehm showed that feuding was a way of controlling, as well as expressing, violence, and that its eventual transcendence by the Montenegrin state did not result in the death of the traditions concerning it and values belonging to it. Blood-feuding presents us with a situation in which the legitimacy of the violence involved is on the whole less contested than in many other contexts, where both sides recognize the right of the other to exact revenge, and the place of the concept of "honor" in this process (for another historical study, see Miller 1990). However, this legitimacy is not historically static, and this is the point we wish to stress. At the same time, we also wish to emphasize the point made earlier – that revenge cannot be consigned to a position of peripherality in the analysis of violence generally. Rather than being confined to a few acephalous societies, most of them now transformed and "modernized," revenge is a form of behavior that has a perennial capacity to re-emerge in the fluid circumstances of state control. It is important, therefore, to study it and trace its coexistence with modern conflicts in various parts of the world.

In terms of its possible historical development, Raymond Kelly has carried out an interesting exercise, based on cross-cultural sample materials, in which he takes the practice of vengeance as a central feature (Kelly 2000). Noting that we need to distinguish between different categories of "violence" and between violence and war, Kelly (2000: 60) traces a possible set of transitions (or at any rate typological contrasts) in responses to homicide:

> (1) no counteraction, (2) the legitimation of capital punishment through public opinion in the absence of specification of a part or entity responsible for its achievement, (3) the stipulation of relational, kin-based vengeance obligations that generate a de facto vengeance group and (4) kin group responsibility for carrying out vengeance against the malefactor (alone) vested in the extended family and/or kindred of the homicide victim. The transition to kin group member liability – in which the malefactor is the preferential but not the only recognized target of vengeance (stage 5), or in which any member of the killer's group is susceptible to vengeance (stage 6) constitutes a watershed in that these stages are restricted to societies with segmented organization.

Stages 5 and 6 correspond broadly to a state of blood-feud, which Kelly accepts as a kind of war because it involves "preplanned armed conflict between political units." Societies of the Papua New Guinea Highlands, we may note here, definitely belong to the category of societies with "segmental organization" (and tend to correspond also with the earlier typology by Otterbein 1993 of societies with "fraternal interest groups"). Kelly further points out that these stages of "development" are generally correlated with the transition from foraging to agriculture. Groups with fixed resources of some considerable fertility are able to engage in fighting against others more easily; and, we may add, have a strong motivation to defend these resources against attack rather than moving away, although the availability of places of refuge elsewhere can also be an important factor.

Kelly's use of the term "capital punishment" for vengeance killings executed by parties of kin, sometimes against neighboring communities but targeting only the killer or putative killer in cases of suspected sorcery or witchcraft, follow the usage of Keith Otterbein (1993), who suggested that this form of action was universal in human societies. Otterbein also noted that a transition to killing any member of a category rather than just the killer represents a massive emotional displacement of feelings onto the category itself. This displacement, we may add, is also fundamental to the extension of such feelings to the nation-state with its ideology of patriotism, and manifests itself sometimes in the actions of transnational terrorist acts aimed at the members of such a nation-state regardless of their own individual actions. It is the dense mesh of perceived interdependencies in the nation-state that provides the grounds for such ideological perceptions, the beginnings of which can be seen in the transition to Kelly's Stage 6.

Kelly bases his own use of the term "capital punishment" partly on the extensive studies by Bruce Knauft of homicide among the Gebusi people, a small group living on the fringes of the Papua New Guinea Highlands in the Strickland-Bosavi region, where the Etoro, a similar people studied by Kelly himself, also live (Kelly 1977, 1993; Knauft 1985). The Gebusi, when first studied by Knauft, had a high rate of homicidal killings resulting from the attribution of deaths to sorcerers. Many of these killings resulted from ambushes, executed either with the help of close kin of the suspect or at least without their determined resistance. We may wish to call such killings "capital punishment," but the semantic interference here is likely to come from the association of such a term with centralized state societies and judicial systems. At any rate, the phrase does point out the association of such "punishment" or "justice" with "revenge," which we ourselves stress. Kelly's treatment also reveals that war, as a development out of blood-feud, is likely to have large elements of revenge ensconced in it in terms of the emotions of those who participate and see their fellow-fighters killed by the enemy. It is all the more striking, then, to consider the complementary point, that blood-feud may be a way of *limiting* conflict rather than escalating it. This also depends on a set of cultural distinctions between blame, responsibility, and liability, a theme we have earlier explored for the Duna people of the Strickland River area in the Southern Highlands Province of Papua New Guinea (Strathern and Stewart 2000f).

In this chapter, we will look at a number of case studies. First we will discuss Christopher Boehm's Montenegrin study and widen it to consider materials on contemporary Albania. Second, we will consider the case of the Kwaio in Malaita, Solomon Islands, studied by Roger Keesing. The blood bounty system among the Kwaio, by which the relatives of a person who had been killed hired others to take revenge, itself had a "fatal impact" on colonial relations, culminating in 1927 in the killing of a British government officer and a subsequent massive revenge reprisal by the British. These events have colored Kwaio history to this day, leading to protracted demands by the Kwaio for compensation. This kind of historical intersection between a pattern of feuding and compensation, and colonial intervention contrasts sharply with Mount Hagen in the Papua New Guinea Highlands, where envy rather than revenge has dominated patterns of interaction and the indigenous revenge system does not involve a full-scale pattern of blood bounty payments.

Finally, we will look at available materials on East Timor and the struggle between pro-Independence and integrationist factions there, culminating in the referendum of 1999 and the withdrawal of Indonesian troops, coupled with violence on the part of pro-integrationist militias. The study shows revenge writ large, cut loose from a specific set of social controls

All of these cases will show how revenge issues, emanating from customary local practices, can rapidly mutate as they become embroiled in succeeding levels of turbulent political conflict. The studies lead easily into a consideration of interethnic conflict, violence, and the state. But before turning finally to these topics, we will include some materials on suicide and a way of interpreting it as an intentional act, one that may also involve notions of revenge.

The examples we use in this chapter are designed to show elements of revenge and its management at work in diverse settings. In historical Montenegro we see it as a part of a coherent political system, transformed over time through the centralization of power. In the Solomon Islands we see it as crucially caught up in colonial and postcolonial history. In East Timor we see it cut loose from both social organization and central control and therefore producing greater risks of outright massacre. These examples bring home the point that revenge may operate either to control levels of killings or to accelerate them, depending on the political and historical contexts.

Montenegro is a part of what remains of the Republic of Yugoslavia, which has its heartland in Serbia and an uneasy existence also in Kosovo. It has a history of seeking or maintaining its autonomy vis à vis others, including resistance to the incursions of the Ottoman Empire. These external conditions have powerfully shaped the ways in which Montenegrin tribal groups have handled their internal affairs. Since the various groups strongly maintained their independence, they pursued blood-feuds among themselves as a way of ensuring their autonomy and equivalence. At the same time they limited the scope of these feuds because of the need to resist the Turks. The final transformation of their own uncentralized system into a central one which proclaimed itself as a Christian state also had much to do with the imperative to unite against external forces. In this final step feuding itself was outlawed. We will see also how feuding and practices of compensation interacted during these periods of historical change. The Montenegrin state was formed in 1851. Boehm's first fieldwork there took place in 1964–66, among a tribe (or *pleme*) of people known as Upper Morača, a group which owned communal forests and summer pasture lands for their livestock. These people belonged to the socialist state of Yugoslavia at the time. Today Montenegro as a whole is reasserting its autonomy within a much weakened overall state structure influenced by the end of Communist rule and a history of conflict with Serbia's politicians the outcome of which is not yet clear. (The fall of Slobodan Milošević has probably modified this situation of conflict.) Boehm's later period of fieldwork in the mid-1970s included archival work which enabled him to study historical records before the mid-nineteenth century and compare them with ethnohistorical materials on feuding.

Boehm calls the mode of living of the Montenegrin tribes prior to their coalescence into a state a "refuge area warrior adaptation" (Boehm 1984: 41). A typical tribe contained various clans, mostly descended from Slavs who came from Russia prior to 1000 C.E. and conquered the ancient Illyrians other than the Albanians. In addition to these older *plemes* there were more recent Serbian immigrants, who had fled from feuding in their own areas or from subjugation by Ottoman lords after violent conflicts. The Montenegrins at one stage paid taxes to the Ottomans, but after 1600 C.E. their Eastern Orthodox Christian bishops played a military role in encouraging them to resist this process and to defend themselves against disciplinary raids by the Turks (p. 43). This pattern of uneasy, fluctuating relations continued "for the next one hundred and fifty years." Montenegrin youths raided Muslim settlements to obtain human heads (p. 46). The unit of settlement was the household, a small patrilocal group which belonged to a clan (*brastvo*). The clans joined together in a *pleme* did not have shared descent, but the *pleme* did have a set of leaders or *vladika*, who could act with the concurrence of the whole tribe to expel traitors (p. 48). States of hostility and feuding between groups were described as *krvna osveta*, "blood revenge," or *u krvi*, in blood (p. 51). Quarrels between people were always at risk of escalating into blood-feud following a killing, partly because of an ideology of honor which declared that it was shameful not to seek revenge. The pressures involved in such a system, Boehm notes, must have been extreme. He cites one case where a mother "showed a container of her dead husband's blood to her young sons to remind them ... they must avenge him" (p. 63). (Similar motifs appear in Iceland, see Miller 1990, and in Mount Hagen in Papua New Guinea, see Chapter 8.) A clear distinction was made in principle here between murder (*ubistvo*) and blood revenge. Accidental killings were also recognized, it appears, and could be "compensated for financially" (p. 66). Vengeance killing was therefore considered legitimate by its perpetrators and by the members of the society at large as its "witnesses," but it could still in turn lead to further retaliation. Although the Montenegrins were converted to Christianity by the tenth century C.E. they blended with it some of their practices, conducting rituals of blood brotherhood and swearing oaths (that might imply vengeance activities) in church (p. 68). Church leaders tended to be the only literate persons, and it was they who campaigned against feuding over the centuries. The code of honor for both men and women was maintained partly by intense local networks of gossip, which functioned in the absence of coercive powers within the tribe. Sensitivity to insult could fuel killings which were regarded as justifiable, but again could be subject to retaliation. Montenegrins, Boehm remarks, were experts in insulting people, but only to a point where they would not react physically. Calculation of this point, though, could be hazardous. Co-villagers might try to intervene in an altercation to stop it reaching the level of a killing. Honor was also involved in cases where a girl became pregnant and her sexual partner refused to marry her which might lead to the sexual partner being killed (p. 102), causing a feuding situation.

Boehm stresses that such killings were seen as morally necessary, but that political circumstances could influence how vengeance was proceeded with, for example whether the killing was between two clans of the same tribe or what the relative size of the clans was. An attack, however, could in all cases be made at once on the house of the killer. If this failed, the attackers could resort to ambushes. Those attacked might flee for refuge, or tribal leaders could attempt to pacify the feud at this stage, arguing that the attackers should accept blood money. The honor code, however, obliged people to feel that it was a dishonor to desist before killing once in relatiation. Still, if their clan was small they were more likely to do so (p. 107). (See Miller 1990: 211, on the reasons why in ancient Iceland people might be reluctant to pursue vengeance.)

Those who fled might be able to return later if they paid blood money and accepted the destruction of their property. Or they could go to the Ottomans and receive land from them. In return they would be asked to raid their own people and bring back a head "to prove that they were worthy of being Turkish subjects" (p. 108).

Within the clan, feuding was not permitted. Between clans of the same tribe, energetic efforts were made to achieve a pacification. Between two clans of different tribes this did not hold, and sometimes any member of the other side's tribe might be targeted, leading to the spread of feuding relations to the tribes at large (p. 109). What would curtail such processes and lead to a settlement would be a raid by the Turks, or simply the threat of such a raid. The Turks both represented a refuge for feuding clans and a force that suppressed the intensity of feuding.

If a pacification did not occur there might be a drawn out period of mutual killing, marked by counting the numbers of house guard dogs killed as well as people. "People" here generally means men. We are told by Boehm that women were not to be targeted. Indeed their killing would not be reckoned as a part of the blood score and was seen as morally dishonorable (p. 111). The two sides would generally not agree to pacify until the agreed score of killings between them was even (p. 113). Reaching this point of equilibrium was hard because each side considered its own grievances to be the greater, and each might try to "pay back in greater measure than was received." Montenegrins recognized the problems of "boiling blood" and its ability to break a temporary truce agreed on as a step to pacification. It might be many years before the wary clans would agree to *miriti krvi*, "pacify the blood" (p. 121).

Here Boehm introduces the institution of the Court of Good Men, composed of *kmets* or "judges" who had to be of high moral status and have a reputation for impartiality. They were charged with helping to settle feuds. The place of religious functionaries was also clearly very important. Boehm notes how a bishop might stand in between fighters urging them to stop and that monks were important as scribes who wrote down pacification documents (p. 122). Also, to test if one side was lying in testimony, its opponents would be enjoined to utter extreme curses, "invoking affliction with disease and absence of male progeny upon anyone who told a lie," and the other side then swore to its own veracity (p. 123). The judges

116

themselves were largely concerned to bring about compromises and, given the context in which honor was at stake, to avoid calling either side guilty (p. 132).

Pacification was difficult to achieve if one side was ahead of the other in killings. It was this side, the "winning" side, that would be enjoined by the judges to sue for peace and to ask the "losing clan" to accept blood money in order to appease its unsatisfied desire for revenge. In one case, which occurred between members of the same village, the "winners" were also told to bring six infants so that a man of the other side would stand godfather to them "and thus cement peace by a spiritual relationship" (p. 134). Their representative was also ordered to "hang the gun which fired the fatal shot around my neck and go on all fours ... to the brothers of the deceased." He did so, saying "take it, O Kum [godfather], in the name of God and St. John." The brothers then took the gun from his neck, kissed him and wept and said "happy be our Godfatherhood." This was followed by a shared feast and then the offer of payment. Weapons were offered, but the recipients took only the gun that had fired the fatal shot, saying that this was for their brother and the other guns should be returned in recognition of the godfatherhoods. Sometimes a large amount of money would be offered, but this too would not be taken. Boehm says that the payment was therefore largely symbolic (p. 135).

It is apparent that much more was involved here than a simple payment of compensation. The occasion was one of an emotional, ritual reconciliation, replacing the emotions of hostility and offering a form of catharsis within the code of honor. Further, spiritual kinship was established by a godfathering. Overall, an equation between persons and guns was also set up. Offering the gun that killed the enemy as a sacrificial gift was a powerful way of making an apology and expressing a willingness to relinquish power and strengthen the other side.

Since godfatherhood was also within the domain of the church, it is evident that in it too we see the power of religious influence in curbing the scale of killings in feuds. If kmets could not settle a feud, they might take the case to a bishop to achieve an honorable arbitration. The bishops also campaigned against the institution of feuding itself. After 1840 Bishop Rade Petrović used his power to end the feuding system by declaring that blood-vengeance killers would be punished by the death penalty (p. 122). The bishop must have been building to some extent on the Montenegrins' fear of being cursed, since bishops were prepared not only to excommunicate those who went against them but also to curse them with a lack of male progeny (p. 69). Even if, as Boehm notes, this did not always stop people from continuing a blood-feud, it must have been a powerful sanction, since feuding itself was a part of the survival strategies of small brotherhoods, and the threat that this survival would be compromised by a curse would surely weigh on people's minds. God provided a symbol of centralized authority which otherwise was difficult to establish.

Montenegro became a part of the Serbian Empire in the late twelfth century C.E. and managed to remain independent after the Turks defeated the Serbs at Kosovo Polje in 1389. Incorporating some Albanian populations of their own, and pursuing feuds based on the same logic as those in Albania, the Montenegrins fought against both Turks and Albanians beyond their borders. Serbia and Montenegro cooperated against the Turks in the Balkan wars of 1912-13, and the area as a whole was incorporated into Serbia at the end of World War II. Its total 1987 population was estimated at 625,000. It has been in the news much more recently owing to its ambivalent relationship with Serbia during the years in which Slobodan Milošević exercised influence in the government of the Yugoslavian Republic as its president, including the period in which Serbian forces drove hundreds of thousands of Albanians temporarily out of Kosovo, provoking military attack by NATO forces during 1999; and subsequently when Serbian-Albanian tensions in Kosovo had been complicated by Albanian attacks on nearby Macedonia, leading to concerns about Albanian expansion in the region. Throughout this period, the news media have said little about internal conditions in Montenegro. It is reasonable to speculate whether unrest there, and elsewhere in the Balkans, might bring with it a return of feuding behavior. If so, we might also speculate that contemporary conditions might make settlements harder to attain, as has certainly happened in Papua New Guinea since at least the 1970s. This is because the increased movements of people and the loss of control over people's actions that goes with this mobility mean that local leaders may not be able to pressurize participants into settling their differences.

For northern Albania, whose tip pushes into the territory of Montenegro, there is some evidence that this has occurred. According to a *New York Times* report of December 26, 1999, in the city of Shkoder on August 3, 1998 a farmer, Shtjefen Lamthi, was shot as a part of a feuding process. His assailant stepped into his path and shot him 21 times with a Kalashnikov assault rifle, then walked away. Though many saw the event, none offered evidence to the police, and his brothers refused to speculate on who might have been responsible.

Albania is a poor country, suffering from environmental pollution and poor nutrition and health conditions, partly the aftermath of failed Communist government efforts to introduce a factory economy. Its new democratic government (established after 1991 when the Communist regime disintegrated) collapsed in 1997, and mobs looted police and army arsenals for weapons, making it difficult for subsequent government authorities to regain control. Bandits have killed members of relief organizations and stolen their vehicles. In these circumstances, the *New York Times* reporter Scott Anderson says, revenge codes have come into play again. Feuding had been banned during the Communist era, with tight state control, but its traditions had remained in the Dukagjin Valley where Shtjefen Lamthi originally came from. His killer, Anderson says, was from the same valley, and he was taking revenge for a killing that happened 13 years before in the village of Thethi, 50 miles to the north-east of the city of Shkoder.

Lamthi's death led to a situation in which his killer's family expected revenge to be taken on them. According to the ideas of the *kanun* or customary law a family is "owned" by the killing unless it takes "its blood back" by killing in return one of the killer's relatives. The chain of killings can continue for a long time. Anderson says that the longest was 240 years. The Communist government itself conducted a battle against this practice, razing the round towers that were built in the past to accommodate families under threat of a revenge killing so that they could wait in safety to hear the terms for a peace settlement. The Communist leader Enver Hoxha ordained that those who took blood vengeance should be buried alive in their victims' coffins (Anderson 1999: 33). Hoxha himself ran a regime of state terror, denouncing anyone who disobeyed him as an enemy of the state. His legacy is therefore not exactly revered. One of his local party members was Preka Lamthi, who became secretary-general for his Thethi region. One day, during a drinking session, a Lamthi family member stabbed a Rrushkadoli man after the latter had insulted his Lamthi hosts by overturning the table at which they sat. Both guests and hosts had transgressed the rules of hospitality.

The Rrushkadoli family waited until Hoxha died and the Lamthi family was no longer so locally powerful. There was an exodus from the villages when Albania was opened up so that movement across the border was easier. Young people rushed to the towns seeking work or emigrated elsewhere. Both the Lamthi and the Rrushkadoli families moved to live near or in Shkoder. But pyramid investment schemes exploded the country's economy in 1997, and large numbers of weapons came into the hands of people now left destitute. One such person, said to be a Rrushkadoli family member, was the man who took his revenge on Shtjefen Lamthi in 1998.

Back in Thethi, Anderson talked with an elder who is sometimes called on to mediate in disputes because of his knowledge of past feuds and how they were settled. This elder clearly resembles the figure of the *kmets* or "judge" in Boehm's Montenegrin ethnography; but he acts alone and without wider support. Anderson also discovered a modern organization, the All-Nation Reconciliation Mission, dedicated to arranging peace negotiations, started by an individual who had himself been involved as a target of a blood-feud, in which he was kept "locked," i.e. unable to move around because of the risk to his life. This man is now the general secretary of the Mission, and he told Anderson that many of the disputes that have recently led to feuds stemmed from the scramble to claim land after the Communist collapse in 1991, fueled in 1997 by easy access to weapons.

The Rrushkadolis themselves professed to want a peace settlement, so as to free them from their "locked-in" status; while Preka Lamthi appeared to be surprised that there were still any "blood" issues between his family and theirs. The ambiguities here indicated clearly that the issues were not over.

Anderson stresses the centuries-old origins of ideas about feuds that lie behind these events. At least equally striking, however, is the intersection between these ideas and a complex, running series of events and circumstances which have conditioned their expression. The Communist Party altered village power structures and destroyed refuge towers; later, economic opportunities made people move from villages to urban centers; subsequently economic chaos led to revolts and the acquisition of weapons. All of these factors severely reduced the likelihood that feuds could be controlled. The new national organization attempts to fill this gap, but faces problems of legitimacy and power.

Boehm's study and this case history from nearby northern Albania both show how feuding systems have interacted with historical events. Boehm's work demonstrates how feuding was both passionately adhered to and prudently kept in check, for good political reasons, and also how significant was the influence of the church. The contemporary study from Albania shows that without such controls feuding becomes in a sense a modern activity itself. In the next case study we will show how a particular construction of ideas about blood-feud intersected with colonial relations between the Kwaio people and the British authorities in the early twentieth century, with long-term effects that are still felt today.

Roger Keesing's work among the Kwaio people of Malaita in the Solomon Islands stretched over many years, from 1962 until his death in 1993. Some two thousand Kwaio people live in the hills above Malaita's eastern coast, clinging to their ancestral land and its ways, while other Kwaio have migrated to the coast and become Christians, joining others of their language group living there. The hill Kwaio have not been exempt from the forces of historical intrusion into their lives, as the extended history in Keesing's last book, *Custom and Confrontation* (1992) shows. Keesing notes that they have been connected to the world economy for more than one hundred years. Early on they worked in sugar cane plantations in Queensland, Australia, and in Fiji. Later they worked on plantations in the Solomons and with American military forces who came to resist the Japanese invasion there during World War II. Young Kwaio men travel to the capital of the Solomons, Honiara, by plane, and seek work or adventure there. Large numbers of Malaita people in general have settled around Honiara seeking land to settle on and opportunities for employment not found at home, leading in the 1990s to further confrontations with the Guadalcanal people themselves who are the traditional landowners in the area and to violent conflict between Malaitans of the Malaitan Eagle Force and Guadalcanal members of the Isatabu Freedom Movement. Young Kwaio men have played a part in the genesis of these most recent interethnic conflicts.

The British government declared protectorate powers over Malaita, Guadalcanal, and other islands of the Southern Solomons in 1893 in order to counter German interests in the North Solomons area (Bougainville). In the 1920s the British instituted a head tax and an alien legal system. In 1927 the Kwaio assassinated two British officers and massacred their police patrol, bringing down severe reprisals, which in turn have led them subsequently to claim compensation from the British for their losses and for the desecration of their ancestral shrines, and after independence in 1978 from their own national government (Akin 1999). The constitution of the hill Kwaio as a cohesive, persisting group has arguably emerged out of these and other struggles they have had with central authorities. Their adherence to ancestral customs may itself not be unconnected to their attempts to wrest what they see as justice from the state for the destruction of their shrines as well as the loss of life at the time of the reprisals.

Keesing recognizes striking continuities in the patterns of Kwaio struggles against the state, centered on issues such as law, taxation, and the power of the British monarchy and the Solomon Islands government against the power of the ancestors (1992: 5). For example, "the son of the leader who assassinated the District Officer in 1927 leads an antigovernment demonstration on the Prime Minister's lawn almost sixty years later"; and does so "clad in the same mode of warrior regalia his father had worn."

It is this "assassination" which is in fact central to our discussion here. Keesing writes (p. 29) that the Kwaio elders themselves see their culture as having two poles: production, wealth, and life; and theft, rape, and killing. Both poles had their own forms of magic and achievement, and some groups specialized in aggressive activities, especially those men who were recognized as *lamo*, "men of violence and presumed ancestrally conferred powers who led in combat and acquired wealth and reputation as executioners and bounty hunters" (p. 30). Killings set blood-feuds in motion, and vengeance could be taken against whole groups, whose members retired into fortified refuge places or went around heavily armed (as in the Balkans practices).

Those involved used magic and also treachery to gain their ends, and epics, called *ai'imae*, were sung recounting the stories of their struggles. Demands for compensation could issue in fights, leaving more dead. Ancestors were invoked in divination to see whether a raid or ambush would be effective. The victims of killings, quite unlike the situation in Montenegro, could be women. Guns, which had been introduced in early days of trading with visiting European ships, were used in these killings. Keesing frequently mentions the institution of the blood bounty. This practice gives Kwaio feuding a twist that is again quite different from the Montenegro patterns. The Kwaio's early access to guns probably also emboldened them in their dealings with colonial authorities.

'Elota, a Kwaio leader whose life story Keesing translated and published (Keesing 1983), remembered the *lamo* as central to these killings, tough characters who were prepared to pursue a quarrel with any outsiders and to threaten to kill them. Such *lamo* were also themselves expected to die violently (p. 54). 'Elota also explained how killings could arise out of a death caused by sickness. His younger sibling died while he himself was still a boy and his parents took a pig, castrated it, and dedicated it as a bounty. "This piglet is for blood – for the death of anyone at all, to avenge my dead child." The pig would live until such a revenge killing had been accomplished, and would then be sacrificed. Two *lamo* men wanted to claim this bounty and asked 'Elota's father about various candidates to be killed, finally suggesting they should kill someone's child, to which the father agreed. The bounty they claimed was 200 valuables (shells and other items) and 30 pigs. 'Elota went on to explain a further twist in his narrative. The relatives of the child who had been killed put up a bounty for the death of one of the killers. The killer then responded to this by himself killing his own cousin (father's brother's son), ostensibly because the boy had defiled an ancestral shrine by defecating in it. He then claimed the bounty from the relatives of the child he had killed, a bounty which they "had put up for his own death." Finally his relatives also claimed a death compensation from 'Elota's father for the death of the cousin. "So my father paid ten valuables as death compensation."

'Elota's examples tell us several things. First, there was a sacrificial aspect to the practice of setting up a bounty. The physical mutilation of the pig marks the future death of a victim, symbolically equating the pig with the victim. The killing itself was therefore seen as in some sense sacrificial. Second, any death could lead to a suspicion that someone was responsible for it, perhaps by mystical means, and to the likelihood that a bounty would be set up for another death "to pay for" the first one. 'Elota does not explain here what was in his father's mind, but perhaps the choice of eventual victim was not random. Third, a *lamo* who undertook a contract killing could receive a substantial amount of wealth for this, as large as any death compensation. Fourth, he could avoid being killed for this by himself executing a kinsman, and could then actually himself claim the bounty. Finally, using the logic of enchained responsibility that is also found in parts of Papua New Guinea, he could *also* claim a share in a compensation payment for the death of the person he had executed, from the family of the man who had originally set the chain of killings in motion.

More generally, the practice of putting up bounties cut the Kwaio revenge system free from the controlling restraints of kin relations. Some men could specialize in the role and acquire wealth in doing so – a sharp contrast with the kin-controlled practices of Montenegro. Killing for revenge almost becomes a commodified practice in Kwaio custom.

Still, the paradigm of revenge held. It was applied also in the context of the labor trade itself, since some Kwaio held outsiders in general responsible for the deaths of young men taken away to work in Queensland or elsewhere who failed to return, and sought to kill outsiders in revenge for this (Keesing 1992: 43–7). Among the Kwaio themselves Keesing suggests that "the Kwaio strongmen [*lamo*] had apparently stepped up the scale of blood feuding at the end of the nineteenth century and early years of the twentieth, partly as a result of the freeing of labor time through the introduction of steel tools, and partly because of the transformation of combat with firearms [brought back by men who had been recruited to work abroad]." One rifle, a Snider, was obtained originally in Fiji; the *lamo* Basiana used its barrel to crush the skull of District Officer Bell in 1927.

Basiana and some of his kin had been made angry when the colonial authorities mounted a revenge raid for the killing of a South Seas Evangelical Mission missionary called Fred Daniels. Kwaio men were upset when the missionary introduced new customs by mixing boys and girls at schools, and when returning converts, who had been away as laborers in Queensland but had once been custom priests, broke ancestral taboos. They killed the missionary to stop these new practices and drive the mission away. In turn the Kwaio oral tradition claims that government soldiers came, set fire to houses, and shot people, men and women, as they came out. The government apparently did this to make the Kwaio respect "law and order." The result was the opposite. The Kwaio, in particular the *lamo*, were affronted. The *lamo* especially might well have seen the British authorities as a threat to their own power.

W. R. Bell was an Australian who was assigned in 1915 to be in charge of a station among the Kwaio, while British officers went to fight in World War I. Bell built up a detachment of indigenous police from north Malaita outside of the Kwaio area, and was concerned for the Malaitans in general and their future. He originally opposed the idea of a head tax, but he was charged with instituting it nevertheless. Bell also sent out a message to the *lamo*: "You have killed, but the killing is over." In 1923 he went on patrol to introduce the tax and to stop blood-feuding. The *lamo* who featured earlier in 'Elota's narrative responded "that he would not pay the tax and would kill anyone who came for him" (p. 59). Bell's party was informed that this *lamo* was collecting the bounty for killing his own cousin, and Bell then sent police in to tell the Kwaio that the law of England had come, people must pay tax, and "eating pigs from blood bounties is finished today." They told Basiana and the other *lamo* to eat their pigs today but to come down to a patrol post and pay tax the next day. Those who did not do so were to be arrested.

The Kwaio, however, were already upset at the deaths the government had caused and "several bounties had been put up for the death of a white man" (p. 61, words of Jonathan Fifi'i). Basiana began to think he could obtain bounty money by killing Bell. He was also angry because Bell had supposedly called him a "bastard" (Fifi'i in Keesing 1992: 61), talk that the Kwaio saw as defiling. Fifi'i recounted Basiana's encounter with Bell in 1926 when he stepped up to pay his tax money. Basiana, according to this account, brought four shillings out of the five that were required and apologized for the shortcoming, saying that he lived in the bush and had not been away on contract labor overseas. Bell brusquely told him to go home and get some pigs for sale to the police, who would give him the fifth shilling required in return. Basiana made the four-hour walk home and took a *dafi*, a crescent shaped pearl shell chest decoration which was consecrated to one of his ancestors. He smashed it, took one of the pieces and laboriously ground it to the shape and size of one of the shillings. He took this back the next day to Bell, saying that the four shillings had pictures of Bell's King on them while the fifth had on it the mark of his own ancestor. "So here are your five shillings – take them!" (p. 65). Bell was angry and called Basiana a bastard, saying "I'll take it now, but don't do it next time."

The District Officer, putatively knowledgeable about the Kwaio, seems to have missed his cue here, a mistake that cost him his own life. Perhaps he did not understand the sacrificial act involved in Basiana's presentation of the shell "shilling" to him. The shell and its destruction were worth much more in Basiana's eyes than a shilling. Presenting it in a shape of the introduced "coin of the realm" was a remarkable act of cultural invention, carrying an assertion of both British power and indigenous power. Had Bell accepted this on its own terms he could have substituted a shilling from other sources for the shell and kept the shell itself as a remarkable memento, removing some at least of Basiana's grounds for resentment. Basiana had exercised his historical imagination. Bell, however, followed the rules, but also clearly saw the act as a challenge to his own domination (as indeed it was).

Keesing continues: "when Bell came to collect the taxes the following year, Basiana smashed his skull with the barrel of the rifle I'alamo [a relative] had brought back from Fiji" (p. 65). Bell was not unaware of this threat to him. He, however, had felt secure because of the firepower of his police with their Winchester rifles. In 1927 on the day of the tax paying at the Gwee'abe station, he kept the police inside the tax house rather than have them man the perimeters of the clearing in front and check on those present. Basiana was able to slip into the line of taxpayers actually holding his rifle and he clubbed Bell with its butt, killing him with a single blow. Basiana's supporting warriors opened fire at the same time, killing Bell's cadet and then all but one of the police and servants in the tax house. Only one Kwaio "warrior leader" was shot in return.

The Europeans in the Solomons feared a general uprising, and some planters (mostly Australians) volunteered to take part in a punitive expedition; the Australian government sent a cruiser to support them. The Europeans, however, found the terrain difficult, and the Kwaio fled in various directions. More effective were the north Malaitan police who had felt some personal loyalty to Bell and had also the motivation of revenging the deaths of their own "fallen comrades" in the attack by Basiana. In many cases these comrades were in fact their own kin, making the exaction of revenge an obligation to their ancestors and the dead themselves. The north Malaitan societies had their own killer-leaders, called *ramo* (=*lamo*), so they shared in the Kwaio's own cultural values placed on killing.

According to oral traditions in their own areas they shot and killed people – men, women, and children indiscriminately – treating their actions as mandated by the colonial power. Some leaders were taken into custody and jailed, returning many years later to join in explicitly anti-colonial struggles. Some voluntarily surrendered, to stop the general carnage and the rape of women as well as the destruction of ancestral shrines. Basiana himself was among these. His two young sons were forced to watch his death. His hanging took place at the government headquarters of Tulagi, and as he was about to mount the scaffold he was said to have cursed the place saying "this place, Tulagi, where you have your flag, will be torn apart and scattered." This was later taken as prophetic of the Japanese attack on the Solomons in World War II, when the British were forced to leave Tulagi when the Japanese bombed and captured it.

In the 1990s, years later, after a further complicated history of protests and efforts at reorganization, and formal independence for the Solomons in 1978, the Kwaio elders continued to compile "lists of people killed by the 1927 punitive expedition, of women raped, valuables stolen, shrines despoiled, property destroyed." From their point of view the desecration of shrines had made the ancestors angry and they would go on wreaking their "vengeance" on the living generations of Kwaio for many more generations. They also pointed out that "the British" killed them indiscriminately, placing responsibility on the colonial power rather than on the north Malaitans (from whom it does not appear that they have mainly claimed compensation). Was this, they pointedly asked, the rule of law, the law of England that caused Bell to tell them that "the time of killing is finished"?

We have seen that theft from outsiders was also a part of Kwaio culture, just as it was among groups in the Papua New Guinea Highlands, where this pattern has fed into contemporary activities of gangs of *raskol*, criminals who attack highway vehicles, break into stores and banks, and kill those who oppose them. Keesing (1992: 177–9) describes incipient patterns of this sort in urban contexts, based on accounts he was given in 1989 by two well-known thieves who had been in the capital city of Honiara on Guadalcanal Island. One of them thought that the other had the power of the ancestors in his body because since the time when they were young and at home they had prayed to these ancestors to help them in stealing activities. The thieves claimed they stole widely from more prosperous Solomons people, shopkeepers, companies, and particularly expatriates. Keesing comments that these activities were annoying, but "recent killings have been vastly more disruptive," especially because of the large numbers of squatters from land-short Malaita as a whole who have settled on Guadalcanal people's land. Malaitans had also come to dominate the Honiara town council. Young Kwaio men were arrested for hacking to death three Barana villagers from near Honiara in 1988. The Kwaio themselves claimed that these killings were provoked by a previous killing of a young Kwaio man at a wedding party. Two Kwaio men who were connected to the descent groups involved in killing Bell in 1927, made prayers and sacrifices and flew in to Honiara to kill the Barana villagers. They did so partly to claim a bounty that had been put up to kill any Guadalcanal person, and to satisfy the promptings of their fathers who had earlier been forced into pacification. Keesing remarks that these kinds of traditions "provide a context in which clandestine murder and blood vengeance can be constructed as assertions of freedom."

The killings of the Barana villagers brought a strong reaction from the Guadalcanal people. They petitioned their prime minister to deal with the squatter problem and with the killings against them by Malaitans. Keesing's narrative ends around this time, but the issues have resurfaced in much sharper form in subsequent years, particularly from 1998 onwards when armed confrontations broke out between paramilitary organizations calling themselves the Malaita Eagles Force (MEF) and the Isatabu Freedom Movement (IFM) of Guadalcanal. Battles between these groups resulted in the toppling of the elected Solomons government, the temporary hijacking of its prime minister Bartholomew Ulufa'alu (himself a Malaitan) by the MEF, and by demands and negotiations back and forth about squatter settlements and land rights. These conflicts were severe enough to involve the concern of international agencies and the governments of Australia and New Zealand. Clearly, at this level, we are dealing both with the political economy of development and change in the Solomons, and with the involvement of factions in national politics. But the thread of vengeance killings also has twisted its way into these events. As we saw also for contemporary Albania (pp. 118–20), where such locally derived concerns are projected into urban, interethnic, and national arenas, disputes become much harder to settle and their effects ramify into contexts where the lives of many other people are also deeply affected. Processes of this kind are invariably marked by a "widening of the vengeance net." We can take these processes, therefore, as a major diagnostic feature of the troubles that revenge activities can implicate. We will find this also in the case of East Timor (pp. 129–31), where we will illustrate it by the conflicts between paramilitary groups that were opposed to the East Timorese people seceding from Indonesia and pro-Independence groups.

East Timor was a colonial outpost of Portugal from 1513 onward, one of the spice islands, valuable for its cloves, nutmeg, mace, and sandalwood. After the entry of the Dutch into this area, Portuguese influence was gradually confined to the eastern half of Timor, an arrangement that was ratified in 1915. When the Dutch colonies became part of the Indonesian Republic in 1945, West and East Timor were accordingly divided. In 1975 the Indonesian government invaded East Timor and forcibly took it over, with the compliance of the international community, owing to fears of the spread of communism. Since that time the Fretilin party in East Timor maintained a guerrilla movement against Indonesian rule. The Indonesian military sought to suppress this movement by force. Narratives by outside observers suggested that the military used rape and torture in pursuit of its aims, and that the East Timorese population had been considerably reduced by deliberate killings. Sonny Inbaraj (1995: 58–104), a journalist who maintained long-term coverage on East Timor, writes that this policy of harassment was put into effect not long after the initial invasion, with aerial bombardments designed to root out Fretilin fighters and to drive the bulk of the population from their mountain homes into the lowland areas where they could be more easily controlled (Inbaraj 1995: 58). Inbaraj states that these operations involved defoliants to lay forest cover bare and chemical sprays to destroy crops and livestock; napalm was possibly among the substances used. The campaign was designed to put an end to Fretilin before President Suharto visited East Timor for the first time. The Indonesian assault forces included in their attack Mount Matebian, an area which is regarded as sacred by the local Tetum-speakers and which villagers were using as a place of refuge. They were forced to surrender when they were starved out. Thereafter the military set up an administration based on counterinsurgency techniques and the surveillance of Timorese officials by Indonesian military personnel. However, the Fretilin rebels never gave up their attempts to resist Indonesian control, and they were supported in this by Timorese civilians who had suffered at the hands of the military. General Murdani, in response, ordered an *Operasi Sapu Bersih* (clean sweep operation) designed to exterminate the rebels, and maintained it until 1985. In response civilian resistance units formed in the capital Dili from 1986 onward. In the same year Portugal joined the European Community and began to lobby on behalf of the East Timorese resistance. Civilian protests were staged after the Indonesian authorities began to take a softer approach.

In 1991 Indonesian troops fired on a civil demonstration in Dili, killing or wounding at least 100 people, and drawing international attention as a result of television broadcasts of the killings. Witnesses declared that the soldiers further stabbed wounded people brought to the morgue or beat them with stones until they died. The military played down the situation and General Sutrisno declared that after the mandatory investigation was over he would wipe out all separatist elements. Inbaraj reports that the editors of the Cornell University *Indonesia Journal* suggested in 1992 that one reason for the military's intransigence was that the middle-ranking army officers were using their position "to milk East Timor while they could through business deals, speculation and racketeering" (p. 101). These officers were annoyed when their operational commander had begun to order a clean-up of corruption in the ranks. In retaliation (revenge) for this the officers sought to have the commander discredited through firing on the crowd at the Dili demonstration. International aid to Indonesia was meanwhile suspended but President Suharto declared he would not bow to this.

The United Nations began to be more involved in 1993 and issued a statement deploring the Dili massacre. The 1996 Nobel Peace Prize was awarded to Bishop Carlos Ximenes Belo and Jose Ramos-Horta, both of East Timor, as a comment to the international community and the Indonesian government. ASEAN, the Association of South-East Nations (including Indonesia) did not, however, pay heed to this. Little further serious change occurred until President Suharto was eventually ousted, and his successor, B. J. Habibie, announced that East Timor could now decide its own future. The vote on this issue, supervised in risky conditions by the United Nations, took place in the summer of 1999.

According to available reports, the military at this time may have countered President Habibie's agreement to allow East Timor to seek self-determination by stepping up an anticipatory campaign, threatening reprisals if the populace chose independence rather than autonomy within Indonesia (*New York Times*, April 6, 1999, p. A3). The military's major strategy appears to have been to recruit unemployed youths and school dropouts and to order "all the pro-integration militia to conduct a cleansing of the traitors of integration: capture them and kill them." The militia not only proceeded to carry out their work of intimidation, but also after the vote they orchestrated violent shows of protest, frightening UN officials (*New York Times*, September 2, 1999, p. A6). Indonesian police mostly stood aside while street battles raged, and foreign journalists and others were threatened. Militia gangs also began to feud among themselves and the UN compound "became a chaos of people running back and forth with sticks, stones, hatchets, and television cameras." In the event the voters overwhelmingly (344,580 to 94,388) chose independence, and the militia stepped up their violence. By September 7, 1999 the UN Security Council sought

Indonesia's consent for an international security force, headed by Australia, to be deployed to restore civil order. Meanwhile thousands of East Timorese fled to West Timor in order to escape the violence in and around Dili. The *New York Times* reported (September 7, 1999, p. A3) that "militias, backed by the Indonesian military, continued their attacks on the people of East Timor on Monday and today, burning homes, killing residents, and forcing many thousands to flee into the barren hills for safety" (report by Seth Mydans, who was covering the elections). Megawati Sukarnoputri, who was at the time expected to succeed Habibie as president, was reported to have blamed the president's administration "and apologized on Indonesia's behalf to the people of East Timor for a quarter century of violence" (*New York Times*, September 7, 1999, p. A8).

The Indonesians at first refused to allow an international force into East Timor. The Indonesian president depended on the army's commander, General Wiranto, for support, and Wiranto could not alienate too many of his own officers on whom he in turn depended. But the "campaign of killing, burning, and forced evacuation, clearly orchestrated by elements of the Indonesian army, continue unabated" (*New York Times*, September 9, 1999, p. A8). Evacuees trucked into West Timor were kept in guarded camps. Eventually they too became subject to the militias' depredations and found difficulty in returning to East Timor later. Some were taken forcibly. A UN spokesperson suggested that these numbered tens of thousands. The UN Secretary-General Kofi Annan warned Indonesian leaders that they might be held guilty of crimes against humanity if they did not allow an international force to take over (*New York Times*, September 11, 1999). The Jakarta authorities finally admitted they had lost control of their own operations (*New York Times*, September 12, 1999), and invited a UN force to enter East Timor (*New York Times*, September 13, 1999). President Habibie also agreed that an international commission should investigate atrocities there. Australia then prepared to lead an international force to restore order and try to supply food, medicine, and shelter for those displaced. The first units arrived on September 20, 1999. They found "block after block of burned, vandalized and roofless buildings, their windows smashed, their contents looted. The home of the Roman Catholic Bishop, Carlos Filipe Ximenes Belo, is a burned shell" (*New York Times*, September 21, 1999). The Indonesian military began to dispute the death toll. Returning Dili residents formed street mobs and beat persons whom they believed to have been militia members (*New York Times*, September 23, 1999). The cycles of revenge continued. As the Indonesian troops (including those who were ethnic East Timorese) left, their commanders indicated that the troops also might wreak what havoc they could. There was suspicion that they in fact incited remaining militias to fire on the incoming peacekeepers, and helped to prevent East Timorese returning from West Timor. Departing from their barracks, the Indonesian troops systematically destroyed buildings and equipment.

Such acts of terror and destruction contrasted markedly with the generally enthusiastic welcome given to the peacekeepers. One report has a photograph of a crowd of thousands led by Bishop Belo, marching in Dili in a procession honoring Our Lady of Fatima (*New York Times*, November 1, 1999). Reports from the year 2000 stressed cautious attempts to rebuild the country's hope and the memorialization of the graves of independence fighters. Subsequently an election has taken place in which the Fretilin party gained a majority, setting East Timor on the path of democratic reconstruction.

The East Timor narrative shows, as we indicated earlier, the workings of vengeance on a massive scale, infecting the Indonesian Army itself. Officers incited local militias first to try to pre-empt an independence vote by intimidation and, when this failed, to punish the voters as they had threatened. While many material, symbolic, political, and historical elements were at work at many different levels, we can see these events as a large-scale drama of revenge played out to its end, to the point where the instigators of violence themselves lost both international legitimacy and prestige in their own society.

In this chapter we have reviewed three case studies of processes of revenge, from controlled to uncontrolled events and results. Montenegro illustrated a vengeance system marked by both its own moral and military checks and balances until it was officially abolished with the creation of the Montenegrin state. As an appendix to this case we considered a report from Albania that clearly showed how revenge activities between families are influenced by wider historical patterns. The case of the Kwaio from the Solomon Islands showed this same entanglement, but almost in reverse: the institution of the Kwaio *lamo* and the bounty system (itself possibly influenced by contact with the outside world through laborers traveling to Fiji and Queensland) became enmeshed with the activities of the British colonial authorities, linking Kwaio and British/Australian history together through a revenge killing and the revenge taken for it. Finally, the case of East Timor has shown the thread of revenge running through the events of independence, causing wide-scale havoc until halted by international peace-keepers. The victims of this violence surely condemned it; its perpetrators were incited to it by claims that it would represent loyalty to Indonesia; but in this instance international witnesses were able to mobilize and stop it.

Before we leave the topic of revenge, we wish to extend the discussion into the domain of suicide, seeing this as an intentional act aimed at bringing about a number of consequences. Suicide has been a long-standing topic in sociology and anthropology studies, ever since the work of Émile Durkheim (1951). Durkheim treated suicide as a mark of social pathology and an index of the kinds of solidarity, or deficiencies in solidarity, present in social contexts. His categories of suicide, (anomic, altruistic, and egoistic), were also intended to mark the sorts of attachments to, or alienations from society that were characteristic of particular countries and their cultures. In considering motivations, Durkheim took these conditions of attachment or alienation as basic factors leading to statistical patterns. He was less concerned to trace the vagaries of individual motivations or their psychological underpinnings. Egoistic suicide resulted from too little attachment to the group; anomic from an inability to realize one's ambitions or from a wish to avoid disgrace; and altruistic from too great an eagerness to serve the group and die for it. (Thus altruistic suicide could not be regarded as a matter of deviance but rather of conformity to a norm.) All in all, suicide was for Durkheim an index of the state of society at large, along with other indices such as religion and the division of labor.

By contrast, in the psychological traditions of writing, the individual pathologies of suicide are considered in depth, while cultural psychologies are explored for their role in generating acts of suicide. In New Guinea studies, for example, shame is frequently cited as a reason why people kill themselves. In Durkheimian terms, we might say that shame-oriented cultures are likely to produce suicidogenic currents running through society, and the level and intensity of these currents determine the incidence of suicide. (For cases see Epstein 1984 and for a representative set of passing remarks on the topic in psychological anthropology see also Ingham 1996:117.)

In Papua New Guinea suicide has been examined through a number of studies. Panoff (1977), who worked among the Maenge of New Britain, recorded examples of suicide that demonstrate the act as having far-reaching consequences. Berndt (1962: 181–201) provides examples of suicide among the Kamano, Usurufa, Fore, and Jate of the Eastern Highlands of Papua New Guinea. His examples demonstrate the importance of shame as one of the decisive factors in the act. Dorothy Counts (1980, 1984) has written about suicide among the Kaliai of West New Britain. She comments that "revenge is an important aspect of the cultural patterns of suicide in many Papua New Guinea societies" and that "in order for revenge suicide to occur there must be a tradition that holds someone other than the victim responsible for it, and the society must have some culturally recognized way of identifying and punishing the guilty person(s)" (1991: 220). Christopher Healey has also notably stressed this kind of approach in his study of suicide among the Maring people who live north of the Hageners in the Western Highlands and Madang Provinces (Healey 1979).

There are clear points of convergence in these varying views on suicide. The avoidance of shame is certainly a motive, for example, of the kinds of altruistic suicide Durkheim mentions at the beginning of his discussion of this category (1951, Bk. 2, ch. 4). Ingham (1996: 117) also refers briefly to another aspect of suicides committed out of shame. He writes: "For the Japanese, suicide may occur when aging or social disappointment damage the self-image; alternatively it may represent *a veiled attack* [our emphasis] against a person or persons seen as responsible for ego's misfortune." In other words, aggression turned against oneself may simultaneously, although indirectly, be turned against another. It therefore can be seen as an act of revenge, motivated not simply by the experience of shame but by the desire to inflict it, to pass shame on. An attack on oneself may be a continuation of an attack on others by other means, removing oneself from conflict but generating new conflict around one's own death.

Plutarch, in his life of Cicero, records that when Cicero was under threat of death from Mark Antony and had been betrayed by Octavius who had previously supported him, he gave thought to the possibility of a revengeful suicide of this kind: "Sometimes he resolved to go into Caesar's [Octavius'] house privately and there kill himself upon the altar of his household gods *to bring vengeance on him* [our emphasis]; but the fear of torture put him off his course" (Plutarch n.d.: 1069). Mark Antony then sent assassins to kill him and they brought back not only his severed head but his hands, with which he had written the Philippics speeches against Antony. Antony thus executed his revenge by dishonoring Cicero's body; while Cicero had thought of using his own death as a protest against Caesar's betrayal of him but had recoiled for fear of being caught and tortured alive, perhaps maimed in the same way his dead body was in fact mutilated.

Contexts of this sort from Japan and ancient Rome fit well with the ethos of societies in the New Guinea Highlands. The category of suicide involved here has been labeled as Samsonic suicide. But analysis of this has not formed a prominent part of the discussions of these Highlands societies, in which assault, murder, and killings in warfare have formed a large part of the stock in trade of ethnography. We have found that suicide of this intentional or possibly intentional kind, motivated by shame but with a latently aggressive or retaliatory aspect, carries a particular salience in contemporary

Duna society in the Highlands of Papua New Guinea (Strathern and Stewart 2000f). The Duna are not alone in showing this context, although the contemporary pattern among them may also be influenced by the stresses of recent social change. The aspect of suicide we highlight, by seeing it as an intentional act with social consequences, may also offer some advantages in the overall analysis of suicide as a cross-cultural phenomenon. We see suicide also as an intentional act that fits with Riches's propositions, since it is certainly an act of violence, surrounded by contested arguments about its legitimacy; but it is its efficacy or otherwise, another of Riches's concerns that we consider has been neglected, that is worth highlighting. We give here a summary of a case among the Duna recorded during fieldwork in 1999.

In mid-1999 a suicide case occurred among the Duna in Nauwa parish, in the Aluni Valley. A young man had some months previously been accused of sexually interfering with a girl of the parish, who was considered to be too young for sexual activity. Neither the young man nor the girl came from the primary agnatic line within the parish. The girl's father came from Kelapo, a distant parish to the south, on the border between the Duna and Huli language areas. He had married the sister of a former Nauwa councillor and agnatic parish member, and had come to live at his wife's place. The young man was also tied to Nauwa as a "sister's son," and his own paternal kin lived elsewhere, near the Lake Kopiago government station. In addition, his actual parents were apparently both dead and he had been cared for by his maternal uncle.

When he was accused, parish councillors and leaders heard the case and stipulated that he should pay compensation, a sum of K300 in money (three hundred kina = c. US$ 100 in late 1999) and a certain number of pigs. He was able to raise half the amount of money and most of the pigs, and the leaders were said to have told the girl's family to acquiesce in the settlement. The young man himself left the parish and went elsewhere, probably back to his paternal area. Some time later, he returned quietly and was taking part in a basketball game with other youths, when he was accosted by an uncle (father's brother) of the girl and abruptly asked when he was going to pay the remainder of the compensation owing for what he had done. The boy made no reply.

That evening calls reverberated throughout the hillsides of the valley system. The boy was lost, and his kinsfolk were concerned. Had he gone to visit kin in one of the other parishes in the vicinity? Early next morning yodeling calls indicated that he had been found dead. He had hanged himself from a tree. Kin from every direction prepared to go to his funeral and circulated a stream of reports. The uncle's demand for further compensation had apparently confused and intimidated the boy and had caused him shame (*itakeu*). His suicide in response to this brought down community condemnation on the girl's family for reopening the claim for compensation. The claim was branded as excessive and demands were turned on the family itself, especially on the father and his kin since it was his brother who had precipitated the crisis by his coercive demand for more. The dead boy's paternal kin came and declared they would take his body and bury it in their own place. The Nauwa kinsfolk resisted this claim and a public debate ensued that involved leaders from all the surrounding parishes. Eventually the boy's body was buried in Nauwa, and the regional leaders decided that a large compensation claim for this death should be made against the girl's father and his kin at Kelapo, and that a delegation of leaders should go with him the several days' walk over to Kelapo to deliver the claim. The sum involved was a conventional 14 × 14 items in money and 200 pigs, according to one report. The father accepted the demand and was permitted to take his wife and children with him to his own place. He reiterated his own perception of an outstanding claim, arguing that the boy had not only interfered with his daughter but had entered his compound without permission to do so. It seemed unlikely that this claim would be recognized. Many commented that it was also unlikely that the Kelapo people would honor the commitment to pay for the boy's death, since they lived so far from Nauwa and had few exchange ties with people there, and since the girl's father himself was said to be an ill-tempered man with little social standing or support.

The case nevertheless shows the reversal of a compensation demand following the death by suicide of someone initially accused. People in the field with whom we discussed this case remarked that the pattern involved was not new but was known from earlier times. The implication is that demands for compensation need to be tempered by reason and moderation because otherwise the emotions of shame and anger that are involved can lead to an untoward backfire. This idea in turn shows that notions of pathways of agency are at work. The boy's suicide was seen as triggered by the excessive and unwarranted act of shaming him on his return to Nauwa. Words are dangerous and powerful and can cause trouble that translates into the need to pay out vital wealth. Much of the pressurizing that goes on between people to make them meet obligations or respond to requests depends on a modicum of shaming. But immoderate shaming causes a peripeteia, a reversal of roles; it carries its own nemesis. In a social context that depends for its continuity on a blend of coercion and persuasion, it is clear that the Duna rules of compensation have enshrined the principle of moderation. When this is breached, and suicide results, the ill effects rebound on those who have shown excessive greed for wealth. A suicide carried out in protest may thus lay a heavy burden in reverse on those who are seen to have brought it on.

CHAPTER 7

Ethnicity, Violence, and the State: Sri Lanka

The topics brought together in this chapter rate as issues of central importance in international affairs today and are intensively written about by historians and political scientists as well as sociologists, anthropologists, and social psychologists (Eller 1999). We cannot aim to synthesize such a large arena of discussion in its entirety. What we will do, instead, is review some of the issues for analysis that have preoccupied writers and suggest anthropological perspectives on them.

David Riches's delineation of violence as a topic was derived from a model of human action seen in terms of individual strategizing. Issues of interethnic violence, by contrast, are usually dealt with in terms of collectivities, collective emotions, and the genesis of senses of shared identity through suffering, conflict, and the like. The weakness of such theories, based on the idea of collective consciousness in the Durkheim tradition, is that they tend to assume from the start what it is they are trying to explore. The weakness of theories based on models of individual action, by contrast, is that it is hard to move from the individual to the collective level. The most careful anthropological approaches, therefore, are those that operate in the intermediate arena between the individual and the collective. Practice theory, for example, does this by assuming that the individual is best seen as part of a social network of interactions and relationships, while also exerting agency within such networks. The network, and the cultural values that are attached to it, serve therefore as stepping stones towards the collective level (see in general Bourdieu 1977). Collectivities are not amorphous, mystical entities, even if they sometimes present themselves as such. They are the emergent outcomes of processes. Adopting this viewpoint, we argue that certain mechanisms come crucially into play in the development of identities. One of these is the influence of leaders; another is the genesis of mythico-histories as noted in Chapter 1; and a third is the cognitive tendency to make a cathexis between actions, cultural items, and senses of identity themselves. Our particular interest, then, lies in the part that violence plays in the overall processes of identity formation. State structures clearly are important in this process because they provide the sources of power through which the three mechanisms we have noted (and many others no doubt) can be brought under personal control and directed to certain ends. As a phenomenon, ethnonationalism is the most common result of the fusion of all these factors and one that easily may come to depend on violence against others. Ethnonationalist movements may also be formed by a state structure (see studies in Levin 1993).

We intend in this chapter to take a case that has become prominent in both the media and in anthropological writings, Sri Lanka, considering how the specific formations of identities have conduced towards the escalation of violence. We will then briefly compare this case with Papua New Guinea in order to show that while the potentials for the creation of lethal, ethnically-based conflicts are there in the Papua New Guinea case, in effect such conflicts have on the whole not emerged. We will relate this contrast to the particular forms of political competition that operate in Papua New Guinea and the particular history of colonial control there. Paradoxically, the supposedly "weak" character of the state in Papua New Guinea may protect it against massive ethnic polarization, while it does regularly pit local and regional groups against the government. Conversely, supposedly "strong" state structures can become vehicles of widespread ethnic violence. It is in the middle ground between the operation of state structures and the pragmatic networks forged at local levels that the seedbeds of violence, or of compromise and peace-keeping, are planted.

Sri Lanka presents a case of the escalation of violence and ethnic conflict that illustrates at least the following themes and challenges. First, the antagonists in the struggle both claim ancient precedents in history as the justification for their position. Their competing mythico-histories parallel in this regard those we found in the case of Rwanda and Burundi. Second, analysts agree that, among the complex catalysts for the development of violence, the effects of the colonial bureaucratic state, which solidified and stereotyped ethnic identities and the territorial framework within which these identities were established, were considerable. Third, they also recognize that, nevertheless, Sri Lanka's transition to independence from colonial rule in 1948 (retaining the name of Ceylon until 1972) was relatively peaceful and that educational and employment opportunities, and political rights had been extended to both the Sinhalese and the Tamil people; the more immediate pathways to violence have therefore been followed in post-colonial times, with a complex history of uprisings, events, and killings. Fourth, as Jonathan Spencer (1990: 2) came to understand in his study of a Sinhala village in Ratnapura District carried out between 1982 and 1984, party politics and with it the potential for violence is widely diffused in both rural and urban contexts. Fifth, the historical intervention of a new cadre of activist Buddhist monks in party politics, based on their version of a Sinhalese mythico-history and an image of the ideal Buddhist state, has provided an unusual element contributing to the violence of politics (and a surprising one, given the putative Buddhist value of peace). Sixth, reprisals taken by the government against Tamil populations in the northern part of the island following the killing of Sinhalese soldiers by Tamil separatists in 1983 led to the igniting of mass populist riots and the escalation of conflict to a level resembling civil war (see history and analysis in Kloos 2001). In this factor we see the powerful role played by emotions of revenge that were triggered by events and were given a justificatory framework through the further ideological manipulation of senses of identity. This last complex of factors has propelled Sri Lanka into an intractable state of conflict which appears to be comparable to similar, but not identical, situations elsewhere in the world (for example, the Middle East, Northern Ireland). Comparability exists here in the intransigent character of the opposition between antagonists and the continuing possibility for violence to break out. We stress again that negative reciprocity or revenge is a major factor in reproducing violence over time, and that the cumulation of acts of revenge over time stacks the odds against peaceful solutions to the issues involved in the conflict. Bruce Kapferer (1988, new edition 1998: xviii) argues that the very violence of modern nationalism is more than a product of certain discourses and "is itself a discursive practice for making the inventions and imaginings of state and populist discourse part of the factuality of lived existence." To this we must add that this factuality includes to a powerful degree emotionality, and if history is made to provide the motor for action, it is the emotion-laden theme of revenge that provides its fuel. Looking at it in this way helps us to construct what Philip Carl Salzman (1998) calls an "anthropology of events," one that shows the dynamic concatenations of events as these are constructed by the participants in them. Kapferer (1998: 220) in his analysis develops the notion of ontology as a significant factor in the syndrome of background causes of violence. He gives this concept a very general meaning: "I use ontology in reference to those constitutive principles of being that locate and orient human beings within their existential realities. Meaning in ontology does not precede the reality of experience but is inseparable from it and is simultaneous with it." If this is so, we would argue that the dynamic of revenge, in its broadest sense, is an important constituent of ontology for some people, precisely because it is enmeshed with other ideas about reciprocity and justice, and even the workings of the cosmos.

It is striking that in the Sinhalese myths which Tambiah, Kapferer, and other scholars all refer to as central to the development of a Sinhalese political ideology, the theme of revenge is found as a central motif, as a part of the wider principle of karma, the unfolding of the consequences of action. Specifically it may appear as a part of a violent process in which the son of a king rebels against his father and is cast out with his followers to the margins of the kingdom because of his immoral behavior, there to become demonic and to attack the state from outside, killing his father and subsequently himself being reinstated as a righteous king. Kapferer mentions one such myth in which "the demon is born the son of the king of Visalamahanuwara ... In dreadful revenge for his father's slaying of his mother, Kola Sanniya moves outside the state and assuming demonic form furiously destroys his father's city. His horror is only ended ... through the intervention of the Buddha" (1998: 89).

Kapferer draws on the chronicles known as the Dipavamsa and the Mahavamsa, which he says were written by Buddhist monks in the fourth and fifth centuries C.E. These narratives include three visits of the Buddha to Lanka, signifying his preparation of the island for habitation by removing demons from it and the appearance in it of the first king. In the ensuing cosmogenesis Sihabahu and his twin sister Sihasivali were the offspring of a rampant lion (*sinha*) and an amorous Indian princess. They were brought up in a cave whose entrance was blocked by a boulder. Sihabahu removed the boulder and traveled with his mother and sister to the borders of the kingdom of his mother's father, the Indian king of Vanga. This king offered a reward to Sihabahu to kill his father the lion, and as the lion came in search for his son to greet him with love, the son, against his mother's pleading, killed him and presented the head to his grandfather, who offered him the kingship in return.

Problems over the succession to kingship seem to be central to this myth and others like it. In these myths there is a problem between father and son, leading to the son's expulsion and his return to the center only through the killing of the father. In the version of the myth that we are looking at, Sihabahu is offered the kingship through his maternal ties, but he has to deny his mother's pleas.

Relations of gender and domestic kinship as against the realm of the state are also encoded here. Most strikingly, order is established only through recurring violence. Sihabahu, however, declines the offer from his maternal grandfather and returns to his lion father's land, where he marries his twin sister (thereby neutralizing the externality of ties otherwise brought with marriage) "and rules wisely and well." They produce 16 pairs of twin sons, including Vijaya and Sumitta.

Vijaya, the eldest son, proves unruly and Sihabahu orders him and his followers to be put to sea in separate boats. They make landfall on Lanka. The crossing of the sea represents a kind of death and rebirth, and their fragmentation and dispersal is akin, Kapferer says, to an act of exorcism of sorcery. First, Sihabahu drives out Vijaya, exorcizing him like a demon from the hierarchical order. Then, on Lanka, Vishnu, acting on the authority of the Buddha, appears as an old man to the new arrivals, "sprinkles them with water and ties a thread around their hands" in a curative rite which effects the removal of their demonic state. Vijaya becomes the new consecrated monarch and establishes a social order based on the founding of the city of Anuradhapura and "the creation of new social units based on marriage to women brought from India" (compare here Guna-wardena 1992). Vijaya has to struggle with the demons of his new land, and he uses his own demonic power to do so, but "in his slaughtering of the *yakkas* [demons] Vijaya in effect encompasses them and moves higher in hierarchy" (p. 57).

Vijaya's kingdom, centered on Anaradhapura, is still a Hindu power. A successor to the kingship is Elara. He is in turn defeated by Dutugemunu and his ten cosmic champions, and the new king constructs a number of public works to the glory of Buddha, thus establishing a Buddhist kingdom. Dutugemunu himself is said to be the reincarnation of a Buddhist novice monk, and his mother Viharadevi has the status of a goddess. When he grows up Dutuge-munu "denies the authority of his father. He refuses to abstain from making war on the Tamils, as his father commands, and sends his father a woman's ornament" (p. 60). The father threatens to bind his now demonic son, who thereupon retires to the margins and contests the rights of his younger brother, who has usurped the symbols of kingly power. He takes back the kingdom, but out of respect for his mother spares the younger brother. Then he wages war against Elara, to whom his father had previously paid tribute, and over-comes him in a cosmic duel, with the aid of his ten champions. He establishes a monument to Elara and ordains worship at it, rein-corporating the dead king into a new realm of his own.

Kapferer argues that "the violence of Dutugenumu – and Vijaya –

is the violence of the sacred. It is the violence of opposition, of birth, and of recreative transformation" (p. 62). It is the ontology implied in such a notion that Kapferer invokes when examining the ideological use of the monks' chronicles in modern nationalism. Elara's army is seen in these terms as a Tamil army and the victory of Dutugemunu as a victory over the Tamils. Kapferer also signals activities of some of the personages in the myths as "evil," and comments that this signifies demonic, outside, and subordinate. The problem, however, for this interpretation is that in these myths the demonic itself is always transformed back again into the righteous and is reinstated at the center of hierarchy. How does this fit with the contemporary struggle between the Sinhalese government and the Tamil rebels? While the rebels may be seen as "demonic" by some, is it the intention of the government to subjugate them, and if so is this intended to be accomplished by transforming them into righteous subordinates? In these myths the demonic "subordinates" kill their "superiors" and themselves gain power, after this ruling as "righteous" Buddhist kings. What appears to have happened is that the reversible or circular dialectic of the myths has been frozen in modern contexts, which refer only to the subjugation of Elara (Tamil, Hindu) by Dutugemunu (Sinhalese, Buddhist). How did this rigidification of the mythic message take place?

The answer appears to be that it took place in the context of modern transformations (see Gunawardena 1992: 81, referring to "the limited expansion of ancient states and the pervasive expansion of European capitalism"). Historical pre-colonial kingdoms in South India and Ceylon were marked, in Stanley Tambiah's phrase (1992: 173) by "galactic politics." That is, numbers of small states, each with its ritual center of power, jostled one another at their margins without any uniform control over their territories. Such a pattern fits the depiction of the margins as "demonic," that is, dangerous and insurgent. Disputes over succession could involve secession or betrayal, pitting sons against fathers, brothers against brothers. Marital alliances and maternal connections would be a vital part of the plays for power, and the roles of women as wives and mothers would have great political significance. Further, "ethnic" identities might in these contexts also be fluid and changing. Over centuries, South Indian immigrant populations blended with the Sinhalese. The outside was indeed taken into the inside. British colonial bureaucratic rule changed this pattern. The boundaries of the colonial state were clearly established. It claimed the legitimate monopoly of the use of force within these boundaries. By census and registration people's identities became fixed and recorded. The advent of print capitalism disseminated ideas about these identities widely. It also caused the wide distribution of ideas from the ancient chronicles, inflected with contemporary overtones, which resulted in popularist versions of perceptions of identities. Commentators all agree that these practices contributed over time to the realignment of identities. However, the British also "educated an English-speaking elite drawn from Sinhalese and Tamils alike" (Tambiah 1986: 65), in order to meet their needs for a number of English-educated white-collar workers who might form a polyethnic national elite, some also educated in Christian schools. Tamils from the impoverished north benefited from the British policy of educational accessibility, and this subsequently led to allegations by Sinhalese nationalists that these Tamils enjoyed an "unfair" educational advantage (Tambiah 1986: 66). However, the Sinhalese of the low-country south-west gained the most benefits from plantation enterprises, as Tamils pointed out, making it necessary for Tamils to enter the professions as an avenue open to them.

The British also brought in large numbers of Tamils from South India to work as laborers on tea plantations in the north. These laborers lived on the plantations in the hills while the independent Sinhalese farmers cultivated rice in the valleys. They were looked down on also by the earlier established Tamils in the north and east (Tambiah 1986: 67). E. Valentine Daniel (1996: 17) notes that these earlier incomers now constitute 12.6 percent of the whole national population, and he calls them Jaffna Tamils. The plantation Tamils speak a distinctive dialect of their own, "less prestigious" than Jaffna Tamil (p. 18). They resent the relative wealth and power of the Jaffna Tamils. They were brought to the island from 1834 onward, and have subsequently, in post-colonial times, been denied citizenship and voting rights. Their large numbers, poverty, and marginalization have clearly conduced to their predicament as people caught in between a South Indian and a Sri Lankan identity. In 1964 by agreement between the governments of Sir Lanka and India, a quota of 525,000 of these people were to be given Indian citizenship and repatriated, while 300,000 were to be given Sri Lankan citizenship over the next 15 years (Daniel 1996 : 222). After the riots of 1983 many of these 300,000 also tried to leave for India; many also emigrated to Britain. Some were subsequently accused of fomenting Tamil insurgency in Sri Lanka.

British colonial influence also included linguistic scholarship. The classification of the Sinhalese language as Indo-European or Aryan was seized upon by Sinhalese nationalists as a mark of their superiority to Tamils. Some scholars, by contrast, have argued that the Sinhalese language was either derived from Tamil (or had at least incorporated many Tamil words and expressions over time), and reflected the close ties and processes of assimilation that had gone on between these categories. Sumantra Bose (1994: 41), taking up a particular position, quotes a Sinhalese linguist, W. F. Gunawardhana, as saying that Sinhalese was actually Dravidian or South Indian in grammar, though its vocabulary was mainly Aryan from North India. Bose also declares that "it has been conclusively established by recent scholarship that the notion that the Sinhalese are of 'Aryan' racial stock, and therefore somehow superior to the 'Dravidian' Tamils, is a racist myth that made its first appearance during the second half of the nineteenth century," produced by Sinhalese nationalists. Remarks of this kind may serve to indicate the minefields of scholarship, myth, and propaganda that surround debates on history and identity in Sri Lanka, just as we saw earlier for Rwanda and Burundi. Colonial scholarship played its part here; post-colonial politicians have seized on "scholarship" for their own ends. The specific basis for the Tamil claim to their own separate state rests on the historical existence of an independent northern Tamil kingdom based on Jaffna up to the seventeenth century C.E. It was the traces of "galactic polities" of this sort that British colonial power temporarily obliterated; and it was these traces that the Liberation Tigers of Tamil Eelam uncovered again as the basis for their separatist movement.

Bose implicates the Sinhalese–Buddhist political movement in this development of a claim of Aryan identity (p. 42). Tambiah (1992) has discussed the involvement of the organizations of Buddhist Sinhalese monks in politics in Sri Lanka in considerable detail, aiming to answer the question of why it is that supposedly peace-loving Buddhists could become involved in violence. By 1956 Sinhala Buddhist nationalism had come to the fore, Tambiah says (p. 42), along with a push to replace English with indigenous tongues, especially Sinhalese, as the national language. A Committee of Inquiry, in a report titled *The Betrayal of Buddhism*, called for a "restoration" of a Sinhala Buddhist polity and the Sinhalese language. The government of S. Bandaranaike accordingly submitted a piece of legislation to parliament to establish Sinhalese as the only official language, excluding Tamil. Sinhalese vigilante groups formed and staged violent attacks on Tamil minorities. In response, the Federal Party proclaimed an objective to set up an autonomous Tamil linguistic state within the Federation of Ceylon (p. 48). Buddhist monks in turn stepped up their demand that this objective should be denied. They entered the political arena, then, through the linkage made between language, religion, and education, because of proposals to create scholarships favoring the Sinhalese. In 1958 the government sent new buses to the Tamil-speaking north with Sinhalese letters on the licence plates. Federalist Party members defaced these and replaced them with Tamil letters. Sinhalese gangs once again took reprisals, and monks (*bhikkhus*) again took part in protests in support of them. Serious rioting and disorder, with assault, arson, and looting against Tamils then ensued (p. 53). It was in this context, Tambiah says, that the Buddhist nationalists began to bring forward the myths from the old chronicles in support of their political aims, claiming that their movement was designed to support these traditions. In fact, Tambiah says, they were using these traditions to support their own political aims, thus fetishizing "culture" (p. 60).

Sri Lankan politics took a turn towards continuing violence from that time, marked especially by riots in 1981 and 1983. Armed insurrection by Tamil youth began in the early 1970s, Tambiah says (p. 70). The government of J. R. Jayawardene passed a draconian Prevention of Terrorism Act in 1979, and the Sinhalese Army increasingly came into conflict with Tamil insurgents. In 1983 Tamils belonging to the Liberation Tigers of Tamil Eelam ambushed an army truck, and killed and mutilated 13 soldiers, in northern Sri Lanka (Kloos 2001: 188). Grief and rage greeted this event, and soon after the funeral in Colombo street fighting broke out in which mobs (unchecked or even encouraged by government politicians) inflicted great damage to Tamil-owned properties in the central business and market areas. The participants included some militant monks.

It is from this time on that we can also see clear elements of revenge attacks coming into play. "In 1985 Tamil militants took the fateful step of attacking for the first time Sinhalese civilians in the vicinity of the sacred Bo Tree in the historic city of Anaradhapura ... Increasingly, Sinhalese civilians, monks, and Buddhist temples became the targets of Tamil militant attacks" (Tambiah 1992: 75). The Sinhalese Army had itself destroyed Tamil Hindu temples and killed their priests. Religious buildings and organizations were now targets on both sides. This brought the monks even more clearly into the field of politics as militant Buddhists harking back to the Mahavamsa and aiming to protect the "Sinhalese homeland." One political party, the JVP (Janata Vimukthi Peramuna) particularly incorporated monks into its membership and pursued a policy of violence that eventually led to a reaction by the government and the suppression of JVP violence. Some of the monks retreated from politics at this time. But Buddhist nationalism, which was fueled by their intervention, has of course remained. Tambiah gives a very thoughtful review of the elements in these interventions that depended on the chronicles, and adds his own historical reconstruction of the development of Sinhalese identity (1992: 129–81), including "a dialogue with Bruce Kapferer."

Given Kapferer's reliance on the power of "ontology," Tambiah asks how, if there has been a long-standing antagonism to a South Indian presence, can it be "that there are so many south Indian peoples and their religious cults and practices which have been successfully incorporated within the Buddhist cosmology?" (p. 167). His implication, with that of a number of other scholars, is that the politicization of Buddhism in the way we have sketched here is a modern phenomenon. He also suggests that Kapferer, in invoking the idea of the "state" in his analysis, may have projected the modern concept of the state back onto the ancient galactic politics, which were quite different in their structure and ethos. Modern nationalist ideology, therefore, cannot really be equated with more ancient conceptions. Tambiah thinks that Kapferer's concepts of hierarchy and inclusion may therefore be inappropriate to the ancient polities (p. 175). This is a telling point. Of course it does not preclude the possibility that, nevertheless, Buddhist nationalists have invoked ancient precedents for their modern actions. Nor does it deny that modern ideology does relate in some way to ancient ideas. However, the logical gaps apparent in the Buddhist nationalists' ideological use of these myths indicate in themselves the disparity between the myths and their own situation and aims, as we have earlier noted.

In any case, the rise of Buddhist nationalism evoked *pari passu* the rise of Tamil nationalism. While Kapferer argues that in ontological terms Sinhalese nationalism is inclusive and hierarchical, it is nevertheless the case that at the level of practical politics it has also been exclusive. In August 1983 an amendment to the Sri Lankan Constitution was passed depriving MPs who refused to take an oath against secession of their seats in the governing body. This provoked in turn the armed responses the government identified as "terrorist" in character. The "Tamil Tiger" movement was thus able to take on the political mantle of representing the Tamil cause. Bose (1994: 83) points out that a generational and geographical turnover was involved here. The new militants were young school drop-outs from Jaffna with few ties to the elite in Colombo. They were faced with resolute opposition from the Sinhalese military. Those suspected of being insurgents could be rounded up and tortured. Daniel (1996: 139) describes how one young man, whom he calls Benedict, was taken by the army in Batticaloa in eastern Sri Lanka. Under torture another boy named him as a militant. According to his own account he was then "beaten with two-foot-long plastic pipes filled with sand. Beatings with sand-filled pipes have an unusual capacity to cause pain without breaking the skin as easily as do other implements." Benedict claimed he did not give in. The Tamil "commanders" of training camps for recruits to fight against the army also indulged in torturing their own recruits. Valentine relates how one man left the camp without permission to see his pregnant wife. On his return the commander hammered a nail into the sole of his right foot to prevent him from escaping again, then had his legs broken to make sure.

The "rationality" of such actions is questionable. What they rather illustrate is the lengths to which violent action can go when unchecked power is involved and there are no dissenting witnesses. The Tigers also nailed blackboards to trees at pathway intersections and wrote on them the names of those who had been killed. The blackboards were wiped clean when an Indian peace-keeping force arrived in 1987. Daniel goes on to report narratives of "rampages" that the soldiers went on "whenever a soldier was killed" (p. 184), another indication of the reverberations of revenge, and of exacer-bating circumstances in the Tamil homelands. This was at a time when, as Eller (1999: 138) notes, the Tamil Tigers had taken virtual control of the Jaffna Peninsula. The Indian Army was called in to pacify the Tamil guerrilla fighters but a multi-ethnic state was to be reconstituted as a part of the intergovernmental arrangement by which the troops were brought in. The Sinhalese rioted at the pro-spect of a return to a multi-ethnic state and Tamil fighters inflicted losses on the Indian troops. A long civil war ensued, and continues. A Tamil Tiger plot caused the assassination of the Sri Lankan President Premadasa in 1993, and the organization maintains a form of con-trol in Jaffna which has been called a rule of terror (Eller 1999: 139). The *New York Times*, October 11, 2000, p. A3, reported that at the time of a presidential election "60 people have died in suicide-bomb attacks by Tiger rebels, as well as in incidents involving partisans of the major political parties: for example, vote rigging, ballot box stuffings, bombing, intimidation and killing." Another report from July 25, 2001, p. A3, reported on a suicide attack by rebels on the island's only international airport, which is heavily guarded. The President, Chandrika Kumaratunga, ordered an investigation to determine how the Liberation Tigers could have breached security in this way. The air force despatched fighters to carry out retaliatory raids on Tiger posts in Jaffna. The rebels had managed to destroy three of twelve Airbuses and eight military aircraft. Thirteen rebels and seven soldiers died. "Some of the rebels were suicide bombers who detonated explosives attached to their waists." This was in pursuit of their policy statement which claimed that "as a nation we have the inalienable right to self-determination ... the right to secede and form an independent state" (Bose 1994: 14). Meanwhile on the Internet various debates are posted with conflicting claims on behalf of both sides. Many of these debates go back to the Mahavamsa and to arguments about priority of origins. The debates chime oddly against the clatter of gunfire. A *New York Times* article from July 25, 2001, gives an estimate of some 60,000 persons as the death toll in the conflicts. Whether this is reliable or not, it is clear that when both sides see themselves as waging a justifiable war, the casualties accordingly rise to the level of a full-scale international conflict. In this context there is no triangle of performer, victim, and witnesses. Both sides are performers and see themselves as victims, and the citizens who are witnesses are all implicated in one way or another. Paradoxically, when both sides inject maximum meaning, and therefore justification, into their actions, the outcome appears, at least to outside observers, to border on the category of "senseless violence": senseless not in the sense of lacking meaning but in the sense of losing the very effectiveness which David Riches says is inherent in violent activity. Too much meaning can mean too little sense.

At a broader level, it is also clear that what is particularly difficult about internecine violence is that there is no third party that can effectively mediate, or certainly arbitrate, in the dispute. Both sides claim sovereignty and both may resent terms of peace-keeping that would thwart them. The intractability of the dispute is then symbolized dramatically – and in this regard successfully – by the appearance of suicide bombers, as we have seen here for the Liberation Tigers and as is seen also in the Middle East with Palestinian suicide bombers, who attempt to justify their cause by killing themselves while killing others. The same point holds for the problems of dealing with radical Islamic movements and their terrorist activities in general. The difference between suicide in this context and contexts in which only the suicide dies is that, as a marker of a warlike state of relations, suicide bombers aim to kill as many of their enemies as possible, using their own bodies as weapons and targeting civilian, as well as military, targets.

Conflicts such as those that have taken place in Sri Lanka are common around the world, and can occur whenever there are major ethnopolitical divisions within a state as one section seeks to secede from the state or two sections vie for control over it to the point of lethal combat. These conflicts may represent an aftermath of colonial dispositions, or they may have ideological causes. Other conflicts result from the coincidence of politics with religious divisions, such as the fighting between radical Muslim groups and Christians in Ambon, Indonesia, and conflicts between Muslim and Christian groups in Nigeria. These conflicts are all examples of major schisms in society.

But there can be a high rate of conflict and violence in a state without these taking a schismatic form. For example, violence and warfare have been an integral part of the history of New Guinea societies, and problems of violence continue to plague the contemporary scene in Papua New Guinea. Yet, overall, we argue, history there has taken the form of negotiated compromises. Ethnic and intergroup contexts of conflict and killings abound. They have not, however, to date led to large-scale ethnocide or to massive polarizations at the national or state level. (There have, on the other hand, been numerous micronationalist/separatist movements in the past, and a protracted state of conflict over one province, the North Solomons, which has led to armed conflict between government forces and a Revolutionary Army since 1988. The dispute appears recently to have been settled without a full-scale secession but with the granting of considerable autonomy to the North Solomons and the opportunity of a future review that might lead to further political change. The conflict arose largely out of economic and ecological problems surrounding the Bougainville gold and copper mine, and ethnic images of difference between North Solomons and other Papua New Guinea people were called into play as a result of these problems.) It is in the mythico-history of what the "nation" is that the clue to historical differences partly lies; so it is in the conditions of production of mythico-history that clues to the trajectories of violence can be found. Where this history definitively excludes a category of people who nevertheless have an experiential and material stake in the nation's resources, the probability of widespread violence increases. After it has taken place, memory and revenge can perpetuate it.

The specific historical form of contemporary politics in the Highlands developed in the years after Papua New Guinea's independence in 1975, and consists of a grafting of ideas about elections, democracy, and parliamentary government into "cultures of exchange" (see Chapter 4). The result has been a massive emphasis on electoral bribery, segmentary factionalizing, and florid personal ambitions which operates to create considerable interest in the political process at local levels and to recreate local processes at national level. At the national level coalition governments have regularly struggled to create consistent policies or competent forms of administrative activity. They have been obliged to enter thoroughly into patronage and faction-based politics in order to stay in power. This process then constrains and channels the impact of government at the local level and tends to worsen the instability and dissatisfaction with politics at this level. The question of the overall identity of Papua New Guinea and its citizens arises from a downward historical spiral in governmental effectiveness and the increasing difficulty of creating a national image. It is evident that people are using versions of Christianity to create a framework outside of secular factionalism and in dialectical response to the daily consequences of that secular factionalism. The idea of the "Christian country" has come forward as a possible solution to the dilemmas of localism on the one hand and state-based corruption and opportunism on the other. Fortunately, there are to date no major divisions between world religions at work in Papua New Guinea.

Anthropologists studying Papua New Guinea societies have sometimes seen warfare and exchange as aspects or moments of wider cycles of political processes. Since the creation of the colonial state warfare between clans has been reclassified as "violence" in the sense that its legitimacy is contested. It has also become an always present possibility or reality, along with the dangers of being attacked by criminals on highways. Electoral or post-electoral violence has become an expected part of the five-year political cycle, in spite of the regular deployment of police on these occasions. Politicians are said to use local gangs of dissidents to disrupt one another's meetings and also the conduct of polling. Papua New Guinea overall has a very high rate of rape and violence against women that is partly a product of new urban conditions and partly a continuation of earlier intergroup and interethnic practices (see numerous papers in Dinnen and Ley, eds., 2000). As people turn to Christianity, they attempt to place a boundary between themselves and all these sources of violence. The mainstream churches are also drawn more and more into the heart of politics, including its oppositional contexts.

What kinds of narratives about violence have been created in these contexts? While the narratives of gang members tend to be based on the model of interclan warfare, in the sense that violence against outsiders can be justified, Christian leaders oppose such violence and attempt to create a picture of a universal society based on non-violence. There is a struggle developing between clan-based and church-based ideologies which could lead, in the slightly longer run, to the creation of church-based political parties that could directly enter politics. Predictably, the place of violence in social relations at large has varied with the correlative place of exchange within the same contextual field, and both violence and exchange are linked to the scale of social relations generally. The people's own internal narratives and interpretations are further correlated here. The fear of millennial "end times" in the 1990s, for example, has been correlated with the realities of danger in social life as it is in the present, while the hope for millennial change for the good similarly springs from those same realities. The paradoxical situation in Hagen today is that people who were rapidly "pacified" just as rapidly became "unpacified"; also that a people whose lives were focused on the exchange of material goods are seeking solutions to their problems through a religion that stresses the spiritual as opposed to the material realm. These paradoxes, however, disappear when we realize that initially pacification was highly superficial: people accommodated to it because it suited them to do so. And they have also begun to weave the spiritual and the material together in projects to build Christian churches and organize exchanges around them.

Sinclair Dinnen has discussed problems of violence in Papua New Guinea in terms of the idea of the "weak state," which we discussed in Chapter 4. One aspect of the "weak state" is that governments find it hard to maintain or establish control over citizens' actions. But this, as we have noted, does not necessarily lead to major schisms within the state itself. The considerable diversity of languages and cultural traditions in Papua New Guinea, and the lack of any large-scale traditions of domination or hegemony by one group over another, lead equally to difficulties in creating a nation-state ideology and to a relatively stable adherence to forms of parliamentary competition and coalition-based government in which personal and regional autonomies can be both expressed and retained (see Strathern and Stewart 1999e). It is in those post-colonial states with pre-colonial patterns of centralization, domination, and large-scale ethnic interactions that the greatest likelihood of schismatic movements inhered, as the Sri Lankan case has shown. These pre-colonial patterns provide a kind of substrata of conditions or tinder on which the fire of post-colonial conflicts can feed and burn. In Papua New Guinea it is as though the tinder were scattered in small amounts everywhere: fires of conflict burn, fueled by local conflicts or confrontations with the state or capitalist enterprises. They constitute serious and debilitating problems but they are unlikely to engulf the nation-state as a whole unless other factors such as massive economic dislocations also come into play. Of course, the unexpected often emerges. Papua New Guinea, like other places in the world, is a nation-state at risk.

CHAPTER 8

Conclusions: Toward an Eclectic Synthesis

In these conclusions we will point to, among other things, the importance of practice theory as a means of entry into the difficult topics we have explored. Practice theory can accommodate the insights of approaches that stress individual action and convert these into terms compatible with theories of collective action. As a theory of action it needs to be supplemented by forms of macrotheory that deal with state structures, and all discussions of its application have to be set into the context of history. Practice theory also cannot work unless the concept of culture is fed into it; culture includes elements such as ethos and emotion which are important in understanding violence.

There are further points we wish to stress. The first is the role of narratives that we discussed in Chapter 2. Lisa Malkki's discussion (1995) of the narratives made by Hutu refugees in Mishamo remains one of the most compelling demonstrations of this point. It is in narrative that every element we have identified becomes synthesized and communicable. Second, narratives can deceive as well as inspire and illuminate. In the context of violence they tend to explain, justify, and motivate people towards violence, while also claiming that violence is the most effective way for them to act. In the longer run, however, violence may cost too much and cause too great an unfavorable aftermath. The limiting case of suicide shows this in an ironic way. Its cost to its perpetrator is as great as any cost could be, the loss of one's life. Yet the cost is paid all at once and the ensuing consequences can be unfavorable only to the living. In fact, when the person committing suicide does so not only out of a wish to exact a kind of revenge but also out of a belief that suicide, while pursuing a sacred cause of harming others will lead to a reward in the afterlife, it becomes the most potent weapon of violence imaginable (Appleby 2000: 25; Juergensmeyer 2000: 198). More usually, the perpetrators of violence live on to suffer a nemesis from the revenge of others or simply from the unintended consequences of their own acts. Revenge, often contrasted with justice, may thus, from another perspective, coincide with it, as we have stressed already in Chapter 6.

Finally, we suggest that acephalous societies may have some advantages rather than disadvantages vis à vis centralized ones in the settlement of disputes including the handling of violence. The projection of disputes in terms of sorcery and witchcraft can be considered in this context. Our observations here turn ideas of the evolution of society upside down: "primitive" societies, rather than being forms to be transcended, may themselves provide valuable models for contemporary postmodern society on how to reintroduce community-based elements into dispute resolution, and on the mediation and transformation of violence into positive forms of exchange.

Violence and practice theory

Throughout this book we have concentrated on case history examples, considered in some detail, from different parts of the world. Obviously, we have not intended any kind of full coverage. Everywhere problems of violence exist and everywhere they tend to have complex historical causes that challenge the ability of a nonspecialist to understand and present them. There are, for example, the immensely protracted, intricate, stubborn, and ramifying problems associated with the Middle East, in part centered on the struggles between the Israelis and the Palestinians, problems that in their secondary aspects reach into widely separated parts of the globe via divisions between the Islamic worlds and the worlds of Judaism and Christianity. This conflict, and its global consequences or concomitants, exhibits for anthropologists familiar problems of the role of religion in conflicts and of the pathways of escalation in violent struggle. We have taken up these problems in relation to other case studies, for example Sri Lanka. We have not dealt with them for the Middle East because of the enormous complexities involved. For similar reasons we have not tackled the general region of the Balkans and the struggles surrounding the break-up of Yugoslavia and the troubles in Bosnia and Kosovo. This region also shows the intertwining of religion with politics and the difficulties of controlling the escalation of conflicts, the same patterns that we find elsewhere. We have discussed the blood-feud in Montenegro, however, with a contemporary case history drawn from Albania (Chapter 6).

Practice theory can help us to approach some of the problems inherent in the study of violence because it enables us to chart a course in between a number of more oversimplified approaches. One theoretical approach, for example, might tend to concentrate on the individual and on an idea of human nature as inherently violent. The task of social control would thus be to constrain this ineluctable human nature in the interests of the social group or society at large. Another approach might suggest that the problem is, rather, located in collectivities, and the ideologies and forms of collective consciousness which they exhibit. Here the individual is lost in the group and the group takes on an existential presence that itself becomes the explanation for behavior. While it might be possible to suggest that collective behavior is itself founded on a form of ineluctable and irreducible human nature found in all individuals as a kind of unconscious program, these two levels of theory tend generally to be opposed and are therefore hard to reconcile with each other. In both cases the appeal may not be to a form of human nature but to forms of culture as supplying the needed explanatory factors.

Practice theory stands in between individualist and collectivist conceptions of social action. In this theoretical orientation social action is seen as precipitated in networks of interaction between socially constituted persons who have motivations and agency, and who act neither simply as individuals nor as members of collectivities but in between these two levels. Social action therefore partakes of both individual and collective concerns but it is always an expression of agency on the part of the social actors. The traits of agency may include strategizing and manipulation, but they also include emotional factors, values, social pressures, memory, and historical consciousness. Essentially practice theory makes the picture of the human actor a complex one and therefore tries to remain true to the multiple dimensions of life experience as people themselves know it. The presence of meaning in action is therefore also fundamental to this approach. Narratives, with their various orientations and biases, are themselves forms of practical action and play an important part in conflicts (Brass 1997: 6).

In relation to violence, practice theory cuts through debates regarding the rationality or irrationality of violence. Violent action (like any other form of action) can, and usually does, exhibit a combination of elements that can be variously labeled as rational or irrational depending on the perspectives applied to it. Violence is neither entirely rational and explicable as such, nor entirely irrational. What is important is to discern the ways in which it can be seen as either one or the other, and in particular to recognize that it is in the evaluative narratives that develop around it – with their concerns for praise and blame, and the difference between the viewpoints of perpetrators, victims, and witnesses – that attributions of rationality and irrationality arise, as do the attributions of good and evil associated with it.

The rationality argument is closely related to arguments about meaning. A number of recent treatments of violence have helped to reverse the notion that violent action is meaningless. Meaningless means irrational. It also means that the action is to be condemned. Various contributions to two different collections of papers on violence (Aijmer and Abbink 2000; Schmidt and Schröder 2001) argue vigorously, however, that violence is not meaningless, but has meanings and that we must understand what those meanings are, whether our purposes are theoretical or practical. Such a step is separate from any evaluative judgement. To say that violence is meaningful does not amount to an endorsement of it, although that might appear to be the case, since to say that it is meaningless is usually a way of condemning it, or of declaring that it has no role to play in social life. In turn these arguments also tend to depend on what it is that we are calling violence, as well as on our deeper interpretations of it. The problem of definition was rightly pointed to by David Riches (1986), and he came up with a set of definitional suggestions and characterizations derived from but independent of what he called an "Anglo-Saxon folk model." The crucial elements in his definition were that violence is physical action that harms another person, and that the legitimacy of this act is contestable. In order to make a pragmatic use of Riches's approach, we need not question too strongly his construct of an "Anglo-Saxon folk model" but can accept it as a convenient fiction which can serve as a pointer to the elements of physical harm and contested legitimacy. If we take the second element seriously, however, it follows that violence cannot simply be equated with the use of force, since some uses of force are recognized as legitimate. If this is so, it renders problematic Jon Abbink's (2000: 77) assertion that "Few if any societies are consistently 'pacifist' in rejecting all violent action: in some conditions it is seen and experienced as necessary, inevitable, justified, or even psychologically rewarding." Such an assertion would have to be annotated by remarking that in Riches's terms "justified violence" is force, not violence. These are semantic matters, but they are not trivial.

Perhaps, however, the difficulty can be resolved by noting that, even in cases where physically harmful action is regarded as justified, a certain ambiguity may inhere in it, showing that at some level its legitimacy is questioned. Nevertheless, the definitional stricture needs to be taken seriously, since arguments that "violence is constitutive in society" tend to refer to forceful acts that are recognized as justified rather than to forceful acts which have an effect on social relations and are a part of such relations but are not constitutive of society as such. Looking at matters cross-culturally, it is obvious that the definition of what is justified or not justified can vary enormously, but there is always a distinction made within a given social context which does specify what is justifiable or not. The areas of ambiguity are therefore ones that can always be identified as ones in which arguments about "violence" arise. Abbink, however, wishes to follow a wider or "weaker" conception of violence which can include what an outside observer might call violence even if the actors do not say that the action is contestable. This viewpoint, in which the observer is given the status of "witness" in David Riches's triangle, may be valid from the standpoint of the observer's own ethical and cultural background. If we adopt it, however, we do so at the risk of introducing considerable confusion, since each observer or ethnographer may have a different and unstated calibration of what qualifies as violence. Moreover, we may not know clearly in every instance whether the people themselves (or some fraction of them) see the actions described as contestable or not in terms of their legitimacy. By occupying the position of witness, the ethnographer may unwittingly drive out the local witnesses from the analysis of the situation.

On the other hand, the further parts of the definition which Abbink (2000: 79) uses, that is, "that violence consists of the human use of symbols and of intimidation and/or damaging – potentially lethal – physical force against living beings to gain or maintain dominance" are uncontroversial. We would only add here that hostile magic and witchcraft or threats of supernatural force generally must surely be potentially included within our purview. Too much stress on, or too narrow a conception of, the idea of physical force would exclude these topics and so impoverish the wider analysis. There are also creative studies which use a broad definition of violence in order to point to historical or universal processes (Bloch 1986, 1992); and others that link violence to the prehistory and history of sacrifice (Burkert 1983, 2001; Girard 1977). We recognize the importance of these studies in their own right and their relevance to our overall themes.

In his analysis of his own field materials Abbink discusses the use of force among the Chai-Suri agro-pastoralists incorporated into Ethiopia in the early twentieth century, who resemble the well-known Nuer people of the Sudan in having "a warrior ethos" (p. 79) and a cultural focus on cattle. The ethnographic data Abbink presents are recognizable as belonging to a range of East African pastoralists such as the Nuer or the Mursi, who stress male prowess in fighting and the value to society of sacrificing cattle at ritual moments of the life-cycle and the installation of religious leaders. Abbink also notes the idea of purification: "People involved in homicide or in handling corpses at burials but also in adultery are to be temporarily isolated and cleansed" by the blood of a sacrificed animal (p. 83). Abbink speaks here of these acts, including homicide, as forms of "transgression." We might ask if the symbolism employed implies that there is some ambivalence about killing in terms of its legitimacy, or whether it is simply a notion of ritual danger. This point cannot be settled here.

Interestingly, when Abbink does clearly talk about the contestability of some forceful acts, he does so in the context of history and social change, for example the Sudanese civil war which has so deeply affected the Nuer (see Hutchinson 1996), the incidence of periods of drought and famine, the decline in the authority of the Ethiopian state, and in particular the rapid spread of automatic weapons that has led to an increase in the intensity of fighting (especially between the Chai and their neighbors the Dizi) and to an increase in tensions between the youths in junior age-grades who tend to own and use these weapons and their elders. Senior men and women in the society contest or criticize the legitimacy of the exercise of force against the Dizi, of the robbery of former bond friends, and the duels in which only large poles were in the past supposed to be used (p. 95). Abbink points out that new processes of this kind are common in the disturbed conditions in Africa and elsewhere today (pp. 98–9).

This analysis suggests that acts of physical force were regarded as legitimate in the past because they were contextually restricted. The breaking of these restrictions as a result of historical change has ensured that violence as the contested use of force has entered the scene.

Violence and meaning

In his preface to the co-edited volume on 'Meanings of Violence', Abbink notes that violence and threats of it are communicative acts, based on the human capacity for symbol-making. He argues that "one has to view ... with reserve" (2000: xii) the moral responses which violent acts tend to elicit among people, and instead to step back in order to describe the empirical variations in the incidence of violence. Of course, in terms of David Riches's scheme, the moral responses of witnesses are integral to the task of analysis itself, and are highly important for understanding the secondary consequences that flow from violence, since revenge is based on both moral and emotional considerations. And moral responses are often precisely the index of the contested legitimacy of an act of force and therefore enter into the definition of violence itself. There is also a risk, in adopting a distanced standpoint and stressing the role of meaning, of appearing to condone acts which in other contexts the social scientist might condemn. This is one of the problems we have seen earlier (Chapter 4) with a "cultural" approach to criminology. Abbink, however, frees himself from these difficulties by disavowing any view that "culture" itself explains violence (p. xii) and by noting that "ethnological, criminological and psychological" approaches are also of value. He also rebuts any idea that a focus on meaning entails a cultural-relativist view, citing studies of the symbols and metaphors to be found "in the violent practice of Basque youth throwing bombs and liquidating innocent victims" (p. xiii) or in football hooliganism (an example of the latter can be found in Dunning *et al.* 1986; Abbink cites Zulaika 1989 on Basque terrorism). Such studies do not imply approval of terrorism or hooliganism. They do imply that a proper understanding of how people become drawn into and subsequently sustain these acts depends on a study of their associated meanings. Abbink is further at pains to recognize that the psychobiological dispositions of humans may be involved in the problem of violence (pp. xiii-xiv). He stresses that study of the communicative role of violence is needed, because such a study locates the phenomenon in its historically and culturally contingent contexts and enables us to study it comparatively.

In his Introduction to the same volume, Göran Aijmer elaborates further on the issue of meaning. He outlines three orders of society that may be involved. First there is the symbolism of iconic codes, beyond the explicit use of language. This domain he calls the *imaginary order* (Aijmer 2000: 3). He notes that it may contain messages that have strong expressive force. Such messages and the symbols that carry them would correspond to Victor Turner's category of multivocal symbols (Turner 1969). It is important to note here that the expressive force involved depends on the emotional charges that these symbols, in their specific contexts of usage, are capable of evoking. An example would be the spontaneous expressions of culturally articulated emotion that are mediated by the purchase and display of national flags in times of crisis. A second domain is that which Aijmer calls the *discursive order*, the domain of international performative acts, to which, we may note, practice theory is addressed. Discourse in this broad sense can contain a measure of alterity that challenges conventional patterns. Nigel Rapport's (2000) contribution to the volume examines this point, looking at this alterity as itself a form of "violence" and looking at its creative aspects, that is the ways in which alterity may contribute to socially adaptive renewal. Clearly this particular vision of the "violent" aspects of creativity pushes the envelope of meanings for the term violence itself in "creative" directions in order to highlight aspects of human agency and being in the world. If all creativity were subsumed under violence in this way the envelope would be stretched beyond its capacity. What Rapport stresses, however, is the transgressive force of creativity, which goes beyond conventions. In elements of transgression, violence and creativity overlap, but we suggest that they are not isomorphic. Third, and finally, Aijmer recognizes an *ethological order* of society, based on "the fact that all human activities have a biological/genetic dimension" (p. 4), processed in memory, thinking, and sensory experience through the brain and the nervous system. Elements such as pain are constitutive of the experience of violence, while these ramify into the iconic and discursive realms of order.

The theoretical schemes put forward by both Abbink and Aijmer take into account a diversity of influences, while concentrating on communication and meanings. Since meanings are involved – and one realm in which symbolic meanings are typically encapsulated and enacted is the realm of religion and ritual – it is evident that the relationship between ritual and violence is implicated in such an approach. It is also evident that the approach sets itself as a major task the job of dispelling notions that violent behavior is meaningless. Anton Blok (2000: 23) signals this issue in the title of his contribution, "The enigma of senseless violence." Blok begins his paper by pointing out that people accustomed to living in state societies are socialized into regarding violence as "anomalous, irrational, senseless, and disruptive," as something that has to be brought under control; whereas in the experience of members of acephalous or stateless societies it may be regarded as normal and/or normative in certain contexts. This observation is insightful and helps Blok to enter into his own discussion. As we have seen, it can readily be agreed that acts of violence can be construed as communicative and meaningful. Whether they are best seen as "rational" or not is a separate issue, and the whole discussion on this point would depend on the definitional stances adopted. Moreover, simply to argue that violence is meaningful does not negate the point that it is disruptive, especially since its explicit purpose, on which its meanings depend, is precisely to be disruptive. As for the question of violence being "senseless," meaning and sense are not necessarily the same. The meaning of "sense" in the word "senseless" has to do with ethics as well as with meaning. Blok (2000: 30) cites the case of terrorism which he declares, quoting Zalaika's study of Basque terrorists, involves "the manipulation of the psychology of violence by inspiring fear among potential victims." That is the case. But terrorism may also provoke an entirely different response among the kin and fellow-citizens of those who are its immediate victims: a stiffening of resolve, a closing of the ranks, and a determination to fight back, which in the end may engulf the terrorists themselves and their cause. In these circumstances can terrorist attacks simply be regarded as a set of rational means directed to an end? In their massive disregard for human life they tend to provoke massive and emotional responses, and themselves to be fed by emotional intensities that enable such a massive disregard for life to come into being in the first place.

The domain of meaningful action can contain demonstrations and threats of rebellion and protest and also of state intimidation. Blok remarks that these are expressed most clearly through "the medium of the human body: shaven heads, stigmas, brandings, mutilations, decapitations, exhumations, display of corpses and denial of decent burial" (p. 34). All of these actions amount to a denial of ordinary personhood to people, or as assumptions of an extraordinary form of such personhood. We should also note that violent intentions may be concealed and the body can be used as a means of screening such intentions from view.

In some state societies, where the state is internally divided between opposing factions and state authority is itself hard to maintain, a point can be reached in which a certain level of violent activity comes to be regarded as "normal." This is not the same as a "normative" set of ideas about the regulation of physical force and its exercise between autonomous groups, since the legitimacy of the violent acts is still contested, but is nevertheless strongly maintained by the opposing sides in relation to their own actions, and as strongly denied by each in relation to the other. This in itself makes the resolution of the conflicts involved between the parties moot. One of the studies in Aijmer and Abbink's edited volume is by Gerard Martin (2000) on violence in Colombia. Martin suggests that in Colombia we can speak of a "tradition of violence" rather than a "culture of violence," and that this relates to the idea that violent acts can be performed largely with impunity. The weakness of the state authority goes along with the organized presence of guerrilla forces, bandits, and death squads. The tradition that gradually builds up in such circumstances consists of "the heritage of violence, the social memory of very strong experiences with violence and terror" (p. 178). This is an important point which must apply in many places. The meanings that violent acts entail over time sediment themselves into the memories of people and become a part of tradition. The perspective here belongs to both victims and witnesses. The meanings to the performers of violence may be different and in fact may amount to a different tradition. In the Colombian case the complex of experiences is signaled by the category of *La Violencia*, belonging to the period of 1946–63. In this period "both sides gave in progressively to apparently aimless cruelties, atrocities and sadism. Rape, castration, killing of foetuses, profanation of corpses became frequent. Victims were not only killed but tortured and disfigured, their corpses cut into pieces" (p. 171). The social background to these events was one in which the killing of families "put thousands of traumatized people on the road ... some of them, mostly men, joined more and more unstructured roaming gangs that operated now for reasons of vengeance, greed, or survival" (p. 172). At the same time many of these killings were made in a ritualized manner in which the victims were denounced and dehumanized for being members of a rival category (such as conservative or liberal), shot, decapitated, and mutilated, so that the killers seem to have shared a common symbolic universe (which one might perhaps label as "cultural").

With such memories, it is unsurprising that traditions of violence came to predominate. Such a combination of extreme social breakdown, unbridled gang activities, imputations of ideological difference as constitutive of identity, and ritualized patterns of killing that suggest an aura of sacrifice, certainly adds up to a situation in which violence, while still experienced as abhorrent and traumatizing, has become "normal." Parallels can be found in contexts of genocide elsewhere, and also in other contexts that amount to civil war or involve entrenched aspects of social division in them. The categorization of victims as members of an opposed class of persons, and therefore as deserving their death, is familiar enough and is perhaps the more intense and brutal because the killings are personal and individual rather than massive and conducted at a distance as in contemporary large-scale warfare.

This feature of the Colombian situation is also known in contexts of state terror. The mere fact that state agents may claim a monopoly on the legitimate use of force does not mean that we cannot speak of some state actions as violence, because a legal or a political claim may simply amount to the ability to carry out an act with a reduced chance of retaliation, rather than an accepted moral privilege. The term "legitimacy" here must be construed widely in order to recognize that the victims of state terror may experience such actions as illegitimate and unacceptable. In turn, resistance movements may be labeled by state authorities as "terrorist" in order to highlight the point that they regard these actions as illegitimate. Such contrary imputations of meaning are characteristic of the intersection of violence and politics everywhere. (See, for example, the studies in Sluka 2000a, including Sluka's own paper on Northern Ireland, and George Aditjondro on Indonesian state terror in East Timor, Sluka 2000b and Aditjondro 2000.)

One problem inherent in writing about terror in contexts of ideological polarization is that fieldwork can usually be conducted on only one side of the divide; the other side is invariably seen as demonic and unjust, while the side worked with sees itself as both just and victimized. Analytically, however, the reason why conflicts are so protracted and violent is precisely because both sides see themselves as victims and as having justice on their side. This is certainly the case in Northern Ireland. The situation is not, however, the same for East Timor, where the power of the Indonesian military was brought against the civilian population in the name of stamping out guerrilla warfare by the Fretilin resistance movement – the same movement that in 2001 emerged finally as the majority party in a democratic election following the referendum in which the people opted for independence. Aditjondro extends anthropological studies of ritualization to the practices of the Indonesian troops. In the course of discussing the mechanisms of political murder, torture, and rape Aditjondro mentions the element of "depurification of the bodies of East Timorese women" (p. 172). Such depurifications included both rape and torture. Women were, Aditjondro says, abducted, kept as sex slaves, and used as spies. He argues that these practices were used as "a weapon ... to subdue the local population," and also as "a weapon to destroy the opponent's culture, by biologically depurifying their ethnic constituency" (p. 174). Whether we speak of culture and biology here, or simply of weapons of subjugation, it is quite apparent that state terror also depends on the communication of certain meanings. Under these circumstances, to say that an action is "meaningful" carries no weight for assessing it in the observer's ethical terms.

It is important, however, in analytical terms, to probe the imputations of meaning to violent acts, seen in a communicative context. A fundamental point, which may be at risk of being missed, is that the communicative intention of a performer of an act may be perceived quite differently by the recipient, as well as by witnesses. The performer may intend to intimidate the victim (in the case of violence) and instead meet with retaliation. Witnesses may also condemn the action. The meanings conveyed by the performer are therefore understood, but their further implications and intentions are rejected. In other cases the parties may also place entirely different meanings on the act because of their markedly different world views. Thus a terrorist may see an action as a part of a holy crusade, while witnesses are divided between seeing it as a demonic manifestation of evil or as the partially justified expression of resentment by an oppressed minority. Different political positions underlie such differences of interpretation. To say that a violent act is meaningful, therefore, may be only the beginning of an analysis of the confusing and conflicting elements of meaning that are involved. Understanding the political identities implicated and at stake is essential here, because this enables us to probe below the claims of universalism that sometimes underlie people's evaluations.

Another recent set of studies contributes further to themes of this kind (Schröder and Schmidt 2001). The editors of this collection distinguish between operational, cognitive, and experiential approaches to the study of conflict and violence. Operational approaches deal with measurable material and political causes; cognitive ones with cultural constructions of meaning; and experiential ones explore individual subjectivities, they say (p. 1). To these distinctions they add their own scheme of a dialectic between "violent imaginaries and violent practices." They suggest that "violence needs to be imagined in order to be carried out" (p. 9). This act of imagination draws on historical memories, traditions, and codes of interpretation and thus emphasizes "the historicity of present-day confrontations." The authors include war in their formulations here, and point out that states cannot wage war without recourse to "narratives, performances, and inscriptions," which present a dichotomized view of reality as means of motivating citizens to fight for their country. Nationalism and ethnic ideologies therefore feed on such processes (p. 11).

A virtue of Schröder and Schmidt's treatment is that they have taken to heart the reasons behind David Riches's triangle of violence and note that all of those positioned in the triangle "are caught up in their own interpretive frameworks and their own agendas" (p. 12). Moreover, victims may become perpetrators, and witnesses become participants over time.

The imaginary does not necessarily lead to the implementation of violence in practice. The authors do not elaborate this point, but simply observe that human agency and purposive planning is needed before imagination becomes reality. Here is in fact an important question: What are the conditions under which the imaginary turns into practice? And does practice always depend on an imaginary realm of ideas? We must observe that, as with all questions of history, several factors have to come into play together for violent practices to emerge; but the imaginary, and thus the realm where prime meanings are located, seems indeed to be significant. From this point of view we might conclude that it is the very density or saturation of meaning that provides the most explosive conditions for violence, especially when these are linked to identity (Bowman 2001); and further, that when explosions occur, their ramifying effects far exceed any theory that imputes rationality or instrumentality as the chief explanation of violence. It is in this regard that we may suggest that what is meaningful can still be "senseless," since its unanticipated outcomes make nonsense of any idea of rational benefits gained by the performers. On the other hand, some violent acts of terrorism may even exceed the expectations of their perpetrators in the damages they cause, while at the same time, and by the same token, generating such a huge backlash that many other interests of their perpetrators are undermined and destroyed in the longer run.

Taken together, the studies in the two collections edited by Aijmer and Abbink and by Schmidt and Schröder provide a very useful and thoughtful update on many of the problems broached in Riches's earlier volume (1986). Riches's work, and especially his Introduction to that volume, is frequently cited as having provided a challenging framework of ideas and propositions from which to approach the study of violence. Aijmer and Abbink's volume adds a stress on meanings as constitutive, and Schmidt and Schröder's formulations enable us to fit war into the overall perspective.

Their realm of the imaginary clearly corresponds to the world of meanings. Their recognition of a dialectical relationship between the imaginary and practice enriches the concept of practice which we ourselves have put forward as helpful in understanding violence. It should further be added here that the realm of the imaginary tends to be highly gendered. Many studies point out that constructions of maleness often invoke ideas of strength, aggressiveness, and the ability to fight in combat, and that such constructions tend to create a bridge to realms of gender relations (see the studies in Harvey and Gow 1994, especially Moore). Moore's essay seems more concerned with reiterating certain messages about the fluidity and constructed character of gender relations in general than with exploring violence in particular, but she does offer the useful generalization that where the categories "women" and "men" are constructed "as mutually exclusive and hierarchically related, the representation of violence is highly sexualized" (p. 154); and that this itself raises a problem of explanation, with which she leaves the reader. An overall answer to such a question would probably have to begin from the observation that gender, like the body in general, has historically been taken as a source of metaphors regarding social relations in general, perhaps because of the deep experiences of being within the life-cycle that are tied up with it. This point brings us to a further recognition of the themes of subjectivity and the emotions discussed in Chapter 5.

Violence, emotion, and subjectivity

Veena Das, Arthur Kleinman, Margaret Lock, Mamphela Ramphele, and Pamela Reynolds have brought together three sets of studies that concentrate on everyday aspects of the subjective experience of violence – to a considerable extent seen from the viewpoints of its victims. The first volume deals with suffering, the second with questions of subjectivity in general, and the third with the processes whereby people try to rebuild their lives following acts, events, and times of violence (Kleinman *et al.* 1997; Das *et al.* 2000, 2001; see also Das 1990). We pick out first a few studies from the Das *et al.* 2000 volume that deal with cases also discussed in the present book.

Allen Feldman contributes a chapter called "Violence and vision: the prosthetics and aesthetics of terror," relating to his work in Belfast, Northern Ireland. Feldman's work is centered on the analysis of actions by what he calls the counterinsurgency state and the reactions of dissident and struggling political factions within the state structure (compare Sluka 2000a, 2000b). He notes the surveillance by camera of the neighborhoods where paramilitaries are known to live (Feldman 2000: 47), including the idea of the intrusion by the state into people's domestic space (just as, we might add, the paramilitaries themselves do, as Feldman's 1991 book *Formations of Violence* portrayed). He argues that network-based rumor with its free-floating qualities can be seen as a form of resistance to panoptic surveillance by the state. The pictures of wanted persons on walls of conference rooms indicate the construction of political subjects in "a circuit of visual prosthetics" (p. 49); and this construction in turn exists within a "violent imagination" that includes "projected yet nonexistent national entities such as a United Ireland or a British Ulster" (p. 50). Discussion of a photograph taken by a blinded former Loyalist paramilitary leads Feldman into an extended consideration of "scopic regions" and "scotology." (The odd resonance of the latter term, which means the study of blindness, with both "scatology" and the term for Scottish persons – i.e. Scots – might give us some pause here.) He notes that in the urban life of Belfast the emphasis on "telling" the identities of Catholics and Protestants through appearance and bodily comportment has privileged the visual sense. Actual attacks on persons and buildings are made with an eye to the pictures of the damage that will appear later in the news media (p. 55), a point that probably applies widely to the psychology of terrorist attacks. One Republican paramilitary told Feldman that repeated acts of violence were necessary "because people forget." In this way violence comes to function as collective memory. Wall graphics are explicitly designed to impress images of fear and domination. Narratives of death by assassination have a cinematic quality, conveying a form of aesthetic realism and a kind of truth-claiming, a sort of "iconic capture" of the world (p. 61). Rumors of a killer known as "The Jackal" evoke the idea of a predatory animal that seeks its victims by night, "an eater of carrion" (p. 68), injecting elements of fantasy and insult into the claims of truth and "realism." Feldman stresses that he is not attempting here to aestheticize domination but instead is identifying acts of aestheticization as intrinsic to power, and also attempting to bring into view "the eye, neither totally blind nor all-seeing, that weeps with memory in the face of violence" (p. 73). His closing remark brings out the sense of the aftermath of violence and the sedimentation of experience into grief as well as reactive anger. One would only wish to add here that the Northern Ireland situation is not simply one of a dominant state and its surveillance of "the people," but a complex, many-layered historical and political confluence of factors in which every side has suffered and therefore may be involved in the weeping.

Jonathan Spencer (2000) in the same volume recounts the story of a friend in a Sinhala village in Sri Lanka in the early 1980s who refused to become a terrorist in spite of seeing himself as a youthful radical. The setting is July 1983 after Tamil separatists had attacked a Sinhalese government patrol in the north, violence was unleashed against Tamils, whole areas of housing were destroyed, and "up to three thousand people killed" (Spencer 2000: 121). Spencer stresses that these retaliatory attacks were orchestrated by government politicians and executed by "young men attached to the ruling party" (p. 122). This orchestration depended partly on the spreading of rumors that disguised Tamil Tiger fighters were "on their way to attack symbolically important Sinhala targets in the South" – rumors that Spencer later found repeated ones that had occurred in earlier times of crisis, for example in 1958. Tamils who attempted to escape were "identified" as terrorists and therefore killed in stylized (ritualized) ways, showing that the acts were intended "as punishment for the collective errors of the Tamil people."

On the other side of the picture, Spencer makes it clear that the LTTE (the Tamil Tigers movement) "emerged after twenty years of state repression, sometimes violent, of peaceful Tamil protest" (p. 125). He is also concerned to point out that at the time of the events in 1983 he received a variety of comments, rather than a single monolithic view, from his Sinhala acquaintances. In other words, while there was a tendency to collapse all the complexities of social life into the one-dimensional perspective of ethnicity, this was not the universal pattern. However, after the Sinhalese government reprisals against the Tamils in 1983, the LTTE "developed a highly elaborate cult of martyrdom ... around the figures of its dead cadres" (p. 126). The death of a hero was elevated to become a significant historical event and was said to awaken (give life to) the national soul of the Tamil people. Here we see the characteristic conflation of the themes of martyrdom and sacrifice – someone dying so that others might live (examined in terms of its possible evolutionary background by Barbara Ehrenreich in her book *Blood Rites: Origins and History of the Passions of War*, 1998; and, in relation to symbols such as national flags, in *Blood Sacrifice and the Nation: Totem Rituals and the American Flag* by Marvin and Ingle 1999).

The external struggle between the Sinhalese government forces and the Tamil Tigers was accompanied by bitter internal struggles among different Sinhalese political parties themselves over perceived injustices and accusations of state terror. Spencer's friend, to whom he gives the pseudonym Piyasena, was arrested in 1984 during a time of student unrest and the government crackdown on protests, followed by the village party boss filing a complaint against Piyasena. Spencer helped get Piyasena freed from detention. In 1991 Spencer returned to the field and found that his friend had refrained from joining an opposition party called the JVP (Janata Vimukti Peramuna, People's Liberation Party), which advocated selective violence in pursuit of its causes. He persisted in this refusal in spite of the radicalizing effect of his arrest and his continuing observation of government actions. At this level, then, Spencer's narrative of subjectivity is intended to show that not every member of a collectivity chooses to adopt the course of violence, even if they feel that they have reasons to do so.

At a wider level, Spencer quotes an interesting distinction made by Das and Bajwa (1993) between two actors' models of a link between violence and the community. In one model, martyrdom is central and through it "violence creates a community of common substance based upon an idiom of sacrifice" (Spencer 2000: 133), as we have also noted above. In the second model "violence creates a community based upon the agonistic exchange of killings in the cycle of vengeance." We might comment that the second model is the one we find exemplified in New Guinea, with the proviso that exchanges also provide for phases in which life-giving wealth is exchanged rather than death-dealing blows. As we have also noted, the LTTE ideology was built on the notion of martyrdom, making feasible the phenomenon of the suicide attack which has become a general, deadly, and intractable feature in other contexts, such as the Israeli-Palestinian conflict and the activities of extremists worldwide who operate under the banner of an Islamic Jihad or "holy war" against the West, in particular the United States. In all cases, the notion of martyrdom is most appealing to those who claim to be historical victims and to have been subject to oppression, thus justifying their terroristic response against the civilian populations of their enemies.

The distinction between "martyrdom" and "revenge" is a useful one, because it implies that the first pattern is conducive to the escalation or prolongation of a struggle seen as having a definite hoped-for transformative outcome, for example the creation of a new nation-state (or more broadly, a new world order). The second pattern might be seen, in contrast, as contributing to a relatively steady state of exchanges of killings without any envisaged transcendent ending. Martyrdom might seem to belong to the idiom of the nation, exchange to the idiom of the clan or tribe. However, these two patterns, although apparently separate, are often linked. Acts of martyrdom may be committed in the name of taking revenge for earlier deaths; feuding deaths can escalate into ascriptions of martyrdom in any instance where one side comes to feel beleaguered and the deaths of its members galvanize those remaining into fighting harder for their survival. Elements of reciprocity enter into both the martyrdom and the feuding complexes.

Spencer also makes another fruitful observation, here drawing on the work of a Sri Lankan anthropologist, Sasanka Perera (1995), to the effect that coping with the traumatic results of nationalist struggles may require not just "forgetting" but ritual actions. People may turn to possession, oracles, and sorcery in this context (see also Kapferer 1997). In Tamil communities on the east coast of Sri Lanka, in a context of torture, sudden death, and disappearance, people have turned to oracles at local goddess temples where mediums in trance "embody, interpret, and acknowledge the injury of war" (Lawrence 2000: 179). Correspondingly, there has been an overall revitalization of these goddess cults in general in the region.

The significance of this point goes well beyond the immediate context of Sri Lanka. In general, the emotional issues surrounding violence have to do not only with its motivations but also with its aftermath, most particularly the grieving for the dead and their reconstitution in memory. People come together to establish and consecrate such memories and to transform the dead into objects of memory, including acts of "forgetting" aspects that are not consecrated (*de mortuis nil nisi bonum*, "say nothing about the dead but what is good"). People also further transform their grieving into resolutions regarding future action. Each public commemoration fixes such resolves in the minds of its participants, as well as definitively labeling the character of the death itself. It is in this way that grieving is turned into a revenge activity, and it is no accident that in situations of conflict deaths resulting from such conflict are mourned with massive public rituals. In this temporal extension of acts of violence into other acts, the triangle of violence model has to be extended into recognizing that the "witnesses" are those who generate the next stages of actions, whether these involve revenge or forms of "healing." It is these emotional extensions of violence that make violent conflicts so difficult to bring to an end.

The third volume edited by Das, Kleinman and their colleagues contains a number of studies of how people do attempt to find "healing" or ways in which to reconstitute their lives. One of these studies is also by Perera. Perera's study relates to the period 1988–91, when southern Sri Lanka experienced a violent insurrection led by the JVP, and a brutal counterinsurgency campaign led by the state. The omnipresence of death prompted narratives of seeing the ghosts of people who had perished in the terror, and of living people who had experienced terror and had become possessed by spirits capable of malevolent activities (Perera 2001: 158).

These narratives emerged from a context in which social trust had collapsed because of the practice whereby masked men helped the army to identify people for interrogation, torture, and murder. People did not know if these informers were their neighbors or relatives, or only strangers. For these reasons, those who suffered most tended to keep silent, for fear the terror might return, and also because of their feeling that others would not understand. (She cites Last 2000 on Nigeria on this latter point; see also Daniel 1996: 135–53, reprinted in the same volume.)

Perera's general point is that popular religion plays an important role in helping people to cope with terror. This is surely true because at such times religion and ritual – standing outside immediate rationalities – offer frameworks of understanding, explanation, evaluation, and orientation through the use of symbols that encode forms of belief about ultimate forces and meanings in the world. In Sri Lanka, ritual specialists and spirit mediums helped to address the problems of what had happened to people who were missing and to suggest ritual measures for their return or if they had died, to make them more comfortable in the afterworld. Clearly, the notion of an afterworld is itself an important part of this whole complex of notions. It can help to ease the pain of grief for those who believe that their dead kin have gone to "a better place," or that they themselves can perform rituals to help the dead find peace. It can also, however, produce anxiety through notions of conscience and guilt in relation to the deaths of kin, including the commonly experienced guilt felt by survivors. Spirit beliefs can also engender doubt about the secret identities of people themselves. Perera (2001: 163) cites Warren's (1993) work on Guatemala in this context, where ideas about people who could transform themselves into animals and cause mischief revealed doubts regarding neighbors.

Perera notes that one of the effects of terror is the disappearance of people, and that "when the body is lost, the normal expression of grief is further subverted in many cultures of terror" (p. 166). In these circumstances, the resort to the supernatural knowledge of the spirit mediums becomes more likely.

Ritual practices and religious notions are also clearly needed in times of terror because after the immediate terror is over, people may find that secular and governmental assurances are often inadequate. This holds both in cases where the terrorist attacks have been made by external agents working secretly to undermine a society's confidence, and also in cases where state terror has been exercised and people have "to live with torturers and murderers" (p. 190). People have lost faith in secular instruments of law and politics, or they feel that these need to be underpinned by religious guarantees of "truth," and so they turn to ritual. In Sri Lanka, Gananath Obeyesekere (1993, quoted in Perera 2001) found that the use of sorcery shrines to exert vengeance against wrongdoers was widespread even in peaceful times. It is reasonable to suppose that with the complete collapse of trust in the state apparatus, including the police, recourse to spirit sources of intervention would increase, especially among poor populations in the south of Sri Lanka who had little access to the centers of power.

The problem of revenge arises here, as it does in all contexts of the aftermaths of acts of violence. Perera notes that "revenge is not compatible with Buddhism, and most victims of terror in the south were Buddhists" (p. 194). Some people in her Sri Lankan study cited the Buddhist dictum that "Hatred begets more hatred." This is reminiscent of the well-known adage attributed to Mahatma Gandhi and repeated by a paramilitary in Belfast quoted by Feldman that "an eye for an eye will make the whole world go blind" (Feldman 2000: 50). In the Sri Lankan case, Perera argues that the question of taking revenge impinged on matters of conscience. However, the narratives of ghost stories and possession enable people to project their hatred and their expectations of justice and revenge onto a supernatural plane "in a socially and ritually accepted fashion" (p. 194). This argument presumably applies to much of the material on sorcery analysed by Kapferer (1997), also with regard to Sri Lanka.

Perera's ethnography of the everyday experiences of people contributes movingly to a cadre of in-depth studies that portray the ways people cope with violence and its memories, and also the ways in which they are enmeshed in the wider arenas of politics. Many of these studies have been located in violence-torn parts of Africa, creating a new genre of Africanist ethnography, and concentrating on aspects of violence from war to witchcraft. We may cite here, for example, Hutchinson 1996 on the Nuer of the Sudan; Heald 1989 on the Gisu of Uganda; Ferme 2001 on the Mende of Sierra Leone; Nordstrom 1997 on Mozambique; Geschiere 1997; and White 2000. David Lan (1985) earlier made a notable study of guerrillas and spirit mediums in Zimbabwe, reminiscent of the role of Nuer prophets in organizing political resistance. These studies contribute, in Nordstrom's words, to "a different kind of war story" in which the experience of violence is central, as are the problems of writing about it. The same problems are explored by Daniel (1996). A similar experiential approach attempts to understand how people create or recreate their worlds that have been shattered by violence. Here we see the idea of creativity against violence in counterpoint to the notion that violence is itself creative or that all creativity contains an element of violence. Where the established has already been ruptured, it is creativity's task to remake order and meaning, not to disrupt a conventional order. Perhaps we may cite here the kind of ritual inventiveness displayed when, after the terrorist attacks of September 11, 2001, the American national anthem was played at the Changing of the Guard at Buckingham Palace by order of the Queen, to stress in this unconventional way the feelings of solidarity and sympathy for the victims linking the two polities and their people.

Violence, revenge, and conflict resolution

Earlier in this chapter we pointed out the practical intertwining of ideas about martyrdom and ideas about revenge. When these are found conjoined, the greatest potential for lethal violence is unleashed, especially if religious ideas of truth and the imperative to establish truth in the world are involved. Where martyrdom is conceived as a passive or non-violent act of dying for a cause without causing the death of others, it operates in a sacrificial domain where the martyr is the sacrificial victim. However, where martyrdom is a part of a violent act, others are seen as the necessary sacrifices that must be made if "truth" is to prevail. The martyr becomes a killer, sacrificing others (or punishing them) as well as becoming a sacrifice. In systems of revenge, ideas of sacrifice may also be present, but they do not operate within such a highly charged set of religious notions. Nevertheless, religious ideas also underpin the imperatives of revenge. Often it is the ghosts (or memories) of the dead that spur on their living kin to exact revenge on the enemies who have killed them. This obligation may be expressed in terms of the ghost of someone recently killed "going ahead" of the spears or arrows of kinsmen, enabling them to target their enemies accurately. That was how it was phrased in the Mount Hagen area of Papua New Guinea in the past. We begin this section, then, with some further remarks about the significance of revenge and exchange, blending it in again later with the theme of martyrdom, since both involve the idea of violence as "sacred duty" (Appleby 2000: 81).

At the outset it should be noted that in Hagen, as in many other places, revenge had to be taken for deaths attributed to sorcery as well as for deaths caused by physical fighting or assaults. Since sorcery might come from remote kin or affines, the retaliation might also be by sorcery rather than physical assassination or collective attacks. Ongka-Kaepa, in his autobiography, gives a detailed account of the elaborate ritual procedures that surrounded this potentially lengthy process (Strathern and Stewart 1999b: 57–62). In his examples, the revenge taken was by physical attack on the suspected sorcerer. After finding out by clandestine enquiries who the sorcerer might be, the relatives of the dead man would challenge their suspect to come forward and take a divination test – making fire with a firethong and dry leaf tinder. A leader on the suspect's side might say that if the divination indicated guilt, then they would pay compensation in pigs and shell valuables. On the occasion Ongka recounts, if the suspect succeeded in making fire, he was considered innocent and went free. Ongka comments: "Perhaps he had cooked a pig as a sacrifice for his own ghosts and obtained their support!" However, he continues, "If fire would not come or the thong broke, they would exclaim and set upon him at once" – thus abrogating the idea of accepting compensation instead of killing the suspect. Up to this time the relatives would have maintained a state of mourning, which they would end only after revenge had been successfully taken. They would publicly bring out the imputed sorcery stuff which they had earlier removed from the dead man's stomach in an autopsy, describe how they had tracked down the sorcerer and had established "who had rejoiced and decorated themselves after his death." "Now," they said, "we will come out of mourning. We will take the cassowary plumes, ax, and other relics of our man and wear these at dances" (p. 59). The cycle would not end there. The new killing might provoke a round of fighting with deaths. Or the kin of the new victim might bide their time. They would target particularly one man on the other side who had been the guardian of the bones of the man originally killed, looking after them in a special spirit house. After revenge had successfully been taken "the guardian of the secret spirit house would decorate himself with fine plumes and remove the skull and jaw of the dead man and place these carefully in the crook of a tree. Then he set fire to the spirit house." Meanwhile, the kin on the other side took an old broken spear or stone axe of the new victim and told his son to keep it secretly, transferring it later to his own son if he did not succeed in taking further revenge himself. Later, "at a bridewealth occasion, or a funeral, they were to go out and see a relative of the other side who was just like their own man who had been killed, in appearance and size, and they were to strike him down. When they had done this, they too could take out the relic they had kept, display it, and finally burn it."

Ongka's account continued, with further permutations, amounting to a number of cycles of revenge, with the possibility of compensation, and with ritual acts of reporting to the ghosts on the success of the revenge taking and an act of symbolic consumption of a victim's flesh. Pigs' livers were cut up and eaten and their parts were called parts of the victim's own body (p. 60). Ongka's narrative conveys the sense of expected negative reciprocity over stretches of time between people bound into these revenge cycles. By implication, such cycles could continue only between small-scale, neighboring political units that were not traditional major enemies and existed in a fluctuating state of hostility and exchanges of wealth. Any escalation of the numbers of deaths beyond the slow intergenerational pattern of killings would have disrupted the fragile political equilibrium between the sets of people involved. At this level, we are in the world of revenge and exchange, a world of temporal extension and contingency, but not in a world further disrupted by alterations of its major parameters. However, ritual practices and relationships with ghosts were seen as integral to the whole process.

Hallpike (1977: 194), at the end of his chapter on compensation and vengeance among the Tauade people of the Goilala area in Central Province, Papua New Guinea, provides the following generalization: "Gift-exchange ... can flourish in a situation of open hostility, since the giver of a *thing* has by that very act put himself in a position of superiority to the recipient. The sanction for an effective system of gift exchange is ridicule ... The satisfaction which this will give to the initial donor is sufficient recompense for the lack of a reciprocal gift." Although Hallpike does not explore in depth the possible ritual and religious correlates of ideas about revenge and exchange, he provides a useful formulation that applies to Mount Hagen and to many other areas in the Highlands of New Guinea. We might comment that the idea that gift-giving confers superiority on the donor is an idea of a cultural or ideological order attached to certain values rather than an absolute sociological principle. For Hagen, at any rate, it is correct, but we have to explore what kind of superiority is at stake here. The superiority involved is not necessarily one that implies clear power or domination aside from the symbolic realm to which it belongs. In the conventional formulation the giver gains prestige, or at least avoids losing it, and this translates into symbolic capital (Bourdieu 1977), which in turn over time may be used to call on material support in further exchange activities. The recipients of a gift are not subjugated by it, but they are in a sense put to work in order to raise further wealth items with which to reciprocate later. Seen in model terms, such a systemic sequence is therefore self-sustaining, although in the practical exigencies of economics and politics the sequence is quite likely to be disrupted. What is sustained while the sequences last is a relatively steady state of relationships without any sharp metamorphoses from one overall state to another. Gifts also assist recipients, since they can disburse them in turn in other directions, helping themselves to raise the wherewithal to make a return later. This point makes it clear that ridiculing a partner who has failed to make a gift may not be a sufficient recompense, unless this also translates into some other positive advantage. The system has to run on success, not failure.

Finally, there is the question of whether gift exchange can truly function in situations of open hostility. Perhaps this is how it functioned among the Tauade when Hallpike studied them. The political relations there do seem to have been highly atomistic and alliance relationships were not strongly developed. In Hagen, alliance relationships were stronger and more durable, and buttressed both by traditions of intergroup relations and the constant renewal of network ties at an interpersonal level, all expressed in the idiom of exchanges of wealth. Moreover, the situation went with an ideological development of notions about exchange that were encountered by observers in the context of initial colonial pacification and the early influence of Christian missions. In this development, revenge killings were seen as replaced by compensation payments which were then followed by sequences of reciprocal competitive exchanges that stabilized intergroup relations. Such sequences were not expected to occur between major enemy groups from the past, so that there was a major fault line in the expansion of peaceful reactions by wealth exchanges. And the agonistic element in exchanges did partially preserve or recreate feelings of hostility. In spite of this, historical and ideological shifts did occur – gift exchange was seen to depend on, and to create, a transformation away from "open hostility" into declarations of alliance. At a later point again this process of self-induced pacification was broken by renewed bouts of fighting (see Strathern and Stewart 2000a for a fuller account). Finally, Christian religious ideas were imported in attempts to shore up efforts at peace-making, reaffirming the importance of ritual and religion that had been prominent earlier (see Strathern and Stewart 1999b).

This historical sequence indicates that, over certain runs of time in Hagen, exchange largely replaced violence rather than simply coexisting or alternating with it. Exchange became a major component of conflict resolution. Revenge activities were suspended. In the exchanges involved what was stressed was not any kind of punishment or justice exercised against killings, but the symbolic transformation of killings into the exchanges themselves. Revenge was transmuted isomorphically into the movement of pigs and valuables (shells or money) between the parties, as though it were hidden in the exchanges of these forms of wealth. But killings were not abolished and could always emerge again at a later point.

It is important to stress the point that exchanges of wealth in Hagen did not function in such a way as to obliterate the possibility of activities of revenge re-arising out of fresh killings, deaths, or injuries. Compensation payments, as ordered by courts, might be seen as forms of punishment, or as the execution of justice, but to label them in this way is a state-centered view. From the viewpoint of a centralized political and juridical system, it is necessary for "revenge" to be cycled through the state level itself and so become transmuted into "justice." The state thus claims justice as something pertaining only to itself. Only the state can "do justice." This hardly fits with the views of people paying compensation in Hagen. Such acts may be seen as taking place nowadays in the framework of the nation-state, but their meanings are situated primarily at a local, intergroup and interpersonal, levels. To take revenge for a killing would be to re-establish parity, make things *kapokla*. Exchange also makes things *kapokla*. Exchange and revenge are commensurate in some ways. It is only if a state-based ideology is adopted that they are rearranged in a hierarchical way, so that exchange is established as "justice" and revenge is decried. Matters are complicated by the fact that "justice" is executed separately against individual citizens and takes the form of trial and punishment. In long-centralized societies the direct option of conflict resolution by exchange is largely absent. Citizens have to depend on the "justice system" for the enactment of both "justice" and "revenge," without any means of directly transmuting their revenge in other directions. While we are accustomed, perhaps, to thinking that conflict resolution is more highly organized in centralized societies, we should note that in some ways uncentralized societies have an advantage – they are able to settle disputes by self-help and to transmute revenge into payments and exchanges over time.

However, once we are dealing with the development of "martyrdom" as a concept (and this is linked to an untransmuted ideology of revenge conflated with justice) the greatest potentialities for violence are unleashed. This is not simply a matter of the intrusion of religion or the idea of a divine mandate, though the latter is important. The idea of sacrifice also underpins the nationalistic sentiments of the members of contemporary democratic states, and therefore is not peculiar to states labeled as "undemocratic" or "fundamentalist," or to certain world religions as opposed to others. What happens in the conjunction of an ideology of martyrdom and an ideology of revenge is that intellectual and emotional processes are brought together with peculiar intensity in favor of an ideal view of the world as a whole, a view that its protagonists consider can only be brought about through struggle. Exactly the same processes enter into the construction of religious movements dedicated to peace rather than to violence; and violent movements may have as their final rationale the creation of a single world order in which "religious truth" will govern and itself bring about peace. Violence and non-violence become in some ways like mimetic alterities of each other, caught in parallel visions of a *telos* in history, distinguished only by their methods. In the face of such complexities we may well conclude that the transition or alternation between revenge and exchange is a more straightforward way of handling conflict than the ways envisaged in globalized notions of martyrdom and sacrifice (particularly those that involve notions of the revolutionary replacement of one world order by another). Ideas of revolution in turn depend on absolute distinctions between "good" and "evil," often equated with "truth" and "falsehood." These symbolic structures of thought do not usually have a central place in the cultural worlds of people who practice their own local religions outside of the sphere of globalization. Since that sphere extends almost everywhere today, it is evident that, in this sense, globalization itself brings about the greatest of threats to the globe.

Two recent books examine the question of the relationship between religion and violence. In Chapter 3 of *The Ambivalence of the Sacred*, R. Scott Appleby (2000: 81–120) discusses the syndrome of violence as a sacred duty, associated with patterns of religious extremism. He points to an important feature of religious zealotry that leads to an escalation in violent actions. This is the rationale of "emergency," which Appleby identifies in extremist versions of Muslim, Christian, Hindu, Jewish, and Buddhist religious movements (p. 82). Such movements may be in conformity with secular politics or at odds with the political leaders of the day, but in any case have their own effects. Appleby cites the case of the Zionist elders of the Ichud Rabbanim who invoked the idea of emergency or *pikuach nefesh*, "a situation that threatens the existence of the Jews," in unilaterally rejecting the Oslo Accords by which certain lands would be returned to the Palestinians (p. 88). He places this alongside the case of the teachings of Sayyid Qutb who joined a radical group, the Muslim Brotherhood in Egypt, "after returning from three years of study in the United States" (p. 91). This movement had been formed in 1928 with the aim of expelling the British colonial power and establishing Shari'a or Islamic Law in Egypt.

Qutb wrote a treatise called *Milestones* which created a manifesto for Sunni Muslim extremism. He claimed that some of his fellow Muslims were in Jahiliyya, a "state of ignorance of the guidance from God," and urged that they should return to the "pure" sources of religion in order to derive principles for life and to cut themselves off from the sources of pollution. The document goes on to state that "true Muslims" must withdraw from such polluting contexts and prepare themselves for a struggle that would be an "offensive *jihad* against infidels and apostates around the world," in order to abolish *jahili* society. Qutb buttressed his position by advocating the practice of "using one's own judgement" *(ijtihad)* in the absence of textual guidance, and invoking the circumstances of "exceptionalism" in order to justify his extremist interpretation of the idea of *jihad* itself. The Prophet's prohibition of fighting, he claimed, was meant as only a temporary stage in a long journey to extend the borders of Islam, an extension that might require physical struggle (for which we may read violence). Appleby points out that extremist religious leaders often use ambiguous language, and so avoid responsibility, but "Qutb uses inflammatory language easily construed as legitimating deadly violence against Islam's numerous enemies" (p. 94). He goes on to note that Qutb influenced numbers of extremist movements, the "Taliban of Afghanistan, the Harkat Mujahedeen of Pakistan, and the Armed Islamic Group (GIA) of Algeria" and also the networks sponsored by Osama bin Laden, which include al-Qa'ida, an organization founded in 1988 to help drive the Soviets from Afghanistan and which has since assisted movements in Bosnia, Chechnya, Tajikistan, Somalia, Yemen, and Kosovo, and trained people in the Philippines, Algeria, and Eritrea (p. 95). In February 1998 bin Laden announced the creation of a new alliance, "the

International Islamic Front for Jihad against the Jews and Crusaders." Given these kinds of categorizations and this dispersal of the networks that live by them, the problem set by extremist and terroristic religious movements becomes deep-seated. Religious ideas and values which Appleby also examines in depth, can equally be made the basis for militant movements for peace preaching a politics of forgiveness and reconciliation based on love and an acceptance of internal pluralism. To a large extent this is because violent extremists tend to operate in secrecy and their leaders tend to ensconce themselves in remote and isolated areas such as Afghanistan, where they can remain relatively impervious to the effects of contrary communications with the outside world, though not necessarily beyond the reach of attack.

Mark Juergensmeyer (2000) has written on "the global rise of religious violence" in which he also makes use of the sometimes contested term "cultures of violence." He deals with matters that have recently come close to the lives of the American people such as bombings at abortion clinics by "soldiers for Christ," and the bombing of the Oklahoma City Federal Building by Timothy McVeigh. Sectarian conflicts in Belfast, the assassination of Yitzhak Rabin in Israel and associated justifications for violence, and the Aum Shinryko assault using the nerve gas sarin on the Tokyo subway are also detailed. He includes a discussion of the first World Trade Center bombing in 1993. In the second part of his book Juergensmeyer proceeds to interweave an extended discussion of these various cases under a number of shared headings, a strategy which has the merit of making it clear that the world views involved are in analytical terms not peculiar to any single case or any one part of the world. His categories have to do with violence as a stage performance (the "theater of terror"), with the idea of a cosmic war, martyrs and demons, warriors' power, and the mind of God. In his chapter on cosmic war he indicates that terrorist groups themselves may see their activities as war, and cites the case of Osama bin Laden who proclaimed in a religious statement *(fatwa)* in February 1998, prior to the bombing of the American embassies in Kenya and Tanzania, that "the world is at war," a war he claimed was started by the Americans and was being waged against "God, His messenger and Muslims" (p. 145). The statement claims a status of victim and asserts that the war involves Muslims as a whole. It is clear from this how important it is to negate these rhetorical claims, which are designed to set up the conditions for a global struggle, and in which a certain construct of "America" is set up as "the enemy" (p. 178). This view of "America" appears to be shared by Sheik Omar Abdul Rahman who, in a speech at the end of his trial after he was convicted of conspiring to bomb the World Trade Center, "predicted that a 'revengeful' God would 'scratch' America from the face of the earth" (p. 179). From bin Laden's viewpoint, America is seen as the "biggest terrorist in the world." We see here the phenomenon of war by semantics, in which both sides consider that the other represents terrorism while their own represents justice. The point is not trivial, since meanings carry intentions and meanings can be dangerous in their implications. Juergensmeyer provides a reasoned discussion of how "America" has come to stand in the position of "the enemy" in this discourse. Rhetorically, the purpose is to satanize or demonize the opponents and thus delegitimize them (p. 183), making force used against them seem fully justifiable (and therefore not "violence"). The further claim is made that options other than the use of force are foreclosed (p. 185). This corresponds to the "exceptionalism" motif or doctrine remarked on by Appleby. Finally, the whole cosmic picture is linked to an idea exemplified by what the leader of Hamas (a Palestinian Muslim movement) told Juergensmeyer: that to die by a suicide bombing "is better than to die daily in frustration and humiliation" (p. 187). The same leader said that Islam in general is about the defense of "dignity, land, and honor." (Interestingly, after the destruction of the World Trade Center, Hamas announced that it was suspending the use of suicide bombings since under the circumstances these would be counterproductive.) Frank Stewart (1994: 139), writing about the concept of honor in general, notes that in some societies "honor may be viewed as more valuable than life itself." He points out that traditions of this kind belong to both European and Arab Bedouin societies, and goes on, interestingly, to note that in European traditions honor was often retained "by trying to kill the man who impugned it, whereas among the Bedouin he does so by getting from him a massive award at law." He goes on: "Bedouin law is ... fundamentally directed towards the peaceful settlement of disputes, and it uses a variety of devices, some of them exceedingly subtle, to discourage the use of force." Such an observation can be juxtaposed with the ideological scheme mentioned above, making it clear that it has been fashioned from a new and globalized dialectic of "Islam" versus "the West/America," which does not in any way correspond to customary Bedouin Arab ideas about honor and law. Ethnographic perspectives of this sort are very useful in assessing the extent to which claims of tradition and authenticity of vision, in fact, rest on new ideological presuppositions and are not simply inherited from the past but are forged in contemporary conflicts and therefore cannot be taken as overall signs of ethnic or religious identity. They may, however, as Juergensmeyer suggests, correspond to personal feelings of empowerment on the part of "the perpetrators of religious violence," who also through their acts challenge the basis for the authority of the secular state by claiming the right to kill its members, and to be prepared to lose their own lives in doing so.

In the last analysis, Juergensmeyer lays the greatest stress of all on the idea that violence itself has been ordained by divine mandate and therefore has been "conceived in the mind of God" (p. 216). Given the insistence of monotheistic religions on the absolute transcendence of the deity, this notion represents a powerful nemesis on that proposition. Juergensmeyer argues further that "in spiritualizing violence, therefore, religion has given terrorism remarkable power" (p. 217). Here, and throughout his book, we have to read "certain kinds of religious traditions" for what he calls "religion in general," but with this proviso we find that he has formulated important cultural conditions under which the massive disaster of September 11, 2001 occurred – when terrorists found a new way to complete their 1993 project of destroying the World Trade Center and ushered the world into a new epoch of struggle and uncertainty comparable in scale to the Cold War period that had only recently ended. As we have seen, the idea of spiritualizing violence is not sufficient in itself to impel people into violent actions. Instead, the impetus to violence is also created in situations of perceived inequity and struggle existing on a range of other fronts – in social, economic, and political circumstances that conspire to the same end. If this is so, it follows that the impetus may also be countered in a number of ways, in addition to criticizing the authenticity of the ideology of violence itself. If the social conditions for violence can be reduced or ameliorated, this will provide one pathway, though by no means an easy one, to do so.

In the end, one of the greatest difficulties to be faced in both understanding and tempering violence in society comes from the fact that the problems are not peculiar to violence as such. The same human propensities and ideological patterns feed into the causes of both security and insecurity in life. In this book we have been concerned to reach that point of understanding. Yet we know that the settlement of conflicts without the actual use of physical force (if sometimes with the threat of it) is equally an intrinsic fact of social life and of human capacities to create it (Caplan 1995). What is needed next is to put together what we know about conflict settlement processes with what we know about the practices of violence and the emotions that feed into violent actions. In this way we can perhaps learn how violence itself can be transcended. The political practice in the New Guinea Highlands of transmuting revenge into competitive exchanges of wealth represents a limited example of the process which worked only in a particular local and historical context. In the contemporary field of international politics, analogs of such transmutations which can be sustained over time and adapted to local circumstances need to be continuously sought so as best to negotiate dangerous altercations and to reduce heightened and protracted acts of violence.

References

Abbink, Jon (2000) Restoring the balance: violence and culture among the Suri of Southern Ethiopia. In G. Aijmer and J. Abbink (eds.), *Meanings of Violence*, pp. 77–100. Oxford: Berg.

Abbink, Jon (2001) Violence and culture: anthropological and evolutionary-psychological reflections on inter-group conflict in southern Ethiopia. In B. E. Schmidt and I.W. Schröder (eds.), *Anthropology of Violence and Conflict*, pp. 123–42. London: Routledge.

Aditjondro, George G. (2000) Ninjas, Nanggalas, monuments and Mossad manuals: an anthropology of Indonesian state terror. In J. Sluka (ed.), *Death Squad*, pp. 158–88. Philadelphia: University of Pennsylvania Press.

Ahmed, Akbar S. (1976) *Millennium and Charisma among Pathans: A Critical Essay in Social Anthropology*. London: Routledge and Kegan Paul.

Aijmer, Göran (2000) Introduction. In G. Aijmer and J. Abbink (eds.), *Meanings of Violence: A Cross Cultural Perspective*, pp. 1–22. Oxford: Berg.

Aijmer, Göran and Jon Abbink (eds.) (2000) *Meanings of Violence. A Cross Cultural Perspective*. Oxford: Berg.

Akin, David (1999) Compensation and the Melanesian state: why the Kwaio keep claiming. *Contemporary Pacific* 11(1): 35–67.

Amarshi, Azeem, Kenneth Good and Rex Mortimer (1979) *Development and Dependency: The Political Economy of Papua New Guinea*. Melbourne: Oxford University Press.

Appleby, R. Scott (2000) *The Ambivalence of the Sacred: Religion, Violence, and Reconciliation*. Lanham, MD: Rowman and Littlefield.

Banks, Cyndi (ed.) (2000) *Developing Cultural Criminology: Theory and Practice in Papua New Guinea*. Sydney: Sydney Institute of Criminology Monograph Series no. 13.

Barnes, John A. (1962) African models in the New Guinea Highlands. *Man* (o.s.) 62: 5–9.

Barth, Fredrik (1959) *Political Leadership among Swat Pathans*. London: Athlone Press.

Barth, Fredrik (ed.) (1969) *Ethnic Groups and Boundaries*. Oslo: Universitetsforlaget.

Berndt, R. M. (1962) *Excess and Restraint: Social Control among a New Guinea Mountain People*. Chicago: University of Chicago Press.

Bloch, Maurice (1986) *From Blessing to Violence*. Cambridge: Cambridge University Press.

Bloch, Maurice (1992) *Prey into Hunter: The Politics of Religious Experience*. Cambridge: Cambridge University Press.

Blok, Anton (2000) The enigma of senseless violence. In G. Aijmer and J. Abbink (eds.), *Meanings of Violence*, pp. 28–38. Oxford: Berg.

Boehm, Christopher (1984) *Blood Revenge: The Enactment and Management of Conflict in Montenegro and Other Tribal Societies*. Philadelphia: University of Pennsylvania Press.

Bonnemère, Pascale (1994) Suicide et homicide: deux modalités vindicatoires en Nouvelle-Guinée. *Stanford French Review*.

Bose, Sumantra (1994) *States, Nations, Sovereignty: Sri Lanka, India and the Tamil Eelam Movement*. New Delhi: Sage.

Bourdieu, Pierre (1977) *Outline of a Theory of Practice*, translated by Richard Nice. Cambridge: Cambridge University Press.

Bowman, Glenn (2001) The violence in identity. In B. E. Schmidt and I. W. Schröder (eds.), *Anthropology of Violence and Conflict*, pp. 25–46. London: Routledge.

Brass, Paul R. (1997) *Theft of an Idol: Text and Context in the Representation of Collective Violence*. Princeton: Princeton University Press.

Breton, Stéphane (1999) Death and the ideology of compensation among the Wodani, Western Highlands of Irian Jaya. *Social Anthropology* 6(3): 297–326.

Brown, Paula (1995) *Beyond a Mountain Valley: The Simbu of Papua New Guinea*. Honolulu: University of Hawai'i Press.

Buckley, Anthony D. and Mary Catherine Kenney (1995) *Negotiating Identity: Rhetoric, Metaphor, and Social Drama in Northern Ireland*. Washington, D.C.: Smithsonian Institution Press.

Burkert, Walter (1983) *Homo Necans*, translated by Peter Bing. Berkeley: University of California Press.

Burkert, Walter (2001) *Savage Energies: Lessons of Myth and Ritual in Ancient Greece*, translated by Peter Bing. Chicago: University of Chicago Press.

Cairns, David (2000) The object of sectarianism: the material reality of sectarianism in Ulster Loyalism. *Journal of the Royal Anthropological Institute* 6(3): 437–52.

Caplan, Patricia (ed.) (1995) *Understanding Disputes: The Politics of Argument*. Oxford: Berg.

Carrier, James (ed.) (1992) *History and Tradition in Melanesian Anthropology*. Berkeley: University of California Press.

Cecil, Rosanne (1993) The marching season in Northern Ireland: an expression of politico-religious identity. In S. Macdonald (ed.), *Inside European Identities*, pp. 146–66. Oxford: Berg.

Counts, Dorothy (1980) Fighting back is not the way: suicide and the women of Kaliai. *American Ethnologist* 7: 332–51.

Counts, Dorothy (1984) Female suicide and wife abuse: a cross-cultural perspective. *Suicide and Life-threatening Behavior* 17: 194–204.

Counts, Dorothy (1991) Suicide in different ages from a cross-cultural perspective. In Antoon Leenaars (ed.), *Life Perspectives of Suicide: Time-Lines in the Suicide Process*, pp. 215–30. New York: Plenum Press.

REFERENCES

Csordas, Thomas J. (1994) *The Sacred Self: A Cultural Phenomenology of Charismatic Healing*. Berkeley: University of California Press.

Daniel, E. Valentine (1996) *Charred Lullabies: Chapters in an Anthropography of Violence*. Princeton: Princeton University Press.

Das, Veena (ed.) (1990) *Mirrors of Violence: Communities, Riots, and Survivors in South Asia*. Delhi: Oxford University Press.

Das, Veena and R. S. Bajwa (1993) Community and violence in contemporary Punjab. In D. Vidal, G. Tarabout and E. Meyers, (eds.), *Violences et non-violences en Inde*, pp. 245–59. *Purusartha* no. 16.

Das, Veena, Arthur Kleinman, Mamphela Ramphele, and Pamela Reynolds (eds.) (2000) *Violence and Subjectivity*. Berkeley: University of California Press.

Das, Veena, Arthur Kleinman, Margaret Lock, Mamphela Ramphele, and Pamela Reynolds (eds.) (2001) *Remaking a World: Violence, Social Suffering and Recovery*. Berkeley: University of California Press.

Declich, Francesca (2001) When silence makes history: gender and memories of war violence from Somalia. In B. E. Schmidt and I. W. Schröder (eds.), *Anthropology of Violence and Conflict*, pp. 161–75. London: Routledge.

Dinnen, Sinclair (2000a) Violence and governance in Melanesia: an introduction. In S. Dinnen and A. Ley (eds.), *Reflections on Violence in Melanesia*, pp. 1–16. Sydney: Hawkins Press.

Dinnen, Sinclair (2000b) Breaking the cycle of violence: crime and state in Papua New Guinea. In C. Banks (ed.), *Developing Cultural Criminology: Theory and Practice in Papua New Guinea*, pp. 51–78. Sydney: Sydney Institute of Criminology Monograph Series no. 13.

Dinnen, Sinclair (2001) *Law and Order in a Weak State: Crime and Politics in Papua New Guinea*. Pacific Islands Monograph Series 17. Honolulu: University of Hawaii Press.

Dinnen, S. and A. Ley (eds.) (2000) *Reflections on Violence in Melanesia*. Sydney: Hawkins Press.

Donnan, Hastings and Thomas M. Wilson (eds.) (1994) *Border Approaches: Anthropological Perspectives on Frontiers*. Lanham, MD: University Press of America for the Anthropological Association of Ireland.

Donnan, Hastings and Thomas M. Wilson (1999) *Borders: Frontiers of Identity, Nation and State*. Oxford: Berg.

Douglas, Mary (1966) *Purity and Danger: An Analysis of the Concepts of Pollution and Taboo*. London: Routledge and Kegan Paul.

Douglas, Mary (ed.) (1970) *Witchcraft: Confessions and Accusations*. ASA Monographs 9. London: Tavistock.

Douglas, Mary (1991) Witchcraft and leprosy: two strategies of exclusion. *Man* 26 (4): 723–36.

Douglas, Mary (1996) *Thought Styles: Critical Essays on Good Taste*. London: Sage.

Dunning, Eric, Patrick Murphy and John Williams (1986) 'Casuals', 'terrace crews', and 'fighting firms': towards a sociological explanation of football hooligan behavior. In D. Riches (ed.), *The Anthropology of Violence*, pp. 164–83. Oxford: Basil Blackwell.

Durkheim, Emile (1951) *Suicide: A Study in Sociology*, translated by John A. Spaulding and George Simpson. New York: Free Press. [First published in 1897.]

Ehrenreich, Barbara (1998) *Blood Rites: Origins and History of the Passions of War*. New York: Henry Holt.

Ellen, Roy (1993) Introduction. In C. W. Watson and Roy Ellen (eds.), *Understanding Witchcraft and Sorcery in Southeast Asia*, pp. 1–25. Honolulu: University of Hawai'i Press.

Eller, Jack David (1999) *From Culture to Ethnicity to Conflict*. Ann Arbor: University of Michigan Press.

Epstein, Arnold L. (1984) *The Experience of Shame in Melanesia*. London: Royal Anthropological Institute, Occasional Paper no. 40.

Evans-Pritchard, Edward E. (1940) *The Nuer: A Description of the Modes of Livelihood and Political Institutions of a Nilotic People*. Oxford: Clarendon Press.

Evans-Pritchard, Edward E. (1976) *Witchcraft, Oracles and Magic among the Azande*. Oxford: Oxford University Press. [Abridged version; 1st edn. 1937]

Feil, Daryl K. (1987) *The Evolution of Highland Papua New Guinea Societies*. Cambridge: Cambridge University Press.

Feldman, Allen (1991) *Formations of Violence: The Narrative of the Body and Political Terror in Northern Ireland*. Chicago: University of Chicago Press.

Feldman, Allen (2000) Violence and vision: the prosthetics and aesthetics of terror. In V. Das *et al.* (eds.), *Violence and Subjectivity*, pp 46–78. Berkeley: University of California Press.

Ferguson, R. Brian (1995) *Yanomami Warfare: A Political History*. Santa Fe: School of American Research Press.

Ferguson, R. Brian and Neil L. Whitehead (1992) Introduction. In R. Ferguson and N. Whitehead (eds.), *War in the Tribal Zone: Expanding States and Indigenous Warfare*, pp. 1–30. Santa Fe: School of American Research Press.

Ferme, Mariane C. (2001) *The Underneath of Things: Violence, History, and the Everyday in Sierra Leone*. Berkeley: University of California Press.

Finney, Ben R. (1973) *Big-Men and Business: Entrepreneurship and Economic Growth in the New Guinea Highlands*. Canberra: Australian National University Press.

Foucault, Michel (1972) *The Archaeology of Knowledge*. London: Tavistock.

Frankel, Stephen (1986) *The Huli Response to Illness*. Cambridge: Cambridge University Press.

George, Kenneth (1996) *Showing Signs of Violence: The Cultural Politics of a Twentieth-Century Headhunting Ritual*. Berkeley: University of California Press.

Geschiere, Peter (1997) *The Modernity of Witchcraft: Politics and the Occult in Post-Colonial Africa*. Charlottesville: University Press of Virginia.

Girard, René (1977) *Violence and the Sacred*, translated by Patrick Gregory. Baltimore: Johns Hopkins University Press.

Glasse, Robert M. (1959) Revenge and redress among the Huli: a preliminary account. *Mankind* 5(7): 273–89.

Gluckman, Max (1955) *Custom and Conflict in Africa*. Oxford: Oxford University Press.

Goddard, Michael (1992) Big-men, thief: the social organization of gangs in Port Moresby. *Canberra Anthropology* 15(1): 20–34.

Goddard, Michael (1995) The rascal road: crime, prestige and development in Papua New Guinea. *Contemporary Pacific* 7(1): 55–80.

Goldman, Laurence (1983) *Talk Never Dies: The Language of Huli Disputes*. London: Tavistock.

Goldman, Laurence (1993) *The Culture of Coincidence: Accident and Absolute Liability in Huli*. Oxford: Oxford University Press.

Gunawardena, R. A. L. H. (1992) Conquest and resistance: pre-state and state expansionism in early Sri Lankan history. In R. B. Ferguson and N. L. Whitehead (eds.), *War in the Tribal Zone*, pp. 61–82. Santa Fe: School of American Research Press.

Hallpike, Christopher R. (1977) *Bloodshed and Vengeance in the Papuan Mountains: The Generation of Conflict in Tauade Society*. Oxford: Clarendon Press.

Harris, Rosemary (1972) *Prejudice and Tolerance in Ulster*. Manchester: Manchester University Press.

Hart Nibbrig, N. (1992) Rascals in paradise: urban gangs in Papua New Guinea. *Pacific Studies* 15(3): 115–34.

Harvey, Penelope and Peter Gow (eds.) (1994) *Sex and Violence: Issues in Representation and Experience*. London: Routledge.

Heald, Suzette (1989) *Controlling Anger: The Sociology of Gisu Violence*. Manchester: Manchester University Press, for the International African Institute.

Healey, Christopher (1979) Women and suicide in New Guinea. *Social Analysis* 2: 89–107.

Hide, Robin L. (1980) Aspects of Pig Production and Use in Colonial Sinasina, Papua New Guinea. Unpublished Ph. D. dissertation, Columbia University, New York.

Hutchinson, Sharon E. (1996) *Nuer Dilemmas: Coping with Money, War and the State*. Berkeley: University of California Press.

Inbaraj, Sonny (1995) *East Timor: Blood and Tears in ASEAN*. Chiang Mai: Silkworm Books.

Ingham, John M. (1996) *Psychological Anthropology Reconsidered*. Cambridge: Cambridge University Press.

Juergensmeyer, Mark (2000) *Terror in the Mind of God: The Global Rise of Religious Violence*. Berkeley: University of California Press.

Kahn, Miriam (1986) *Always Hungry, Never Greedy: Food and the Expression of Gender in a Melanesian Society*. Cambridge: Cambridge University Press.

Kapferer, Bruce (1997) *The Feast of the Sorcerer: Practices of Consciousness and Power*. Chicago: Chicago University Press.

Kapferer, Bruce (1998) *Legends of People: Myths of State: Violence, Intolerance and Political Culture in Sri Lanka and Australia*. Washington, D.C.: Smithsonian Institution Press (first published in 1988).

Keesing, Roger M. (1983) *'Elota's Story: The Life and Times of a Solomon Island Big-Man*. New York: Holt, Rinehart and Winston.

Keesing, Roger M. (1992) *Custom and Confrontation: The Kwaio Struggle for Cultural Autonomy*. Chicago: University of Chicago Press.

Keiser, Lincoln (1986) Death enmity in Thull: organized vengeance and social change in a Kohistani community. *American Ethnologist* 13: 489–505.

Kelly, Raymond (1977) *Etoro Social Structure: A Study in Structural Contradiction*. Ann Arbor: University of Michigan Press.

Kelly, Raymond C. (1993) *Constructing Inequality: The Fabrication of a Hierarchy of Virtue among the Etoro*. Ann Arbor: University of Michigan Press.

Kelly, Raymond C. (2000) *Warless Societies and the Origin of War*. Ann Arbor: University of Michigan Press.

Ketan, Joseph (1998) "The name must not go down": Political Competition in Mount Hagen, Papua New Guinea. Unpublished Ph.D dissertation, University of Wollongong.

Kituai, August I. K. (1998) *My Gun, My Brother: The World of the Papua New Guinea Colonial Police 1920–1960*. Pacific Islands Monograph Series, no. 15. Honolulu: University of Hawai'i Press.

Kleinman, Arthur, Veena Das, and Margaret Lock (eds.) (1997) *Social Suffering*. Berkeley: University of California Press.

Kloos, Peter (2001) A turning point? from civil struggle to civil war in Sri Lanka. In B. E. Schmidt and I. W. Schröder (eds.), *Anthropology of Violence and Conflict*, pp. 176–96. London: Routledge.

Knauft, Bruce M. (1985) *Good Company and Violence: Sorcery and Social Action in a Lowland New Guinea Society*. Berkeley: University of California Press.

Knauft, Bruce M. (1999) *From Primitive to Post-colonial in Melanesia and Anthropology*. Ann Arbor: University of Michigan Press.

Lan, David (1985) *Guns and Rain: Guerrillas and Spirit Mediums in Zimbabwe*. London: James Currey.

Last, Murray (2000) Reconciliation and memory in postwar Nigeria. In V. Das *et al.* (eds.), *Violence and Subjectivity*, pp. 333–66. Berkeley: University of California Press.

Lawrence, Patricia (2000) Violence, suffering, Amman: the work of oracles in Sri Lanka's eastern war zone. In V. Das *et al.* (eds.), *Violence and Subjectivity*, pp. 171–204. Berkeley: University of California Press.

Lemarchand, Rene (1994) *Burundi: Ethnocide as Discourse and Practice*. Cambridge: Woodrow Wilson Center Press and Cambridge University Press.

Levin, Michael D. (ed.) (1993) *Ethnicity and Aboriginality: Case Studies in Ethnonationalism*. Toronto: University of Toronto Press.

Lewis, I. M. (1970) A structural approach to witchcraft and spirit possession. In M. Douglas (ed.), *Witchcraft: Confessions and Accusations*, pp. 293–310. London: Tavistock.

Lewis, I. M. (1989) *Ecstatic Religion* (2nd edn.) London: Routledge.

LiPuma, Edward (1994) Sorcery and evidence of change in Maring justice. *Ethnology* 33: 147–64.

Lock, Margaret and Nancy Scheper-Hughes (1987) The mindful body. *Medical Anthropology Quarterly* 1 (1): 6–41.

McFarlane, Graham (1986) Violence in rural Northern Ireland: social scientific models, folk explanation, and local variation. In D. Riches (ed.), *The Anthropology of Violence*, pp. 184–203. Oxford: Basil Blackwell.

Malkki, Liisa (1995) *Purity and Exile: Violence, Memory, and National Cosmology among Hutu Refugees in Tanzania*. Chicago: University of Chicago Press.

Maquet, Jacques (1961) *The Premise of Inequality in Rwanda: A Study of Political Relations in a Central African Kingdom*. London: Oxford University Press.

Martin, Gerard (2000) The 'tradition of violence' in Colombia: material and social aspects. In G. Aijmer and J. Abbink (eds.), *Meanings of Violence*, pp. 161–92. Oxford: Berg.

Marvin, Carolyn and David W. Ingle (1999) *Blood Sacrifice and the Nation: Totem Rituals and the American Flag*. Cambridge: Cambridge University Press.

Marwick, Max G. (1952) The social context of Cewa witch-beliefs. *Africa* 22: 120–35.

Marwick, Max G. (1970) Sorcery as a social strain gauge. In M. G. Marwick (ed.), *Witchcraft and Sorcery: Selected Readings*, pp. 280–95. Harmondsworth: Penguin.

Merlan, Francesca and Alan Rumsey (1991) *Ku Waru*. Cambridge: Cambridge University Press.

Middleton, John (1987) *Lugbara Religion*. Washington, D.C.: Smithsonian Institution Press.

REFERENCES

Middleton, John and David Tait (eds.) (1958) *Tribes Without Rulers: Studies in African Segmentary Systems*. London: Humanities Press.

Miller, William Ian (1990) *Bloodtaking and Peacemaking: Feud, Law and Society in Saga Iceland*. Chicago: University of Chicago Press.

Moore, Henrietta (1994) The problem of explaining violence in the social sciences. In P. Harvey and P. Gow (eds.), *Sex and Violence*, pp. 138–55. London: Routledge.

Murphy, Liam (2000) The name of our God is dialogue: millennial visions in Northern Ireland. *Journal of Ritual Studies* 14(2): 4–15.

Nordstrom, Carolyn (1997) *A Different Kind of War Story*. Philadelphia: University of Pennsylvania Press.

Obeyesekere, Gananath (1993) *Sorcery, Premeditated Murder and the Canalization of Aggression in Sri Lanka*. Colombo: Studies in Society and Culture.

O'Hanlon, Michael (1989) *Reading the Skin: Adornment, Display and Society among the Wahgi*. Bathurst: Crawford House Press.

Otterbein, Keith (1993) *Feuding and Warfare: Selected Works of Keith Otterbein*. New York: Gorden and Breach.

Panoff, Michel (1977) Suicide and social control in New Britain. *Bijdragen Tot de Taal-land-en Volkenkunde* 133: 44–62.

Perera, Sasanka (1995) *Living with Torturers and Other Essays in Intervention: Sri Lankan Society, Culture, and Politics in Perspective*. Colombo: International Center for Ethnic Studies.

Perera, Sasanka (2001) Spirit possession and avenging ghosts: stories of supernatural activity as narratives of terror and mechanics of coping and remembering. In V. Das *et al.* (eds.), *Remaking the World*, pp. 157–200. Berkeley: University of California Press.

Plutarch (n.d) *Plutarch's Lives: The Lives of the Noble Grecians and Romans*. Translated by John Dryden and revised by Arthur Hugh Clough. New York: Random House (The Modern Library).

Purkiss, Diane (1996) *The Witch in History: Early Modern and Twentieth-Century Representations*. London: Routledge.

Ranelagh, John O'Beirne (1983) *A Short History of Ireland*. Cambridge: Cambridge University Press.

Rapport, Nigel (2000) 'Criminals by instinct': on the 'tragedy' of social structure and the 'violence' of individual creativity. In G. Aijmer and J. Abbink (eds.), *Meanings of Violence*, pp. 39–54. Oxford: Berg.

Read, Kenneth E. (1955) Morality and the concept of the person among the Gahuku-Gama. *Oceania* 25: 233–82.

Read, Kenneth E. (1965) *The High Valley*. New York: Scribner's.

Read, Kenneth E. (1986) *Return to the High Valley: Coming Full Circle*. Berkeley: University of California Press.

Riches, David (ed.) (1986) *The Anthropology of Violence*. Oxford: Basil Blackwell.

Riebe, Inge (1987) Kalam witchcraft: a historical perspective. In M. Stephen (ed.), *Sorcerer and Witch in Melanesia*, pp. 211–48. New Brunswick: Rutgers University Press.

Robbins, Joel, Pamela J. Stewart, and Andrew Strathern (eds.) (2001) *Pentecostal and Charismatic Christianity in Oceania*. Special Issue of *Journal of Ritual Studies* 15(2).

Salzman, Philip Carl (1998) *The Anthropology of Real Life: Events in Human Experience*. Prospect Heights, IL: Waveland Press.

Scarry, Elaine (1985) *The Body in Pain*. New York: Oxford University Press.

Schmidt, Bettina E. and Ingo W. Schröder (eds.) (2001) *Anthropology of Violence and Conflict*. London: Routledge.

Schröder, Ingo W. and Bettina E. Schmidt (eds.) (2001) Introduction: violent imaginaries and violent practices. In B. E. Schmidt and I. W. Schröder (eds.), *Anthropology of Violence and Conflict*, pp. 1–24. London: Routledge.

Scott, James C. (1985) *Weapons of the Weak: Everyday Forms of Peasant Resistance*. New Haven: Yale University Press.

Sillitoe, Paul (1979) *Give and Take. Exchange in Wola Society*. Canberra: Australian National University Press.

Sillitoe, Paul (1981) Some more on war: a Wola perspective. In R. Scaglion (ed.), *Homicide Compensation in PNG*, pp. 70–81. Port Moresby: Law Reform Commission Monograph 1.

Sluka, Jeffrey A. (ed.) (2000a): *Death Squad: The Anthropology of State Terror*. Philadelphia: University of Pennsylvania Press.

Sluka, Jeffrey A. (2000b) "For God and Ulster": the culture of terror and Loyalist death squads in Northern Ireland. In J. Sluka (ed.), *Death Squad*, pp. 127–57. Philadelphia: University of Pennsylvania Press.

Southall, Aidan W. (1956) *Alur Society: A Study in Processes and Types of Domination*. Cambridge: Heffer and Sons.

Spencer, Jonathan (1990) *A Sinhala Village in a Time of Trouble: Politics and Change in Rural Sri Lanka*. Delhi: Oxford University Press.

Spencer, Jonathan (2000) On not becoming a "terrorist": problems of memory, agency, and community in the Sri Lankan conflict. In V. Das *et al.* (eds.), *Violence and Subjectivity*, pp. 120–40. Berkeley: University of California Press.

Stephen, Michele (ed.) (1987) *Sorcerer and Witch in Melanesia*. New Brunswick: Rutgers University Press.

Stewart, Frank Henderson (1994) *Honor*. Chicago: University of Chicago Press.

Stewart, Pamela J. (1998) Ritual trackways and sacred paths of fertility. In Jelle Miedema, Cecillia Ode, and Rien Dam (eds.), *Perspectives on the Bird's Head of Irian Jaya, Indonesia: Proceedings of the Conference, Leiden 13–17 October 1997*, pp. 275–89. Amsterdam: Rodopi.

Stewart, Pamela J. and Andrew J. Strathern (eds.) (1997a) *Millennial Markers*. Townsville: Centre for Pacific Studies, James Cook University of North Queensland.

Stewart, Pamela J. and Andrew J. Strathern (1997b) Sorcery and sickness: spatial and temporal movements in Papua New Guinea and Australia. *JCU–Centre for Pacific Studies Discussion Papers Series*, No. 1, 1–27.

Stewart, Pamela J. and Andrew J. Strathern (1998a) Money, politics, and persons in Papua New Guinea. *Social Analysis* 42(2): 132–49.

Stewart, Pamela J. and A. Strathern (1998b) End time frustrations in Hagen: the death of Moka and polygamy: Is there a better world? *Okari Research Group Prepublication Working Paper* No. 6, pp. 1–11. For the session 'Humiliation and Transformation: Emotion, Subjectivity, and Modernity in Melanesia' at the 1998 AAA conference Philadelphia.

Stewart, Pamela J. and Andrew J. Strathern (1998c) Life at the end: voices and visions from Mt. Hagen, Papua New Guinea. *Zeitschrift für Missions- und Religionswissenschaft*, 82(4): 147–64.

Stewart, Pamela J. and Andrew Strathern (1999a) Custom, modernity, and contradiction: local and national identities in the Pacific. *Okari Research Group Pre-publication Working Paper* No 27, pp. 1–16. For the conference on Pacific Identities, Noumea, New Caledonia, July 1999.

Stewart, Pamela J. and Andrew J. Strathern (1999b) Death on the move: landscape and violence on the Highland's Highway, Papua New Guinea. *Anthropology and Humanism* 24(1): 20–31.

Stewart, Pamela J. and Andrew Strathern (1999c) "Feasting on my enemy": images of violence and change in the New Guinea Highlands. *Ethnohistory* 46(4): 645–69.

Stewart, Pamela J. and A. Strathern (1999d) Time at the end: the Highlands of Papua New Guinea. In Christin Kocher-Schmid (ed.), *Expecting the Day of Wrath: Versions of the Millennium in Papua New Guinea*. Port Moresby: National Research Institute, Monograph 36, July, pp. 131–44.

Stewart, Pamela J. and A. Strathern (2000a) Introduction: latencies and realizations in millennial practices. In P. J. Stewart and A. Strathern (eds.), "Millennial countdown in New Guinea", *Ethnohistory*, Special Issue 47(1): 3–27.

Stewart, Pamela J. and A. Strathern (2000b) Introduction: narratives speak. In Pamela J. Stewart and Andrew Strathern (eds.), *Identity Work: Constructing Pacific Lives*. ASAO (Association for Social Anthropology in Oceania) Monograph Series No. 18, pp. 1–26. Pittsburgh: University of Pittsburgh Press.

Stewart, Pamela J. and Andrew Strathern (2001a) The great exchange: Moka with God. Special Issue, "Pentecostal and Charismatic Christianity in Oceania," edited by Joel Robbins, Pamela J. Stewart, and Andrew Strathern. *Journal of Ritual Studies* 15 (2): 91–104.

Stewart, Pamela J. and A. Strathern (in press) Transformations of 'monetary' symbols in the Highlands of Papua New Guinea. For a special issue of *L'Homme* on money edited by Stephane Breton.

Strathern, Andrew (1971) *The Rope of Moka*. Cambridge: Cambridge University Press.

Strathern, Andrew (1974) When dispute procedures fail. In A. L. Epstein (ed.), *Contention and Dispute*, pp. 240–70. Canberra: Australian National University Press.

Strathern, Andrew (1977) Contemporary warfare in the New Guinea Highlands: revival or breakdown? *Yagl-Ambu* 4: 135–46.

Strathern, Andrew (1979) Gender, ideology, and money in Mount Hagen. *Man* (n.s.) 14: 530–48.

Strathern, Andrew (1982) Witchcraft, greed, cannibalism and death. In Maurice Bloch and Johnny Parry (eds.), *Death and the Regeneration of Life*, pp. 111–33. Cambridge: Cambridge University Press.

Strathern, Andrew (1984) *A Line of Power*. London: Tavistock.

Strathern, Andrew (1992) Let the bow go down. In R. B. Ferguson and N. L. Whitehead (eds.), *War in the Tribal Zone*, pp. 229–50. Santa Fe: School of American Research Press.

Strathern, Andrew J. (1993a) *Voices of Conflict*. Pittsburgh: Ethnology Monographs no. 14.

Strathern, Andrew (1993b) Violence and political change in Papua New Guinea. *Pacific Studies* 16(4): 41–60.

Strathern, Andrew (1996) *Body Thoughts*. Ann Arbor: University of Michigan Press.

Strathern, Andrew and Pamela J. Stewart (1997a) Introduction: Millennial markers in the Pacific, pp. 1–17. In Pamela J. and A. J. Strathern (ed.), *Millennial Markers*. Townsville: JCU, Centre for Pacific Studies. Reprinted, 2 May 1999, *World*

Anthropology the AnthroGlobe Journal [electronic journal]
http://anthroglobe.com/docs/articles/7.pdf.

Strathern, Andrew and Pamela J. Stewart (1997b) The problems of peace-makers in Papua New Guinea: modalities of negotiation and settlement. *Cornell International Law Journal* (3): 681–99.

Strathern, Andrew and Pamela J. Stewart (1998a) Embodiment and communication: two frames for the analysis of ritual. *Social Anthropology* 6 (2): 237–51.

Strathern, Andrew and Pamela J. Stewart (1998b) Seeking personhood: anthropological accounts and local concepts in Mount Hagen, Papua New Guinea. *Oceania* 68 (3): 170–88.

Strathern, Andrew and Pamela J. Stewart. (1998c) The embodiment of responsibility: 'confession' and 'compensation' in Mount Hagen, Papua New Guinea. *Pacific Studies* 21 (1/2): 43–64.

Strathern, Andrew and Pamela J. Stewart (1999a) Objects, relationships, and meanings: historical switches in currencies in Mount Hagen, Papua New Guinea. In David Akin and Joel Robbins (eds.), *Money and Modernity: State and Local Currencies in Melanesia*, pp. 164–91. ASAO (Association for Social Anthropology in Oceania) Monograph Series No. 17. Pittsburgh: University of Pittsburgh Press.

Strathern, Andrew and Pamela J. Stewart (1999b) *Collaborations and Conflicts: A Leader Through Time*. Fort Worth: Harcourt Brace College Publishers.

Strathern, Andrew and Pamela J. Stewart (1999c) *'The Spirit Is Coming!' A Photo-graphic-Textual Exposition of the Female Spirit Cult Performance in Mt. Hagen*. Ritual Studies Monograph Series, Monograph No. 1. Pittsburgh: Department of Anthropology, University of Pittsburgh.

Strathern, Andrew and Pamela J. Stewart (1999d) *Curing and Healing: Medical Anthropology in Global Perspective*. Durham, N.C.: Carolina Academic Press.

Strathern, Andrew and Pamela J. Stewart (1999e) Global, national, local: sliding scales, constant themes. In *Globalizacao e Identidade Nacional*, edited and translated by Joao Barroso into Portuguese, pp. 39–64. São Paulo: Editora Atlas S.A. Publishers.

Strathern, Andrew and Pamela J. Stewart (2000a) *Arrow Talk: Transaction, Transition, and Contradiction in New Guinea Highlands History*. Kent, OH: Kent State University Press.

Strathern, Andrew and Pamela J. Stewart (2000b) Creating difference: a contemporary affiliation drama in the Highlands of New Guinea. *Journal of the Royal Anthropological Institute* 6(1): 1–15.

Strathern, Andrew and Pamela J. Stewart (2000c) Further twists of the rope: Ongka and Ru in a transforming world. In Pamela J. Stewart and Andrew Strathern (eds.), *Identity Work: Constructing Pacific Lives*, pp. 81–98. ASAO (Association for Social Anthropology in Oceania) Monograph Series No. 18. University of Pittsburgh Press.

Strathern, Andrew and Pamela J. Stewart (2000d) Mi les long yupela usim flag bilong mi: symbols, identity, and desire in Papua New Guinea. *Pacific Studies*, 23 (1): 21–49.

Strathern, Andrew and Pamela J. Stewart (2000e) *The Python's Back: Pathways of Comparison Between Melanesia and Indonesia*. Westport, CT: Bergin and Garvey.

Strathern, Andrew and Pamela J. Stewart (2000f) Accident, agency, and liability in New Guinea Highlands Compensation Practices. *Bijdragen* August 156–2: 275–95.

Strathern, Andrew and Pamela J. Stewart (forthcoming) Hagen settlement histories: dispersals and consolidations. In Pamela Swadling, Jack Golson, and John Muke (eds.), *Nine Thousand Years of Gardening: Kuk and the Archaeology of Agriculture in Papua New Guinea*. Adelaide: Crawford House Publishing.

Sykes, Karen (2000) Raskolling: Papua New Guinea sociality as contested political order. In C. Banks (ed.), *Developing Cultural Criminology: Theory and Practice in Papua New Guinea*, pp. 174–94. Sydney: Sydney Institute of Criminology Monograph Series no. 13.

Tambiah, Stanley Jeyaraja (1986) *Sri Lanka: Ethnic Fratricide and the Dismantling of Democracy*. Chicago: University of Chicago Press.

Tambiah, Stanley Jeyaraja (1992) *Buddhism Betrayed? Religion, Politics and Violence in Sri Lanka*. Chicago: University of Chicago Press.

Taylor, Christopher C. (1992) *Milk, Honey, and Money*. Washington, D.C.: Smithsonian Institution Press.

Taylor, Christopher C. (1999) *Sacrifice as Terror: The Rwandan Genocide of 1994*. Oxford: Berg.

Taylor, Lawrence J. (1995) *Occasions of Faith: An Anthropology of Irish Catholics*. Philadelphia: University of Pennsylvania Press.

Trompf, Gary W. (1994) *Payback: The Logic of Retribution in Melanesian Religions*. Cambridge: Cambridge University Press.

Turner, Victor W. (1969) *The Ritual Process: Structure and Anti-Structure*. Chicago: Aldine.

Wagner, Roy (1967) *The Curse of Souw: Principles of Daribi Clan Definition and Alliance in New Guinea*. Chicago: University of Chicago Press.

Warren, Kay B. (1993) Interpreting *La Violencia* in Guatemala: the shapes of Mayan silence and resistance. In K. Warren (ed.), *The Violence Within: Cultural and Political Opposition in Divided Nations*. Boulder: Westview Press.

Warry, Wayne (1987) *Chuave Politics: Changing Patterns of Leadership in the Papua New Guinea Highlands*. Canberra: Australian National University (Political and Social Change Monograph no. 4).

White, Luise (2000) *Speaking with Vampires: Rumor and History in Colonial Africa*. Berkeley: University of California Press.

Wiessner, Polly and Akii Tumu (1998) *Historical Vines: Enga Networks of Exchange, Ritual and Warfare in New Guinea*. Washington, D.C.: Smithsonian Institution Press.

Young, Michael W. (1971) *Fighting with Food: Leadership, Values, and Social Control in a Massim Society*. Cambridge: Cambridge University Press.

Young, Michael W. (1983): *Magicians of Manumanua: Living Myth in Kalauna*. Berkeley: University of California Press.

Zulaika, J. (1989) *Basque Violence: Metaphor and Sacrament*. Reno: University of Nevada Press.

Index